EARTHLINGS

THE BEGINNING

RAY STAR

D0620350

3013030303197 4

Copyright © Ray Star 2021

Published: 2021 by Chronos Publishing First edition published August 2021 1-100

ISBN: 9781914529122 Paperback Edition
ISBN: 9781914529139 e-book
All rights reserved.

The right of Ray Star to be identified as the author of this Work has been asserted by her in accordance with sections 77 and 78 of the Copyright, Designs and Patents Act 1988.

This book is a work of fiction and any resemblance to actual persons, living or dead, is purely coincidental.

No part of this publication may be reproduced, stored in a retrieval system, copied in any form or by any means, electronic, mechanical, photocopying, recording or otherwise transmitted without written permission from the publisher. You must not circulate this book in any format.

Every endeavour has been made to ensure this book is printed on recycled paper where possible, and the author is planting a tree per book sale.

To my sun, my moon, and my stars,

this book, and all that I am, is for you.

CHAPTERS

PROLOGUE...8

PERIDOT 14

HOME 23

THIRTEEN...37

INTRUDER...53

THE LOST BOY 71

THE CRAFT 88

GONE..107

EUAN 124

CHANGES..125

THE TRUTH 139

THE MAINLAND 152

EARTHLINGS 164

THE A.I STATION 174

CAPTURED 184

BONDED 200

FAMILIARS 209

ONWARDS 222

COMPOUND FOUR.................................234

TERRAIN 248

THE H.L.F...265

INTRUSION...276

FREYJA 292

PHOENIX 297

UNVEILING...301

HIDDEN POWER 316

ALLIANCE 326

ALAN...336

AMBUSH 340

THE STAND...352

PHOENIX 360

VALLAEARTHA...364

EUAN 368

ABOUT THE AUTHOR...370

A NOTE FROM THE AUTHOR...371

ACKNOWLEDGEMENTS 372

Prologue

It's official. I hate chickens. Not that I dislike them, no, that I physically have a deep-founded internal hatred towards them. I genuinely despise the evil feathered mother cluckers. You may think that's an odd statement to make, but you're not currently being chased by hundreds of them trying to peck you to death. As bizarre as that may sound, that's my reality at this moment. In their defence, it's not their fault. It's one specific chicken that's really got it in for me and rallied the others against me.

This chicken's name is Alan.

Yep. You heard right.

Alan the chicken.

He's out to get me.

Well, to viciously kill me and broadcast it worldwide, but let's skip the semantics and get back to basics. I'm about to be killed by a chicken named Alan. He's always hated me, from the moment he first laid his beady little black eyes on me, all those years ago. I knew the first moment I saw him, he'd be trouble.

I sound like a mad man if you have a normal life outside of The Resistance, but for me, this is everyday life. You see, I live in a society run by animals. Not cute fluffy kittens, or tail-wagging wet-nosed dogs, but sharp-clawed chickens, heavy hooved cows, furious foxes, and evil elephants. They're angry. Furious in fact. They hate humanity and seek to enslave us.

I'm one of a few trying to revolt, a newly initiated member of the Human Liberation Front. Our aim is to liberate humanity from slavery and give freedom to all. As a result, The Descendants, as they like to call themselves, want me dead. My mission was to attempt to negotiate a way to coexist harmoniously as a bi-species coalition - I nearly had the treaty approved too. The pigs, who are surprisingly forgiving creatures, were so close to signing. Until Alan pecked his way in. Now it's all gone to hell, because this one chicken can't get over the past, and wants me dead.

So, now I'm running for my life. No members of The Resistance to help me, no backup lying in wait, just medium built me. And over a thousand chickens out for blood. I'm lucky the feathered fleabags can't fly, or I'd be a goner already. My legs are bleeding from the ones that've made it close enough to my ankles, but so far, the rest of me is unscathed. I just need to keep moving and get out of here.

"Get him before he reaches the top!" Alan screeches.

Oh yeah, they can talk too. Did I mention that? Horrid squeaky feral noises, worse than nails on a chalkboard.

I'm so close to getting out of this building that I allow a ray of hope to shine through. The Human Liberation Front will come to my rescue if I can just get to the top of these stairs and get their attention. They won't know the treaty's gone wrong. When they hear what's happened, Alan will have a price on his head even bigger than mine.

He's now solely responsible for the potential end of human freedom as we know it, and it's not just humans that will be angry, the dogs, horses and crows will be furious. He'll have nowhere to hide and maybe, just maybe we can salvage the treaty, and save humanity. The fate of the human population as we know it is on my shoulders. I will not fail. Just. Keep. Going. My sides ache, my legs burn, and my lungs feel like they might collapse; one flight of stairs to go, I can't give in, I can make it.

"Argh!" a scream escapes my lips, one of the flock has his beak embedded in my ankle and more are closing in, I kick my leg out, but the mean clucker holds tight; ten stairs, breathe, nine stairs, breathe, eight stairs.

"Do not let him escape!"

I can hear the panic in Alan's voice, he knows if I get out and tell the H.L.F what happened, he's doomed. That thought alone spurs me on. Four steps, three steps, two steps – wham – I boot my leg through the door as hard as I can, chicken attached and all, his neck slices open and my ankle is free.

I burst through the door panting for air, I can't believe I made it, only as I skid around the corner, I'm forced to screech to a halt. I can't believe my eyes. No. How is this possible? I'm on a roof. An exceedingly high roof at that. I ran up a lot of stairs, but I didn't think it was this high, I can't jump down, I'll never make it.

"Times up Euan," sneers Alan, approaching to the side of me, his army of chickens a feathered mass behind him.

I don't know if you can imagine what a sneering chicken looks or sounds like, but it's almost comical if I wasn't most likely about to meet my end. If I die, no one will know the truth. The truth would end with me, and Alan the dirty feathered fleabag will keep control of the humans. Slavery will not cease; our race will continue to be exploited behind closed doors whilst many remain ignorant of our plight and those that do know, being subjected to a death sentence, or worse. I must get out of this, somehow.

"Hey Al, how's it going?" I pant.

"You can't sweet-talk your way out of this one boy, it's just you and me and I have an army behind me, it's time you got what you deserved. Now, how to kill you? Death by pecking, or plummeting?"

"Can I have a moment to decide, I can't rush my own death now, can I?" Surveying the area out of the corner of my eye, I try to stall my impending doom.

There must be a fire escape or a ladder I can climb down, but as I look, there's nothing. Just the doorway I came through, only now there's a hoard of chickens in front of it. I don't fancy my chances. Even if I get back down, I'll be back where I started. Only there's a mass of angry animals at the bottom of those stairs too, thanks to Alan's tirade of lies. He really is one arch-nemesis of a chicken. Unless a miracle occurs, there's no way out, I'm doomed.

"Tick tock boy, my clan is hungry, don't worry, it won't take long to put you out of your misery," Alan jeers, beady eyes gleaming with delight. He can't believe his luck. He's won, and he knows it.

"Even after all these years you won't move on will you, you'll see an entire species put to death for petty revenge?"

"Petty revenge?!"

Anger seeps through every individual feather, Alan seems to grow in size, "Trillions of my kind, not millions, not billions, but *trillions* massacred by your race, and you think this is petty?" he squawks, "no boy, this is blissful, sickly, sweet, revenge, and there's no way in hell I'm letting a puny human like you ruin it. We're finally on top of the food chain and why shouldn't we be? Years of cages, torture and death, no more!"

He paces closer towards me, I can almost smell his rancid breath as he continues to rant, "the other species don't understand, we give an inch - you'll take a mile. Your kind nearly killed the planet with your greed, and now it's thriving you want us to consider letting you ruin it again? Never!" he spits in angst, which is a funny thing for a chicken to do, in any situation other than this.

"You can't blame the entire human population for what older generations did, the people you're punishing now, didn't do anything wrong! We're not all bad eggs Alan," I try to placate him, not realising my mistake, as the all-too-common phrase slips out of my mouth.

"Bad eggs?" Alan whispers in fury, flapping his wings, I notice he has clusters of feathers missing underneath. Puffing his chest out, he closes the gap between us, murder in his beady black eyes.

"Your kind deserve to be in slavery, every single one of you. Men, women, children, even your babies. I won't stop until I've seen it done," he whispers sadistically, then with a gleam in his eye and a snarled rasp, "Time to die boy, peck or plummet you decide, be grateful I'm giving you the choice."

He advances upon me, the flock behind match step for step, hatred in every one of their eyes. I take it back about it just being Alan, these chickens really hate humans. And in this precise moment in time – me.

Pecking will be brutal. No way will they make it quick. They'll peck slowly in private places and thrive on my screams of pain; they think I deserve it. Never mind that I'm not my predecessors and I've never eaten a chicken in my life. That doesn't matter to them I'm just another human and we're all evil in their eyes. I have no choice – I'll have to jump.

I pinch myself, just to check it's not a dream. But no such luck. This isn't a nightmare, I'm not about to have one of those weird falling sensations, then wake up glad it's over, this is really happening. I'm about to be murdered by chickens. I'm scared. My lungs ache from running. My ankle is in agony from breaking down the door. As I look down there's a beak hanging out of it. This makes me smile as sadistically as Alan, at least I took one of the nasty pluckers down with me. Wish it'd been more than one though.

"Times up boy," Alan's voice brings me back to my peril, they advance on me as one, a clan of feral, furious chickens, baiting for my blood.

There's no way out. I cannot let them get me, the enormous impact on morale it would have if the first human negotiator within the revolution of The Resistance was killed by a chicken. I can't be responsible for them getting one over us. I turn, closing my eyes, heart hammering in my chest, sweat drips from my forehead, blood trickles down my ankle, this is so not how I expected to go. Fleetingly, I glance back at my nemesis, today could have changed this way of life if he hadn't interfered. I don't allow him to revel in his triumph, as my final act of defiance I grin, saluting the evil feathered bird as I step to the edge, "Suck eggs Al."

I jump.

As I plummet, fully aware that these last futile moments are all that's left of, let's admit, a pretty depressing life, I think back to the one time I was truly happy and her face pops into my mind. With seconds left before I impact onto the dirt, I do the last thing I thought possible in this moment and smile. Saying her name for the last time, I think of the girl who gave me my only genuine moments of happiness on this earth, "Peridot."

PERIDOT

"Aargh!!" I wake with a jolt, sweat running down my face, tummy in knots. Another falling dream. I hate when I get them. They're worse than monsters under your bed or the boogeyman in your closet. The falling dreams always scare the cripes out of me. Every night this week I've had the same dream, being chased by an unknown enemy and jumping to my death, rather than letting them get me. I always wake shaking and terrified, just before I hit the ground. They're always so real. Taking a moment, I focus on my surroundings to bring my heartbeat back to normal, my mattress feels soft beneath me. I'm in my bed, I'm safe, it was just a dream.

Looking to my right, the moon shines down through my bedroom window, a brilliant orb of translucent white light. Knowing that I won't get back to sleep, I opt for my normal routine for when the reoccurring nightmare makes its way into my dreams. Yawning, I rise slowly and prepare to go for a moonlit stroll in the dark. The moon always has a calming effect on me. Popping on my favourite pair of comfy bottoms, I wrap up in one of my dad's old cosy jumpers, grabbing my dream diary as I go. Quietly as possible, I open my window. Mum freaks out when I go out at night, but there's no point living in the middle of nowhere if you can't enjoy it.

We live on a secluded farm on a remote island just off the coast of England, just me, Mum, Joseph, Ann, and our animals. We grow plants that Mum makes into medicine and herbal remedies. Joseph tends to the crops, Ann home schools me and I care for the sanctuary animals. I'm thirteen years old this week and I've never left the island. If I want to go for a midnight stroll, I'm going to, whether Mum throttles me for it in the morning or not.

Besides, she can only tell me off if I get caught and she rarely catches me. I have it down to a system now. Arranging my pillows under the duvet, I attempt to make a humanish form then step back to admire my handiwork. It's not great, but it'll do if anyone pops their head in to check on me. Carefully, I pop my window securely on the latch, so it doesn't slam shut, then close the curtains behind me to ensure no light shines through.

Gingerly, shimmying down the window ledge, I take my time to dangle down the last drop until my feet touch the ground, then I'm free. As much as I hate the nightmare, I'm always glad when I get to go for a walk in the dark, especially when the moon is at its fullest. Strangely, the vivid dreams only invade my slumber on the days leading up to a full moon. I've never realised that before. Mentally, I make a note to jot it down in my dream diary.

I've always loved to read and write, lucky really, as there's not much else for me to do here other than that or my chores. There are no other children on the island that I know of. Mum's a bit of a recluse, so we don't get visitors. I love where we live, but it's lonely, I'd be lost without our animals. Speaking of which, I'll need to go the long way around the back of the barns so none of them sees me. Last time they noticed me sneaking out and made a racket that woke Mum up. I was on manure duty for a week – I'm not risking that again.

A light breeze guides me along the way, trees gently swishing in the wind. I walk briskly past the back buildings, over the opposite side of the fence and down to the stream. I love our home, it's ever so beautiful, especially at night. I don't understand why mum worries so much, it's not like anyone ever comes around here. The worst thing I'd have to fear is stepping in animal dung, Mum's just a worrier.

I know she's the way she is because she loves me and doesn't want to lose me like we lost Dad, it's made her overprotective over the years, and very firm on my schooling. Ann's a great teacher and I like to learn, but now I'm almost thirteen, I need to live a little too. I'm barely allowed to explore the island, the one time I did try to go outside of our land Mum was furious, I could hear her shouting for hours. Earth knows who to as Joseph and Ann were out; herself in the mirror most likely. I love Mum, but I think losing Dad may have made her a little loopy.

Making my way down the spiralling creek, I finally come to my happy place. A singular aged oak tree, standing alone at the base of the stream. It's the oldest tree I've ever laid eyes on. Its vast trunk towers over me, endless as it rises into the sky. I lean into the bark, taking strength from its sturdiness, the branches sway in the light breeze, welcoming me as it rustles its leafy greens. At my feet clusters of acorns litter the ground, some as old as the tree itself, worn down into the earth over time, others anew, the tops taken off by squirrels harvesting. Its shadow looms over the water as it opens out into a large pool. It's like looking out at the ocean. Deep dark blues and at its furthest point, inky blackness. The moon smiles down at me, glittering off the water's edge.

Slipping off my shoes, I nestle my toes into the damp earth, close my eyes and breathe in deeply. I love this spot, no matter what I'm feeling it gives me peace. I wish I had someone to share it with, but if I show Mum then she'll know my hiding place, so I can't. I bring Phoenix sometimes, our family dog, but it's not the same. I'd do anything to have a friend my age.

As water laps at my feet, the loneliness seeps its way in, as it always tends to when I get lost in thought. Stepping back, I take a seat by the old oak, feeling sadness wash over me. The gnarled bark digs into my spine as if trying to snap me out of it. The thought is preposterous, yet whenever I'm feeling low, sitting here always manages to clear my mind. I lean my head back against the trunk, the tree's vastness making my body and my worries seem small in comparison.

"I know, it's dumb." I sigh out loud.

I shouldn't be this upset over something so trivial, life on the island would be a dream to some, it's just lonely. I'm thirteen this week, I can't be home-schooled forever. I should ask Mum if I can start school for my birthday if I can pluck up the courage. But what if she says no? The tree's bark digs into my spine again. What if she says yes? The question echoes in my mind, not of my own doing, leaving with it the faint hint of hope.

"Thank you," I whisper.

A sudden gust of air whooshes past leaving in its place an upheaval of branches, the old tree creaks deeply, its leaves rustling animatedly in the remnants of wind. I press my hands against the moss-covered base, soft to the touch, as if it were the trees beard. The thought makes me smile, I don't feel as alone anymore.

Opening my dream journal, I begin to write my thoughts down onto the paper. Jotting down my most recent nightmare, I make a note that the moon is at its fullest again. Taking a moment to look up, it almost feels like the moon watches over me. Mum has always taught me to give thanks to the moon, says she's always watching over us, even when we can't see her. I used to think she was crazy, still do most of the time if I'm being honest, but I understand what she means, I really do feel her in this moment. I smile up at the sky getting lost in thought once more, when in the quiet of the night, a twig snaps.

"Which of you followed me this time?" I sigh, looks like it wasn't the moon watching me after all.

Either Joseph, Ann, one of the animals or even worse, Mum. Oh, I'm so on manure duty again.

"I'm coming back now, I couldn't sleep that's all," I grumble, standing up to face whoever followed me.

Turning to face the trees, I'm greeted with emptiness. That's odd. I know I heard something. One of the animals must've followed me down. If I can just get them back unseen, I may still get away with my midnight stroll. Another twig snaps.

"Hello?"

I'm met with silence.

"I know you're there – let's go home for treats."

Still nothing. Strange, all the animals go wild for treats. I'm not scared, I know the boogeyman isn't real, and no one ever comes to our side of the island. Maybe an animal's injured and needs help. Mum won't tell me off for getting up to rescue a poorly animal, this could be my saving grace. I hope they're not too badly hurt. Carefully making my way into the trees, I try to see through the darkness. The moon's bright, but not bright enough to see through all the bushes. It's so dark I can't make out a thing.

"Come on out, so I can help you -"

I hear what sounds like a startled gasp and that's when I freeze. Animals make a lot of very odd noises, but they don't gasp. A trickle of fear edges into my voice.

"Hello, is anyone there?"

"Mum?" I call timidly.

No response, just pure silence and now I'm freaked out. Slowly, I backtrack away from the trees and inch towards the water, leaving my shoes and journal behind. Then, as another twig snaps, I bolt.

Panic courses through my veins as I run as fast as my legs will carry me. I'm a book worm, not overly athletic, but I'm used to running with horses, rolling with pigs and playing round up the rabbits, so when I need to move I can. I'm at the fence in a matter of minutes, hurtling myself over it. My foot catches the top causing me to cry out, the horses neigh wildly, no doubt waking everyone up. The sudden glare of lights switching on from inside the house confirms my worries to be true. Hobbling over the rest of the way, I sneak glances behind to check I'm not being followed, I see nothing. Maybe it *was* nothing?

"Peridot Watkins, what are you doing out of bed?!" Mum strides towards me, Phoenix at her heels.

I'm going to be in so much trouble, she's full named me. She only full names me when she's really ticked off. I need to think of an excuse quickly.

"I heard noises, I thought there was an animal hurt and came over to look, but I got stuck going over the fence," I manage to prattle out, almost coherently.

If I tell her about the weirdness in the woods, she'll put the farm on lockdown, and I won't be allowed any form of freedom, I can't tell her.

"You're bleeding?" she questions, eyes narrowing as she looks pointedly at my ankle. I cross my legs to try to hide the gash.

"Are you sure you weren't taking one of your walks, the moons full?" she gives me the look, you know, that 'mother' look that you can't tear away from.

"No -" I reply a little too hurriedly, "I heard an animal and came to check it out, I don't even have my shoes on, see?" I point, bringing attention to my filthy feet. Trust Mum to notice that I only wander when the moons full, she may be a little eccentric, but she doesn't miss a beat.

"Your feet are wet." she glowers pointedly.

"Erm…" I struggle to think of an excuse quick enough.

"Into your room right now Peridot! Get cleaned up and I'll send Ann in to patch up your foot, where are your shoes?"

"By the pond," I skulk.

"Peridot you must stop this! It's dangerous to be out at night - you have no idea what could be out there!" Her voice becomes shrill, "You know the drill, you're on manure duty this week - yes, even your birthday, and I won't hear another word. When you're older you can go out at night, but not while you're a child, it's not safe!"

She stares at me waiting for my normal tirade of, it's not fair, why me and I hate my life retorts, but I'm still confused by the gasp in the woods, and it sinks in that just this once, she may be right. I nod my head meekly, limping past her towards the house.

She mutters angrily to herself as she wanders off to retrieve my shoes. She's livid, but that was a gentle telling off. She must still be half asleep, I'm sure I'll be in for it properly in the morning. I get to my room to find Ann waiting with a bowl of warm water, a selection of Mum's remedies and bandages at the ready. Phoenix bounds in joining us.

"How did you know I was hurt?" I ask.

"Oh Dot," she fusses using her pet name for me, "I've been caring for animals for years, us humans don't sound that different when we're in pain. Now, pop your foot up, let's have a look."

Slowly, I take a seat at the end of the bed, wincing as I lower myself down. Now my adrenalin has ceased, my foot throbs painfully.

"You really must listen to your mother, it's dangerous at night, you should've at least taken Phoenix with you," she tuts, affectionately patting his head. He lays down by my foot and gives it a lick, making me feel bad for not taking him.

"Sorry boy," I ruffle his ears.

He gives me a 'you went out without me' look, giving my foot one last solemn lick before rolling over. Even Phoenix is cross with me. The events of the night sink in and my eyes tear up. I had an awful nightmare, was scared half to death, ran for my life, nearly ripped my foot off and now everyone's mad at me. Life is so unfair. Ann pulls me into a hug, soothing down my hair just as Mum returns with my shoes, placing them down by the door.

"Mum?" I sniff, about to ask if she picked up my journal.

"Yes Peridot," she sighs, looking defeated and drawn. I take in her eyes and notice dark circles as lines of worry crinkle her forehead. She really does worry about me. Glancing at her hands, I can see they're empty, she doesn't have my journal, I'll go get it tomorrow, she looks like she needs to sleep.

"I didn't mean to worry you. I just couldn't sleep that's all." I try to explain, crying freely now and not for sympathy, I genuinely feel bad. I just wanted to clear my head. Who knew this night would turn out to be such a nightmare?

"Get some sleep," she sighs, giving me a weak smile, "you'll feel better in the morning." She closes the door quietly behind her, leaving me with Ann and Phoenix once again. I hear her make her way back downstairs. The moment she's out of earshot, I burst into sobs.

"Oh Dot, it's okay, your mum will be fine, she has a lot on her mind right now, that's all," Ann tries to soothe me.

"It's not just that," I sniffle.

I want to tell her about the dreams, the loneliness, how hard it is not having any friends or someone my age to talk to, and most of all I want to confide in her about the strange noises in the woods, but I can't. Ann is devoutly

21

loyal to my mother, and I have no doubt in my mind she would tell her about the noises I heard. I can't risk it.

I remain quiet as she wipes down my foot. Ann knows when not to pry and focuses on tending to my wound, a large gash in my ankle weeps freely. She pops one of Mum's tinctures on and the bleeding stops, almost completely, removing a cap from another bottle of what looks like oil filled with leaves and a clear crystal, she smears some across the wound. The pain soothes instantly. I'm always amazed by Mum's remedies; she has one for everything. Ann lifts my other leg to tuck me into bed. Rolling a drizzle of another oil over my forehead, she pops a sprig of lavender under my pillow then quietly leaves the room.

Phoenix jumps up, nuzzling his nose into my neck, I cuddle into him gladly and stroke his ears, looking into his beautiful golden eyes, until I feel the weariness of the night sink in. Phoenix always makes me feel better. I wish I'd gone with him in the first place. Mum's right, going out at night was a stupid idea and tomorrow will be better. I drift into a light slumber, unaware as I do, Phoenix's golden eyes turn a deep shade of purple, and he watches over me until I fall asleep.

HOME

I wake the next morning feeling right as rain. Jumping out of bed I completely forget my bad foot, cursing loudly as it gives way beneath me, forcing me to remember the events from the night before.

"Peridot, do not use that language!" Mum shouts up the stairs, "come down for breakfast, we have a busy day ahead."

Rolling my eyes, I hobble to the shower room adjacent to Mum's and let the water run nice and warm. Carefully stepping in, I let the water cascade down and feel the remaining weariness from the night wash away. Steam rises as the water gradually gets hotter and I relish the feeling as my body warms from top to toe. Grabbing one of Mum's homemade shampoo balls, I lather up my hair and body. The water runs murky, the grime from my midnight escapade washing down the plug.

Slowly, I peel Ann's bandage off my foot and am amazed to see it's nearly healed. What was a large wound is barely visible, with only a slight red mark and bruise remaining, I must've hit it harder than I thought. The bruise aches like mad, I'll need to ask Mum which other remedy I can take to get rid of the pain. Wanting to spend a lot longer under the hot water, I begrudgingly get out, wanting to get back in Mum's good books. I change hurriedly, slipping into a comfy pair of trousers, a baggy T-shirt, warm socks and boots.

Briefly, I check my reflection in the mirror, dark green eyes look back at me, looking tired and not all that different to Mum's. Dark circles are starting to form, the cycle of nightmares starting to catch up with me. Tucking my short brown hair behind my ears, I note that I could do with some sunshine, my skin naturally very pale is missing the trademark freckles that sneak out when the sun shines. Spring, or Ostara as Mum calls it, is only around the corner. With the promise of warmer weather coming, I grab a cardigan on my way downstairs to keep out the chill of March mornings and head to the kitchen.

"Good morning, how are you feeling?" Ann glances up from the breakfast table.

"Miles better after a shower, my foot's still sore though, do we have anything I can use for the ache?"

"I think it's time you learnt your herbology Peridot," Mum scolds, walking briskly into the kitchen. "You should know that a simple yarrow lotion will clear that right up. Did you pop a quartz crystal in the shower with you?"

Drat. I forgot quartz is a universal healer.

"I forgot," I admit, "can you help me make a lotion before I tend to the animals, it's really hurting?"

"Yarrow takes three days to brew," she shakes her head, "I've got some upstairs, I'll bring it down while you eat breakfast. I'm going out today to run some errands, can I trust you to get everything sorted round the sanctuary without wandering off?" Her dig doesn't go unnoticed, and I bite my tongue, resisting the urge to retort. My birthday is in three days. Three days until potential freedom. Of sorts. Do *not* jeopardise it.

"Yes Mum," I relent, avoiding eye contact.

Looking surprised she heads upstairs. Ann gives me a knowing look, serving a plate of pancakes upon the table with a selection of fruit and nut toppings to choose from. I select my favourites, raspberries, blueberries, and pumpkin seeds with a sprinkle of sugar over the top. My mouth salivates as I take a bite, the warmth of the pancakes complimenting the cool sweetness of the fruit perfectly.

"What's the plan today?" I ask between mouthfuls and yummy noises.

"Let's attend to the animals first, then perhaps we'll see if Val's got the supplies for a few basic remedies? You're thirteen in a few days, she's right, it's time we add herbology to the curriculum," she finishes her pancake, getting up to leave her dishes in water to soak.

"I thought Mum would be teaching me herbology?"

"She will in time, I'll do the basics with you then when you've got the techniques down, Val can take over and show you the practical side properly."

"Why does she nag that I don't know which herbs make which remedies if she won't teach me anyway?" I grumble.

"If you listened to what Ann just said Peridot, I will be teaching you, but you need to know the theory before you can jump into the practical. Our craft is difficult to master, you need to be taught efficiently," Mum bristles on re-entering the kitchen to hand me the lotion, "apply before you go outside, let it sink in for five minutes and do the same before bedtime. It'll be right as rain in the morning. No more dramas today please."

With a sigh, she closes the door behind her. I watch her leave, head down walking briskly. She didn't use to be like this, she used to be fun – but that feels like forever ago. When I was little, she would take me with her to find a particular plant she needed for an ointment or tincture. Then she would spend hours going through all her crystals and 'magickal bits n bobs' as she'd call them, explaining the various healing properties and history of our family.

25

We come from an ancient line of healers, it's something Mum is immensely proud of. And she should be proud, there isn't a single health problem I've not seen her cure. People used to bring their animals to us from across the sea and she'd have them patched up and on their way within a few days or in some cases, hours. Those that were too poorly to make the trip back or needed extra attention, we'd home here at the farm which, over the years became a sanctuary. The animals became my friends over time, my only friends, I think to myself sadly.

Not that I don't love where we live, I only wish I had someone my age to share it with, it gets so lonely. Mum's a technophobe and doesn't allow me to watch TV or use the computer unsupervised, says children should be children and play outside. When we have watched a movie, I tend to feel sad afterwards, so many people out there with friends and families and here it's just us, Ann and Joseph. I'm not entirely sure how they knew Mum, but Joseph has something called cancer which Mum needs to give him regular treatment for. They live here with us. I'm so glad they do, I think of them as the grandparents I've never had. My only company. Other than Phoenix and the rest of the animals.

Phoenix pops his head into the room just then, it's strange, but whenever I think of him, he's there. It's like he knows when I need him. He reminds me of a lion with his burnt gold fur, long tail, overly large head and teeth. Even his nose and eyes are golden. My mum calls him a 'red nose', which I've always found odd as it's not red at all, but Mum tends to have odd names for all the animals.

We have horses called Roland and Amy, pigs named Charlie and Chloe and around thirty or so cows, lambs and rabbits ranging from Betty to James and Jessica. No chickens though. I've often wanted chickens, but Mum's adamant we can't have them. Too much hard work she says.

How a little chicken can be harder to care for than a horse or cow is beyond me but that's just Mum - I'm used to abiding by her rules.

Phoenix pads over and sits next to me while I finish off my pancakes. Absently twiddling with his ears, I continue to watch Mum out the window, I can almost see a cloud of stress and worry surrounding her, as she continues to walk briskly down the lane. I don't understand what she can be so worked up about. We live the least stressful life you could ever imagine, in comparison to what I've read in books or witnessed in movies anyway. The older I've grown, the more withdrawn and stressed she's become, continuously fussing about my safety.

I imagine it's hard for her raising me alone. I barely remember my dad, we lost him when I was little, all I have left of him is a few old sweatshirts, a handful of photos and my name. Peridot was his favourite crystal and birthstone. It's a peculiar name to have; I prefer Peri, but I guess Peridot does have a nice ring to it.

Phoenix lays his head on my leg bringing me back to the present. Ann often calls me a daydreamer - my mind wanders constantly. Perhaps that's why my dreams are so vivid, I'm always overthinking things. Saving my last pancake for Phoenix, I pop it on the floor along with a handful of extra blueberries, he wolfs it down tail wagging. Joseph passes the window then, looking in expectantly; our cue to start work. Quickly rubbing on the yarrow lotion, I add my plate to the sink and grab my overalls. The lotion smells awful, but instantly soothes the ache and I'm able to stand on my foot without wincing.

"Any better?" Ann joins me, getting into overalls too.

"Miles better, the lotion smells funny though."

"Don't let your mum hear you say that," she laughs.

"That wouldn't go down too well, would it? What's been wrong with her recently? Her mood swings are getting worse."

"Don't worry about your mum dear, the full moon makes her a little skittish that's all. Shall we tend to the animals? If we start now, we should finish before lunchtime," she replies a little too quickly, popping on her gloves and then handing me a pair.

I'm aware that she's trying to change the subject but I'm grateful for the distraction and put my gloves on also. Phoenix bounds out the kitchen door barking around the various stables to wake everyone up, much to their annoyance - the animals love a lay in. I hear the horses neigh in protest causing me to chuckle out loud. Roland and Phoenix have a love-hate relationship; Phoenix takes great joy in waking him up early, purely for his enjoyment. Gleefully, he bounds back to us looking proud of himself, Ann rolls her eyes shooing him away.

Heading out back I make a start, sorting the various feeds into buckets, placing them onto the carts to wheel over to the stables. Alfalfa hay and carrots for the horses and cows, a mix of grain and veg for the pigs and sheep, then leafy greens and hay for the rabbits. Ann comes over to give a helping hand and together we wheel the cart round to the feeding areas, unlatching the stable doors, so the animals can roam and enjoy their day.

Our land goes on for acres and acres, sometimes we won't see Roland or Amy for a few days, but Ann always says not to worry they'll come back when they're ready, animals need their freedom. Joseph drives over with the compost truck, coming to a halt just short of the barn doors. We use the animal's manure to nourish the soil to grow our crops, as gross as that sounds. Mum says that people used to use chemicals which made a lot of people ill. How poop is cleaner than chemicals I struggle to grasp, but again, you must go along with Mother.

"Morning ladies, how are we today?" Joseph hollers, ruffling my hair as he passes, "I hear you had quite the adventure last night?"

"Morning Joe, news gets around fast huh?"

"It sure does when there's only four of us on the farm. Are you excited about your birthday – the big one three? Not a little girl anymore, time for you to get properly stuck in," he grunts, beginning to shovel heaps of dung onto the compost truck.

"I don't think I can get more stuck in than this," I gripe, sweat trickling down my forehead as I grab a smaller trowel to help him. Manure is so heavy!

"You wait, young lady, you're about to learn what real responsibility feels like," he grins, nudging Ann as he passes. She elbows him in the ribs a little forcefully to which he guffaws to himself. I'm not sure if Joe isn't a bit loopy like Mum, I rarely understand what he's talking about.

"What does he mean?" I ask Ann.

"Vallaeartha just has a few things she'd like to run past you after your birthday that's all, nothing to worry about."

"What kind of things?"

"Things to do with your future dear," she placates, giving me a reassuring smile.

Her response is vague at best, but I can't help but feel hopeful, maybe she's going to ask if I want to go to school. The idea of extra freedom gives me a push to work extra hard. Mum will be pleased when she gets home. My labour doesn't go unnoticed, and we're finished a good hour before lunchtime.

"Why don't you get cleaned up and have an hour to yourself before lunch, we can make a start with herbology after we've eaten," Ann suggests as we trudge back across the field towards the main house.

Heading upstairs, Phoenix at my heels, I run another shower. That's the only downside to working on the farm, it's grubby work, I'm forever caked in various forms of dirt. I think we all shower twice, maybe three times a day. We have a strict rule of no more than five minutes each, except on a weekend where we can have baths. Solar panels provide our energy, but on the winter days where we don't always have hot water, Joseph curses profoundly for all to hear at the cold. He never uses swear words, per Mum's request, and has the craziest outbursts which have us in fits of giggles. He says the most bizarre things to replace curse words.

The shower runs nice and warm today, making me smile, I do love the farm and our life, I just wish I had friends. And that Mum wasn't so moody all the time, I miss the fun we used to have when I was little. Maybe when we have our chat I can see if she'd like to do something with me this weekend. We could go riding with Roland and Amy, we've not done that since I was little and Mum loves to ride.

Stepping out of the shower, I pull on a fresh pair of trousers and jumper. March weather is still brisk, and I won't be working up a sweat like earlier. Slipping on a clean pair of socks I look for my journal. I have a few of them, Mum's always encouraged me to write, says it helps to know who you are as a person to look back and see how you used to be feeling. I find my favourite journal, a beautiful heavy bound book with a tree of life on the front, it was a birthday gift from a few years ago. Jotting down my hopes and fears, I lose myself in thought, and before I know it twenty minutes have passed.

Finishing up, I go to put my journal next to my dream diary, realising suddenly, it must still be by the pond. I'll have to run down and get it. Grey clouds are forming outside, and no way am I losing all the months' worth of dreams I've jotted down. I call out for Phoenix as I head back downstairs, I'm not going alone again even in the daytime, Mum would completely freak out and I don't want to get Ann in trouble.

"Ann, I'm just going for a walk with Phoenix before lunch, is that okay?" I ask.

"Sure, just make sure you're back by one-thirty, we have tomato and basil soup with granary rolls in the oven," she replies in between chopping tomatoes. My tummy rumbles in response, this morning worked up an appetite.

"Okay, I won't be long. Come on Phoenix, walkies!"

Phoenix jumps up nearly knocking me over and bounds out the door, while I jog to keep up with him. He veers towards the stables with mischief in his eyes.

"No Phoenix, we're going to the pond," I holler after him, he does a U-turn, tearing past me towards the trees, much to the relief of Roland, who I can tell saw him coming. He trots over to me whinnying in Phoenix's direction.

"I know, he's pesky to you, isn't he?" I soothe, stroking his long mane.

We've had him for as long as I can remember, a beautiful black stallion, so tall he towers over me. Amy ambles over swiftly joining us, the two are inseparable. She is the complete opposite in comparison to Roland, a brilliant bright white horse with a light blonde mane. She looks like a unicorn minus the magickal horn. She stares daggers at Phoenix, who's barking for me to follow him. Giving Roland and Amy a quick peck on their noses, I hurry after him.

We trek through the tree's, Phoenix stopping to sniff at every other bush and shrub, leaving his scent sporadically as we go. Dogs sure are strange, I'm glad we don't do that. A little further into the woods, we come to the clearing, the pond sparkles under the midday glimmers of the sun as clouds pass over. It's completely different in the day, just as beautiful, but no longer the inky blue-black, instead, crystal-clear water with greenery on all sides. Coming to a halt, I begin to look for my dream dairy. Where on earth has it got to? I know I didn't have it when I ran away.

Thinking back to last night, the memory of snapping twigs and the strange gasps come back to resurface, I hadn't given it much thought since. I wonder if my mind was playing tricks on me where it was dark. Suddenly, Phoenix stops and growls startling me. This is very out of character; I don't think I've ever seen Phoenix growl before - he looks scary. The hair down his spine stands on end, going a deeper shade of burnt gold, his top lips curls baring his bright white, strikingly sharp teeth. He sniffs the air, finds something, and pads towards one of the trees, his growl getting deeper with every step.

"What is it, boy?" I whisper, trying not to let fear show in my voice. I know I'm safe with Phoenix, but I've never seen him act like this and I have no clue as to what he's growling at. Maybe someone or something really was here last night.

"Hello," I call out, "Is anyone there?"

Phoenix barks and I back away, he keeps looking at a certain spot in the trees and I begin to feel afraid.

"Phoenix let's go," I whisper-yell, my diary will have to wait. I can ask one of the others to find it for me. He ignores my request, turning back towards the trees, jumping up at the base of a large bark, still growling deeply. There's an audible sound of surprise and something crashes to the ground with a loud thud causing me to yelp in fright.

That's it, I'm out of here.

"Phoenix let's go *now*!" I yell, hurriedly backing away from the trees and back towards home. Phoenix gives a final bark behind me, a quick peek over my shoulder finds him ambling along at my heels, my dream diary enclosed in his teeth.

"Good boy!" I praise, shakily retrieving it from his jaws. That must've been what fell from the tree. I keep running until we reach the fence, climbing over carefully, not wanting a repeat of last night. I feel safer knowing Phoenix is with me, but still completely freaked out. Someone is at the pond. No doubt in my mind, that was a human sound I heard. Who could be hiding on our land and why? And what's more, why did they have my diary? I curse myself for being a wimp, I should've stayed and spoken to them, I wasn't alone, Phoenix was with me, I probably would've been safe. It wasn't worth the risk, I reassure myself, Mum's always warning me how dangerous strangers can be, they could've been robbers or something.

As the thought registers, panic returns. What do I do? Do I tell Ann? I can't, she'll tell Mum and I'll be on lockdown forever. I'm so close to my birthday and a chance of freedom I cannot, *will not* risk ruining that. Maybe they're just passing through, they could be gone tomorrow? Nervously, I try to convince myself. We're nearly back at the kitchen when Phoenix stops to look back, he's itching to go back and do more barking.

"It's okay Phoenix you scared them off," I whisper, his tail wags feebly in response, but he doesn't stop looking towards the trees, a subtle whine audible above the rustling of leaves in the wind. I can't risk Ann or Joseph following him, I need to distract him.

"Biscuits!" I bribe, in my most animated voice. His head turns in my direction - it works every time, his tail wagging genuinely as he follows me in, all thoughts of intruders lost to the thought of homemade rich teas. I make myself comfy at the kitchen table and pile Phoenix's bowl to the brim to keep him occupied, just as Ann re-enters the kitchen.

"You're back quick, how was your walk?"

"Just what I needed," I manage to smile, "the clouds are greying though, didn't fancy getting soaked again, I've already had two showers today."

She nods in response while dishing up three steaming bowls of soup with crusty bread rolls. I breathe in deeply, the smell of freshly chopped tomatoes and basil making my mouth water.

"Good cooking love," Joseph approves loudly, trudging in from the fields. Taking two bread rolls, he plonks himself down at the table and proceeds to break one into bite-sized chunks that he swirls around in his soup with a spoon. The other he breaks in half, dipping generously in the soup before dropping it into Phoenix's bowl, which I note is already licked clean of biscuits, not a crumb remaining.

"Mm-mmm," he sighs blissfully, "nobody can cook like the Mrs."

He kisses Ann's cheek as she passes, causing her to giggle girlishly in response. I stare momentarily transfixed. They are undeniably in love. Even after forty years of marriage, they remind me of love-struck teens. Ann's light brown skin hides her age well, in contrast to Joe's almost grey-white tones, showing every crease and crinkle as he smiles boyishly in her direction. She continues to grin from his display of affection, as I busy my head in my soup to avoid staring. It's nice seeing two people so at ease and in love with each other, but it makes me sad my dad isn't here. Sipping my soup quietly, I try to stop my thoughts spiralling as they often do when I think of Dad. Joe's appreciative slurps from across the table do the trick and I stifle a laugh as his slurps turn to chomps and he begins inhaling what's left of his bread roll. Joe's eating habits are very vocal, a pet peeve of Mum's, who rarely eats at the table with us due to her disdain of his noises.

"Not hungry my man?" he asks Phoenix, who hasn't touched his roll. Phoenix looks towards the door then back up at Joe and whines. As he does this, Joe drops his spoon splattering hot soup everywhere.

"Cat's whiskers!!" he curses, jumping up and down like his legs are on fire. Ann and I try to hide our giggles as the giant of a man with his wild grey hair leaps around the kitchen like a leprechaun, cursing absurdly all the way to the sink where he proceeds to splash his lap with cold water.

"Pfft," he grumbles, "can't even enjoy a bowl of soup without something needing tending to, we need more men in this rumble stripping house!" he proclaims wildly before stomping out of the kitchen.

"Well, come on then, are you going to show me what's so blooming important or what?!" he shouts. Ann and I exchange a confused glance, until Phoenix bounds out of the door, barking animatedly at Joe as he trudges after him. Ann looks anxious for a moment, then catches me watching and busies herself with her soup again.

"Silly boys," she laughs half-heartedly, stealing glances out the window when she thinks I'm not looking.

This is normal behaviour for Joe, so I'm not concerned. He often speaks to the animals like he understands them. I've walked in on him having a full-blown conversation with Roland many a time, he always stops when he sees me, no doubt embarrassed - but he needn't be, I talk to the animals myself constantly. I just don't pretend they can talk back. I used to when I was little, but I'm getting too old for make-believe now. Maybe I'll start again when I get older like Joe, perhaps he gets lonely here too. He's always going on about how we need men at the farm, but Mum refuses.

Sipping the remnants of soup, I continue to watch Joe pacing behind Phoenix through the window, they reach the fence leading to the woods and I try not to worry. He can take Joe to the pond, but no one knows I was there again so I can't get in trouble. The chances of Phoenix telling him are impossible - he's an animal it's not like he can talk.

THIRTEEN

Three days pass with no more oddities taking place. The farm runs smoothly, other than one incident with one of the lambs and a rabbit. They have acres of land to roam yet seem to prefer to congregate together, which often results in 'squabbles' as Ann calls them. One particular squabble got rather heated, and I had to remove Eugene the rabbit off Crystal the sheep's ear. Crystal had a nasty bite, and I got a mean nibble in the crossfire. Mum tended to both of us whilst nagging me to let them sort it out themselves. Rabbits can be vicious when they want to be, and sheep are more than capable of looking after themselves apparently.

I wake to the sun shining through my window which is rare for March and a grin spreads across my face. Todays the day. The big one-three as Joseph said. I'm going to ask Mum if I can go to school! Phoenix bounds into my room, his tail wagging feverishly as he leaps onto my mattress, smothering me with licks.

"Phoenix enough, enough!" I squeal, ducking under the covers. He goes to the foot of the bed, sneaks his nose underneath, shimmying up to my face still licking like mad. I buckle over in giggles until he gives me room to breathe and give him a hug, "thanks boy, I love you too."

Shuffling out from under the covers I throw comfy clothes on - I'm not expecting any chores today. Mum seems to have forgiven my late-night stroll and has agreed to let me have the day off. I'll wait until we're alone before I ask her about school. Running a brush through my hair I nip to the bathroom, freshen up then skip down the stairs, Phoenix at my heels.

"Good morning birthday girl!" Ann and Joseph welcome in unison, a plate of pancakes stacked high in Ann's hands and a gift messily wrapped in tissue paper in Joe's.

"Thanks, guys," I grin, taking a seat at the table.

"Tuck into these beauties and then we can do presents," beams Joe, ruffling my hair affectionately before passing me the sugar. I go overboard and sprinkle a generous spoonful, skipping the fruit and grabbing dark chocolate spread and chopped nuts. Joe waits until I'm done, gives me a wink then does the same. Ann tuts as we scoff away, sitting down to help herself to a bowl of assorted fruits to add to her porridge.

"I'll have to start calling you gummy if you lose any more teeth," she scolds Joe.

"I don't miss dentists that's for sure," he laughs, chomping away loudly. I wonder to myself what a dentist is as Mum walks in smiling. She surprises me by wrapping her arms around my waist and kissing my cheek,

"Happy birthday sweetheart," she pops a beautiful handmade wicker basket of boxes wrapped intricately in bows onto the table. My eyes widen with joy, I wasn't expecting this.

"Thanks, Mum," my eyes unexpectedly well up with tears as I turn to give her a big hug, burying my head into her midriff.

"Can we spend the day together still?" I ask hopefully, she's barely been home the past few days, staying out late at night, I've heard her getting into bed gone midnight.

"Most definitely," Mum surprises me again. "I have lots to show you now you've come of age."

Before I have time to ponder what she means, the kitchen door opens, Roland and Amy gracefully ducking their large manes into the kitchen. Mum tends not to let animals come into the house, other than Phoenix that is. I remember when I was little, Amy used to try and sneak up the stairs to sleep in my room. I'd hear Ann sneaking her back downstairs so Mum wouldn't wake up and tell her off.

"How do you always know when it's my birthday?" I muse, jumping down from the breakfast table to give them a hug. I wrap my arms around them both, squeezing warmly. They whinny softly and I get a playful nudge from Roland in the ribs, tugging on his tail in response Amy whinnies excitedly, ready to play.

"Not in the house!" Mum intervenes.

Roland and Amy neigh in protest, causing her to huff in exasperation, hands on her hips giving them the look. Roland seems to stare right back at Mum in defiance whilst Amy trots back outside. I head back over to the breakfast table disappointed when she surprises me yet again.

"Let's go for a gallop, shall we?" she proclaims, mounting Roland and patting his side with gusto.

"Jumping jellyfish!" Joe jumps in surprise as Roland doesn't need telling twice, wildly hurtling out of the kitchen, upheaving a mass destruction of dishes in their wake.

"What in the name of?" Joe's jaw drops open as Roland canters at the speed of light, nearing the end of our drive within seconds. Amy bounds back in excitedly, lowering her mane for me to hop on. I don't have the grace of Mum, clambering on awkwardly, but we catch up in no time, Amy's hooves cantering even faster than Roland until we're side by side. Mum grins over at me, calling wildly into the wind, I follow suit, my hair a hurricane, Phoenix at our heels, all of us galloping as one. I laugh with glee, it's the perfect moment, just like we'd do when I was little, although admittedly never this fast. Amy and Roland run so fast my eyes stream. Phoenix begins to lag as we keep going, galloping past the stream, across two meadows and down to the furthest point of our land. A few minutes further, we begin to slow, lightly trotting next to each other, Roland and Amy bumping noses and whinnying softly.

"Not done that in some time, have we?" smiles Mum breathlessly, reaching over to pat my leg.

"I'll say," I grin, "that was amazing!"

I look at a picture in my comfy wear, struggling to stay balanced on the beautiful unicorn-like creature that is Amy. I glance at Mum who in comparison looks like a Goddess, dark hair nearly to her waist, an excited glint in her deep green eyes. We reach the end of our land, trotting to an area I've not passed before. Gazing out across the land, I realise we're nearing the coastline. As we turn the bend I gasp. We've come to a steep cliff overlooking the sea. It's breathtakingly beautiful.

"Wow," I breathe.

"Something else, isn't it?" Mum beams. "I've wanted to bring you here ever since you were little, I'd watch you sneak off to the pond and wish I could show you the sea," she reveals sadly, causing me to look up in surprise.

"You knew I was going to the pond at night?"

"Peridot you're a Pisces, it's in your nature to love water. I send Phoenix out to watch over you when you go for one of your 'secret' strolls after dark, you're not as sneaky as you think," she rolls her eyes making me squirm uncomfortably.

"Why didn't you stop me?"

"I feel bad that you're cooped up on the farm all the time, I know it's hard for you. I knew if I let you venture out too far to somewhere like this, you'd end up sneaking off here alone. It's okay when Phoenix can follow you but say he wasn't around like the other night, you hurt your foot badly, if that had been here you could've died - you nearly hit an artery. I know you find it hard to believe, but I really do keep you on the farm for your safety."

I'm quiet as I let her words sink in. I can't believe she knew I went out after dark so often and simply sent Phoenix to watch over me. Phoenix! I think suddenly, the traitor, I bet it was him hiding in the woods that day. No, it couldn't have been, he was with me the second time and the noise sounded human...

"Peridot?"

Mum's voice startles me, I was lost in thought again.

"Sorry. I was just thinking if you knew I was going out at night, why didn't you talk to me about it?"

"Everyone's allowed some secrets," she replies eyes wandering uncomfortably, "that's sort of what I need to speak to you about. There's a lot I want to share with you, I've been waiting until you were old enough to tell you. Shall we go open your presents and we can have a proper chat about it all later?" she asks tentatively.

"Sure, there are things I want to ask you too," I nod, thinking about school.

Now that she's admitted she feels bad about me being alone, I'm hopeful that's what she wants to talk to me about. She gives me a slightly nervous, encouraging smile and turns Roland towards home. She trots ahead, Amy and I following behind at a gentler pace, much to my relief as my bottom is starting to feel sore. As we near our land, I notice Phoenix pacing by the end of the fence. He barks at Mum animatedly.

"Oh, shush, she's perfectly safe with me," she exasperates as he rushes past her, jumping up at Amy to lick my leg.

"Sorry boy, were we too fast for you?" I tease. He follows us back home and doesn't leave my side until we get back to the breakfast table. Joe looks up as we enter, still attempting to clean the mess of dishes that litter the floor.

"Leave it, Joe, I'll get everything tidied up while Peridot's in the shower." Mum glances at me, "We'll finish up breakfast and then we can do presents, how does that sound?"

I beam back at her in response, before thundering up the stairs, two at a time and careering into the bathroom. Stepping into the shower, I lick my lips and savour the saltiness from the sea breeze, I'm so excited to have a whole day with Mum and to ask about going to school. I wonder what she wants to talk to me about, as the warm water washes over my body. I can't believe she'd been letting me go out after dark all this time and only freaking out when Phoenix wasn't following me. She puts a lot of trust in a dog, it's not like as if something had happened, he could tell her.

I step out of the shower, quickly dry off, pulling on black shorts, a cream jumper, and my favourite over-worn slippers. As it's my birthday, I make an extra effort and apply one of Mum's lip balms and add a sparkly clip to my hair then head back downstairs.

"Oh Dot! You're a little lady already," Ann gushes fondly, passing me the present from her and Joe, "we hope you like it."

I unwrap the paper to find a framed picture enclosed. It's a picture I've not seen before, it's of me as a baby, in between Mum and Dad. I don't know what to say. It's lovely. Mum and Dad look so happy, I'm smiling up at them, while they look down at me adoringly. The frame is a beautiful white with deep blue flowers around the edges.

"Joe carved the frame for you earlier this week, it took me a while, but I found the picture hiding away, I knew I had it somewhere. I painted the frame your favourite colour."

"It's beautiful I love it," I sniff, my eyes brimming with unexpected tears. Joe passes me a tissue.

"Your Dad would've wanted you to have it," he replies earnestly, giving my shoulders a rub.

"You knew my father?" I look at him surprised.

Mum walks in then and gives Joe a look, he shuffles away uncomfortably, opting not to answer as Ann gives me a quick hug.

"Have a nice day with your mother dear, we'll see you tonight for supper."

She heads outside, avoiding Mum's eyes, Joe claps me on the back following after her, Phoenix in toe.

"Shall we finish breakfast? That gallops left me famished," Mum suggests over-cheery. Her smile is forced and not the genuine grin that she had earlier this morning, I know it's hard for her to see Dad, so I pop the frame face down on the table and nod.

"Jam?" she asks, handing me a plate of freshly toasted crumpets. Greedily, I take three, we were only gone for an hour, but riding works up an appetite. Especially when our horses can run like the wind. Spreading on a large dollop of homemade apricot jam, I sigh in contentment.

"That was your dad's favourite too," Mum muses over at me, her smile genuine this time.

"Really?" I smile back. I like talking about Dad. It's so rare that we do.

"Oh yes," she nods, "well, that or a bacon sandwich." She pops her hand to her mouth suddenly, like she's said a curse word or bit her tongue.

"What's bacon?" I ask, ignoring the startled jump, I assume she's burnt her mouth on her crumpet, they are steaming hot. I chomp on mine with my mouth slightly open to let air cool them down.

"Eat nicely Peri," she scolds, nudging my chin.

"I don't want to burn my tongue like you just did," I explain, swallowing hurriedly. Mum looks awkward for a moment, then shakes it off.

"The thing you just asked, is kind of what I need to talk to you about, so I guess it's a good thing it slipped out," she assents.

I'm lost. Mum hardly ever speaks about Dad anymore and when she does, she ends up getting upset or cross. I try to change the subject, not wanting anything to ruin the first moment of quality time we've had together in what feels like forever. "What, bacon? Or eating properly?" I joke.

"A bit of both if I'm being honest," she grimaces.

I stop eating to look at her, baffled by the response when Joe bursts unexpectedly through the kitchen door.

"Val! Come quick, some of the rabbits are hurt, someone's on our land," he thunders past the table, rummaging under the sink and comes out with a strange metal device I've not seen before. Mum jumps up immediately, throws off her shawl, rolls up her sleeves and runs to the door.

"Peri, stay in the kitchen, promise me you will not move from that table!" she instructs, eyes wild, a fierce look on her face as she pulls out what looks like a wooden stick from her sleeve.

"Peridot promise me!" Mum shouts.

"Yes, I - I promise!" I stutter in shock. I've never seen Mum react like this. Joe's already darted back outside as Roland and Grace canter over.

"Everything's going to be fine I promise, please just stay here so I know you're safe, I'll be right back," she insists less aggressively, swinging her leg up and over Amy. Joe mounts Roland with such ease, I would not expect that for a man of his age. His back leg slams the kitchen door shut just as Phoenix bounds in, the door narrowly missing his tail as it closes. I hear them gallop off, as I rush to the window, Phoenix, barks and stands in front of me on all fours. I swear he's telling me to sit down.

"I'm not going outside, I just want to see what's going on," I gripe, my eyes tearing up. Why would we have intruders? I can't imagine anything we have on the farm that would be worth stealing, maybe some of Mum's supplies, her crystals perhaps?

It hits me then. The noises in the woods! What if that was the intruder? I collapse down onto the floor, tears rolling down my cheeks. I'll never forgive myself if any of the animals are hurt, I shouldn't have kept it a secret. I bet that was them hiding, waiting for the right moment. Mum's remedy barn, with all the supplies and crystals, is right next to the rabbits, I bet they got in the way of them breaking in and injured themselves in the process.

I start to hyperventilate, crying freely when Phoenix pads over and sits solemnly beside me. Bringing his face close to mine, he nudges my cheek making me look at him. I meet his gaze, as he leans his nose against mine. A sense of calm washes over me as I stare into his golden eyes. They are ever so beautiful. Like looking into the sun, but without the glare. My mind wanders as I picture a sun setting, my body feels warm and cosy, then oddly, I'm content. I try to fight it, yet sleep finds me.

"Peri, are you okay?" Mum's voice stirs me from a distance. Opening my eyes, I find Phoenix curled up at my feet, his head resting upon my lap. Noticing the time, it's nearly three in the afternoon. I must've fallen asleep as over four hours have passed. Slowly rising, I take a moment to get my bearings, the panic from earlier resurfaces.

"What happened?" I exclaim, jumping unsteadily to my feet, causing Phoenix to wake. Mum wraps her arm around my shoulders, pulling me into a hug.

"Everything's fine, someone came onto our land and tried to break into my supplies, a few of the rabbits were hurt but they're okay now."

"It's all my fault!" I cry, feeling awful. The animals are hurt because of me. Why didn't I tell anyone about the noises in the woods? I've kept it a secret too long, it's time to come clean.

"Don't be silly Peridot, it's not your fault," Mum soothes, stroking my hair.

"You don't understand - that night by the pond, I heard someone in the trees, it's why I got hurt, I ran back afraid!"

"Why didn't you tell me?" Mum stops stroking my hair abruptly to look at me. I squirm uncomfortably at the wrath that's undoubtedly to come, but I'm telling her the truth - even if it does get me in trouble. If I hadn't kept it from her in the first place, none of this would've happened.

"I was scared if I told you, you'd not let me out and I really want to go to school. I love the farm, but I'm so lonely, I want to have friends and I was scared if I told you, you'd never let me leave again," I prattle out amongst sobs as the dam bursts.

Her features remain static, it's impossible to know what she's thinking at my emotional outburst. I flinch inwardly, awaiting the shouts to start, but after what feels like forever, she puts her arm back around my shoulders and leans her head into mine.

"Oh Peri, why does everything have to be so darn difficult?" she utters.

Not the response I was expecting so I remain quiet, aware that her question was more to herself than me. After a moment she rises and begins to pace, wringing her hands nervously as she does. I'm almost stunned into silence. She looks more nervous than I feel, what is she so anxious about? After an eternity of pacing back and forth, she turns to face me.

"I knew this day was coming, I just don't know how to make this work without losing you," she sighs.

46

I don't understand what she means so remain mute. Perhaps she's worried that if I go to school, I won't be at home very often anymore.

"Give me a few days to make some arrangements and we'll figure something out," she concedes, causing an unexpected smile to spread across my face.

"Really? You mean it? I can go to school?" I squeal.

"Let's try and salvage what's left of your birthday, for now, we'll work something out soon, I promise," she replies.

It's vague, but it's not a no, and she's promised she'll sort something. She may be overprotective and drive me round the twist, but I don't think she'd break a promise to me. Warily, I go in for a hug which she reciprocates, holding me tightly. Ann returns then, noticing our embrace and begins tidying things that don't need to be tidied, so as not to interrupt our moment.

"How about a movie?" Mum suggests, pulling back, tears threatening to fall from her eyes also. "You choose a film, I'll rustle up some popcorn and after we can make burritos for dinner, how does that sound?"

I beam happily, that sounds perfect to me. Leaving Mum in the kitchen with Ann, I head to the lounge to find a movie. I select my favourite. An old movie called Matilda. It's about a little girl with special powers, who wants more than anything to have friends and go to school. I can relate to that. Except for the special powers anyway.

Mum joins me moments later with a bowl overflowing with popcorn, Ann with drinks and Phoenix with blankets, causing me to chuckle. I take it he wants to cuddle up on the sofa. I settle in the middle, Mum on one side, Ann on the other and Phoenix sprawled out across the three of us. Any thoughts of the intruder from earlier are forgotten as I become engrossed in the movie, dreaming of going to school and making friends just like Matilda does. Joe pops his head in as the final scene ends, the credits rolling down the screen.

"That girly mush all over and done with?" he teases, "what's for tea I'm starved?"

Heading into the kitchen, Mum makes my favourite, mixed bean burritos with salsa and fried rice. She piles high bowls of spiced beans, steaming fried rice, tomato and onion salsa and a mixed leaf salad. Passing round wraps and spoons we greedily help ourselves, each of our wraps overflowing heartily. I'm still on my first wrap as Joe tucks into his third, wolfing it down with approving chomps and snorts. I can sense Mum resisting the urge to tell him off as his chomps get louder, fully aware he can eat freely tonight without the wrath of Mum or Ann.

"Don't you just love birthdays?" he guffaws, snorting a bean across the table. I burst out laughing as Mum and Ann both look utterly repulsed but end up laughing too.

"You're an animal!" Ann declares.

"I've been called worse," he retorts eyeing Phoenix, who turns his back to the table.

"Sorry Phoenix, a figure of speech," Ann noticeably blushes. I roll my eyes to myself, it's not like he has any idea what they're saying. I pop the last half of my second burrito on a plate for him and he gobbles it up, admittedly, much nicer than Joe ate his.

Ann begins to clear away the table, as the lights dim suddenly, the room going into darkness. After the hubbub with the intruder this morning I nearly fall off my chair in shock, until the sound of three people very poorly warbling the happy birthday song quietens any fears. Thirteen candles glow brightly atop a large chocolate birthday cake. My mouth waters at the scent, the candles causing the icing to melt, a gooey chocolate aroma fragrant in the air. The Happy Birthday song comes to an end, and I make a wish, blowing out all thirteen candles with one breath, hoping more than anything for my wish to come true. The lights return and I admire the masterpiece, the cake is a chocolate sponge, layered between fruity ganache with chocolate icing and strawberries decorating the top. Mum serves us all a generous slice, Phoenix included, and we all make various yummy noises.

A comfortable silence follows as we all revel in our individual stuffed-ness. The madness from earlier that day forgotten. I let my mind wander as to what Mum will arrange for my schooling, I have no idea where the nearest school is. Maybe that's what she meant about losing me, but I'm sure Ann won't mind taking me or in time, if she'd let me, I could ride with Roland or Amy, I could cut across country that way. I'm nervous and excited about what my new routine will be. A yawn escapes my lips as I start to feel sleepy.

"Peri - we forgot to open your presents!" Mum exclaims, rising to get the wicker basket of goodies from earlier. It lands with an audible thud upon the table.

"Merlin's beard! What've you got in there? A basket of rocks?" excites Joe, coming up behind me to poke around. I fly swat his hand away.

"Yes, of sorts," Mum smiles, a twinkle in her eye, "quick open them up," she slides the basket closer towards me.

As I peer in, I notice the time she's put into decorating the basket, each item wrapped in its own tissue paper and intricately made bows, little flowers placed delicately here and there, with singular crystals poking out.

"It's beautiful, thank you so much," I gush, knowing she's put so much effort into the basket.

"Today's a very special birthday Peridot, thirteen is a magickal number," she replies. "Had to make it extra special for you."

I resist the urge to roll my eyes at her wacky beliefs, the moment feels magickal, so in a way, I guess she's right. I take out the crystals and put them aside to add to my collection. I get an assortment each year and have great fun going through Mum's old books, working out which ones she's given me. Next, I get to unwrapping. Mum's gone overboard this year and each present gets a bigger smile than the last. A set of pyjamas, fluffy socks, new slippers, an assortment of hair clips, a tea mug, (freshly made on the kiln), a new journal, and a selection of homemade lotions, ointments, and tinctures.

Coming to the last three presents, each present is wrapped in my favourite colour, a beautiful sea blue with little silver stars drawn on. The first of the three special presents is a beautiful black gown, floor-length with a hooded cape. It feels so soft, I can't wait to try it on. The second is an elongated length of carved wood, with bloodstone and peridots embedded into the handle. Running my hands over the intricate craftsmanship, I'm dumbfounded as to what it is supposed to be but marvel at its patterns, feeling an overwhelming sense of purpose flow through me. I've never felt anything like it. I catch my mum looking at Ann and Joe proudly. I go to ask what it's used for, when she passes me the last present, interrupting my train of thought.

"This is from me and your dad," she unveils, causing me to fall silent, "I've been keeping it safe since you were little," she explains.

I gently unfold the wrapping to find a delicate silver necklace, an aquamarine, emerald and peridot pendant dangling from the chain. It twinkles under the light and my eyes glisten, as tears threaten to fall.

"Oh, Mum. It's gorgeous." I utter breathlessly.

"It is, isn't it?" she smiles, undoing the clasp and fastening it securely around my neck.

"It has special properties designed to keep you safe. Emerald from me with the strength of Taurus to protect you, Peridot from your Father with the logic of Virgo to keep you on your path, and lastly your birthstone, Aqua Marine empowers all the qualities of Pisces, your empathy, intuition, and love for others will be your Inner compass. Wear this necklace always and it'll guide you as you grow older."

I don't quite understand what I need all that for, but I will wear the necklace gladly nonetheless, it's beautiful and I'll cherish it always.

I am officially worn out, as Ann and Joe head outside to put the animals to bed, they wish me one last 'happy birthday' and Mum helps me upstairs with the basket of goodies. After changing into my new pyjamas, I add my new crystals to my windowsill to charge them under the moonlight. I catch Mum smiling,

"See I do listen. Moonlight and sunlight re-charges their energy," I roll off matter-of-factly, as Mum has told me countless times before. She chuckles, coming to tuck me in, placing my presents into the top drawer of my bedside table.

"Always keep these safe Peridot," she gestures to the gown, ointments and elongated wooden ornament.

"What do they all do?" I yawn, sleep almost upon me.

"Think of them as your survival kit and I'll start showing you how to use them soon, I wanted to today but never mind, it'll all come in time."

I have no idea what she means and am too tired to ask more questions, so simply nod my head sleepily.

"Thanks for the presents, I love them Mum," I tell her, my eyes closing before my head hits the pillow. Sleep finds me instantly, I'm out like a light.

INTRUDER

I awake groggily from a deep slumber to a strange sound. I was having another of my dreams, a nice one to begin with. I'd been riding with Mum under the stars, across fields in full bloom, a rainbow of colours shooting past the thundering of hooves, eventually coming to halt at my favourite place, under the old oak tree. I laid with Mum feeling safe in her arms when the dream turned sour. A murder of crows began circling above, screeching loudly before plummeting towards us in an array of soot-black feathers. The largest swooped straight at me, pecking the bark frantically trying to tell me something, only just as the message became clear – I woke up. I shake my head trying to remember the words embedded into the bark but it's no use. The message is gone, the dream has left me flustered, it was so vivid, almost real.

I fumble around for my dream diary, wanting to note the dream down before it evades my memory as dreams so often do. As my eyes adjust to the darkness, I can still hear the noise that woke me, a light tapping on my window. A tree must've fallen in the wind, I hear it howling wildly. We're used to dramatic weather changes on the farm. We're still experiencing the after-effects of something called climate change says Mum but it's getting back to normal, and the weather changes will cease over time. I go to open my curtains and remove the fallen branch that's wrap-a-tat-tatting on the windowpane, only to fall back in shock.

There's a boy at my window.

A real, breathing, dark-haired, little boy.

Rubbing my eyes, I pinch myself to make sure I'm not still dreaming. Ouch - that hurts! My mouth hangs wide open in disbelief. I'm awake. This is real. There's a very wet, very skinny, very scared looking boy at my window. Without thinking, I scramble over and quietly as I can I undo the latch, cold brisk morning air seeps into my bedroom causing me to shiver. The boy's teeth are chattering, his cheeks are sunken, he looks positively awful. I don't know what to do. Or to say. I've never met another child before.

"H- Hi," I stammer.

He looks at me curiously, and replies in kind, "Hi."

We stare at each other for what feels like forever but must be moments. His teeth continue to chatter, and I realise with a start that I need to help him, urgently. His eyes are hollow, face gaunt, his frame painfully skinny, it's a wonder he's still standing through the gale that billows wildly outside.

"Can you climb in?" I whisper.

He looks at me in surprise for a moment, then slowly nods his head. Opening the window fully, I help him clamber inside, taking his weight as he struggles to lift himself up and over. He barely weighs a thing. He lands on the floor with a light thud, hoping the wind drowned out any noise, I hurriedly close the window. I want to get him warm and comfy before I wake the others, I have a feeling he'll be afraid of Mum as she's almost certainly going to freak out.

I grab the duvet off my bed and wrap it around him, tucking every body part in as best I can, hands, feet, right up to his chin. I take in his appearance as I do. He's covered in cuts, bruises and caked in mud. And really smells. I realise with a start, that what looks like crusted mud tangled in his hair could easily be something else, he positively reeks. Trying to withstand the stench and not be rude, I turn on my bedside lamp and pour him a glass of water from the jug on my nightstand.

"What's your name?" I ask tentatively.

He looks down and doesn't reply, but takes the glass of water, gulping it down frantically. I refill the glass for him, "would you like some food?"

He's barely able to keep his eyes open, but he nods slowly, looking at the floor and completely avoiding eye contact. It dawns on me that this boy is afraid of me. I don't understand who he is, how he got here, or how he's in the state he's in, but I want to help him, so I don't pry. I do what Ann does when I go into myself and let him be.

"My name is Peridot," I whisper, slowly getting up and heading towards the door, "I'm going to get you some food, you're safe now," I tell him.

He looks up, finally gaining eye contact. His eyes are a brilliant blue, I'm transfixed for a moment by how beautiful they are, in contrast to the rest of him.

"Please, don't get the witch," he requests fearfully.

I'm stunned for a moment and don't know what to say. This boy has clearly been through something truly terrible.

"I'm going to get you food and then I'm going to help you get better, there are no witches here," I assure him.

Putting the weird comment down to fear and exhaustion, I quickly, quietly as I can, dart downstairs, returning moments later with a loaf of bread and some of Ann's leftover soup. I can't risk heating it and waking anyone, he'll have to have it cold.

I hand him the loaf along with the bowl of soup and he wolfs it down vigorously. I go to shush him as he chomps loud enough to give Joe a run for his money, but then stop myself, as the duvet falls, and I see his frame. He's a bag of bones. I can see his ribs through his top and his arms are skinnier than mine. A startled sound of shock leaves my lips before I can stop myself. The boy looks up, pulling the duvet back up.

"Sorry," he begins to cover up.

"What happened to you?" I ask, unable to contain the horror in my voice.

"I escaped," he states simply.

"I don't understand, escaped from where?"

He stays silent, focusing all his attention on the nearly empty bowl of soup. Trying not to pry too deeply I ask again. "How did you get like this, where are your family?"

"My mum is in captivity, I tried to free her too, but I couldn't, so I ran," he shrugs, not elaborating further.

It's then that he stops eating and tears escape his eyes. I don't know what to say or do. In captivity from who? And where? There's so much I want to ask him, but I don't want to make things any worse, so I don't. I simply sit with him and let him be. It's what I'd want if I was in his condition.

"Thanks," he sniffs, his breathing evening out, "I'll leave soon, I just had to get out of the storm, I was so cold."

"No!" I exclaim, a little too loudly, "I mean, you can't go, you need to rest and get better, my mum's a healer. Try to get some sleep and I'll get her to come to see you in the morning. We'll take care of you."

The boy looks at me with fear in his eyes and tries to get up, "No, not the witch!" he stands, making his way to the window, tripping and falling on the duvet as he does, landing with an audible thud.

It's then that Phoenix crashes into the room on delayed high alert, coming to an abrupt halt as he sees the boy. The hair on his spine arches in a line, his lips curling over his teeth as he surveys him upon the floor.

"Easy boy," I coo, stroking down his fur until he softens, seeming to understand that the boy isn't a threat, but remaining wary non the less. I expect the boy to whimper or cower in fear at Phoenix, but he sits up straight, looks resolutely at him and asks peculiarly, "what's your name?"

I can't help but giggle out loud. Turning away, I put my hand over my mouth to stop laughing. The poor boy, he's delirious, he needs sleep. I really should go and get Mum. I hear Phoenix making what sounds like growling noises at him and go to tell him to stop when the boy continues.

"Hi, Phoenix, I'm Euan."

I look at him in surprise.

"How'd you know his name?"

"He just told me - didn't you hear him?"

I look at Phoenix in bewilderment as he sits next to who I now know to be Euan and starts to sniff him. It's then that it sinks in. The gasp in the woods. The intruder on the farm. It's him. It's Euan.

"You're the one who took my dream diary!" I exclaim "And tried to break in yesterday?"

He looks down nervously, cementing my suspicion. I'm a little relieved if I'm honest - there were no burglars, just a hurt boy looking for shelter. He must've heard me talking to Phoenix, when we went back to get the diary that time. That's why he's so wet and muddy, he must've been camped out by the pond! I try to ignore that Euan is now having a one-sided conversation with Phoenix and decide it's time to wake the adults. Euan is in a bad way and needs help, I have no idea how to use the kit Mum got me for my birthday, I'll have to go get her. I back away slowly so as not to startle Euan further, but stumble into none other than my mum as I do so.

"What on earth is all this racket?" She asks, hands on her hips, looking truly ticked off at being woken so early.

"Erm ... Mum ... meet Euan," I step aside so she can see the boy.

She gasps in shock, whilst Euan looks quite positively terrified at her presence. He darts up trying to get out the window, but Phoenix pulls him back down firmly, teeth in his tattered clothing. He stands protectively in front of the boy looking directly at Mum. I'm shocked as he starts to growl.

"Oh, shush Phoenix, don't be ridiculous," Mum scolds moving towards Euan, placing a hand on his head. Euan cowers away in fear, but she doesn't back away. She removes the duvet and surveys him from head to toe, whispering under her breath incoherently as she does.

"Peri run along and get Ann please - I'll need her help."

"No! Don't leave me with her!" Euan cries out. "Please!" I feel bad, I know Mum can be scary, but he's genuinely petrified, something truly awful must've happened to him for him to react like this.

"I'll be right back I promise, Phoenix will stay with you. Mum's the best healer in the world, don't be scared," I dart from the room before he has time to reply, dashing down to Ann and Joe's cottage on the side of the main house as quick as my legs can carry me.

"What on earth is the matter dear?" asks Ann as she sleepily opens the cottage door,

"Come quickly there's a boy, he needs help!"

"That's impossible Peri, have you had another nightmare? Let's find your mum," she takes my hand.

"No, you don't understand, there's a boy here on the farm! He's hurt, Mum's with him now and she asked for you!" Ann drops my hand and goes quiet as Joe pops his head around the door.

"Told you didn't I – the times coming. Typical women, never listen, just think old Joe's jabbering again," he rolls his eyes handing Ann her dressing gown, already wrapped up in his own, with fluffy slippers to match. I resist the urge to giggle at such a serious time, Joe looks utterly comical in his bedtime attire.

"Come on then lass, lead the way, lets meet this lad at long last, shall we?"

Confused as always by his ramblings I lead the way into the main barn and up to my room, only to find Euan fast asleep with Phoenix curled up next to him. Mum continues to examine him, deep concern etched across her features.

"How did you do that?" I whisper.

"Sorry Peri, I had to use one of the presents from your healing kit, I'll show you how to make a new batch in the week. I think we'll be needing a large supply with this one," she answers, rising unsteadily to her feet.

"Poor lad," Joe looks over him kindly, "he looks broken. Let's fix him up shall we," he heads over to Euan, I expect him to lift him and take him to the spare room, but oddly he begins to hover his hands above his body, not touching him, more as if waving something invisible over him. Mum nudges him with her foot, fretfully looking in my direction.

"Oh, Val stop it woman! You can't keep hiding our ways from her forever, it's time she knew. Now pack it in and let me help the boy!" he proclaims firmly.

"Joseph!" Ann scolds.

"No, he's right Ann," Mum sighs defeatedly, "I think the time's come."

I'm used to everyone talking in riddles around me, but irritation surfaces, wishing someone would speak plainly, so I knew what was going on. I'm distracted momentarily from being angry as I watch Joe, he sweeps his hands in a sideways motion, over and around Euan whilst mumbling incoherently as Mum did earlier.

"I didn't know Joe could heal too," I whisper, eyes glued to the bizarre scene in front of me.

"In a way darling," replies Ann, "Joe is a Seer."

The lights go out and I gasp in awe.

"A Seer? As in he can see the future?"

"Ay lass, in a way of sorts, yes," replies Joe before turning irritably towards Mum, "Val will you turn that codswalloping light back on and get some control woman! If today's the day you deal with this, scaring the breeches off the girl isn't going to help a darn thing."

The lights switch back on, and I stumble back in shock.

"Okay - what's going on?"

"Nowt to worry about lass, you're about to learn some overdue family heritage that's all," Joe pats me on the shoulder as we move towards the door. A stern look exchanges between him and Mum as he does so, she sighs again, seemingly in defeat to head downstairs with Ann. I begin to follow behind them, glancing back at the boy on the floor before I do. I don't know why, but I feel like nothing will be the same after tonight. My heart pounds slightly and I begin to feel anxious.

"None of that now missy, you get a grip as well," Joe commands rubbing my back as he does so. "Val's tough as an ox which means you are too. Now go downstairs and ask every question you've ever wanted to ask, and make sure you get your blooming answers. All of this, treading on glass ends now. There's a change in the wind afoot and you need to be prepared. I'll pop young kiddo here into bed and be down in a minute."

I feel oddly reassured by Joe's words but equally confused at the same time. For once Joe is the only person making sense, but at the same time, making no sense at all. Ask questions about what? What change in the wind? Who is this boy and why is he here? And most importantly, why have I been confined to the island my entire life? With my mind a spin, I realise that I do have questions. A lot of them. After thirteen years, I'm finally going to get some answers.

I make my way downstairs slowly, trying to get a grip in my head of what I want to know. What confuses me the most? That just confuses me more. This has all happened so fast and unexpectedly, I don't know whether I'm coming or going. I can hear Mum and Ann whisper-bickering at the kitchen table and stop to eavesdrop.

"Vallaeartha! You can't keep hiding things from her, Joe's just promised her answers and you said you'd give them to her."

"But it's not that simple, is it? You know quite well she is too young to know everything! I moved us to this island so Peri would have a chance at a normal life and that's what she's getting, I'm not taking her childhood away before she's had a chance to have one. When she's an adult I'll tell her everything, but for now, the basics will do and that's final. I am her mother and it's my decision to make!"

"But my life's not normal." I step into the kitchen, "I'm thirteen years old and I've never left this island! Everyone speaks in riddles around me, I'm not allowed off our land, I don't have friends – I'd never met another child until tonight, that's anything but normal!"

I start to hyperventilate, anger building up inside of me. I've never voiced this out loud, but I'm cross. Mum's constant fussing over my whole life has meant I've barely had a life at all.

"You'll understand when you're older Peridot," she sighs, getting up to leave the table.

"Don't you dare Vallaeartha!" Joe barges into the room, fury radiating from him, "You are going to give this girl some answers – if you don't, I will!"

They stand firm, one in defiance of the other, hands-on-hips, nostrils flaring, waves of frustration seething from them both.

"Please don't fight, just tell me what's going on," I sob.

"If her father were here, he'd tell her," says Joe.

The room falls silent as that bomb drops. Mum looks like she's been slapped in the face. The air in the room gets visibly colder and the lights begin to flicker. Joe takes a step back warily as the floor begins to quake.

"Well, he's not bloody here, is he? I am! Just me!" she shrieks in anguish. The lights go out all at once across the island, animals outside stir, I hear Roland and Amy neighing wildly, along with a variety of animal noises calling frantically into the night. Phoenix thunders into the room from upstairs, howling at Mum, who visibly tries to calm herself. She stays focused on Phoenix, the rumbling starting to settle, lights begin to flicker back on unsteadily, everyone is unearthly quiet. I remain glued to the spot, partly out of shock, and partly convinced I'm having one of my dreams.

"I'm doing what I think is best for my daughter Joseph, if you don't like it, you can leave," tears brim in Mum's eyes, and she looks away. Joe goes to say something, stops himself, gives me a pained look and leaves the barn, closing the door quietly behind him.

I'm so confused. I'm anxious and oddly I'm worried about the boy upstairs, which everyone seems to have forgotten about, even though his appearance is what's caused the outburst tonight. I look over at Ann who smiles encouragingly and nods towards Mum as she seats herself at the kitchen table. My heart hammers as I pull up the seat next to her. I notice the tears brimming in Mum's eyes and I soften a little, it must be so hard not having Dad and I know she's trying her best. Taking a deep breath, I ask,

"Mum, can you please just tell me one thing?"

She looks up at me, apprehension in her eyes.

"What are you trying to protect me from?"

"Oh, Peridot. If only you knew."

Great. I ask a question and receive yet another riddle in return. I know I'm not going to get all the answers I need tonight, but I am not leaving this table until I get something. I need a reason as to why we live the way we do. Why I can't leave the farm, why Mum is so obsessed with my safety and what Joe meant about telling me the truth. The truth about what?

As I'm trying to get a grasp in my head of what I want to say, without it escalating into a row, Ann gets up from the table. She pops her hand on both our shoulders then heads outside to give us privacy. The tension from just now seems to have evaporated from the room somehow. Ann looks back visibly tired and says to Mum.

"The basics are better than nothing Val," then shuts the door quietly behind her.

The room warms, and I feel strangely calm, content even. I glance at Mum who seems to have calmed down too.

"Blooming Empaths," she mutters, shaking her head as if trying to rid her mind of something.

"Fine. They're right. I know they're right. It's just not that easy. If it were, we wouldn't be here, do they not realise I want a normal life for you too?" She sighs.

I stay quiet, as she works out what she's going to say in her head, I know the slightest wrong word and she'll lose it and I'll get nothing, I'm about to get something and something will have to do. For now, anyway.

"Peridot..." she pauses, I tap my foot anxiously, bated breath, scared of what's to come next. What can it be that she's so scared to tell me? Perhaps we're fugitives, on the run from the law. Or worse, someone's out to get us and we need to stay hidden, so they can't ever find us. No other reason could warrant us living on a secluded farm, on an island, in the middle of nowhere with zero interaction from other people for thirteen years.

"Peridot, before I begin, I need you to understand that there are some things I can't tell you - yet," she adds hurriedly, "I want to more than you will ever comprehend, but Peri you are a thirteen-year-old girl and there are some things I refuse to burden you with until you're older. Joe may disagree and say you're ready, but he's not your mother. I am, and I am doing what is right by you, earth be damned." She sighs, head in her hands "For now, I will tell you only what you need to know. When you're older and the time comes, I will tell you the rest. I promise. For now, I will tell you only what you absolutely *need* to know. Do you understand?"

No. I think to myself. No, I do not understand at all, but she's not going to budge, and this is the closest I will get to find out even a smidgen of the truth about my life. So, it'll do. For now. I say nothing and simply nod in agreement.

"Okay then. Here goes nothing. Peri a lot of what I'm about to say will be confusing and you are going to want to ask questions, but I need you to stay calm and ask your questions when I finish talking. Okay?"

I nod again apprehensively.

"Where to start. At the beginning I guess..." she looks confused herself for a minute, then offloads hurriedly, "Peridot, the world outside of this island isn't what you've seen in films or read in books. The world has changed. Dramatically."

Not what I was expecting but I don't interrupt, clinging to the edge of my seat to hear more.

"Something happened many years past, and the world changed," she looks down sadly before continuing, "people aren't sure what caused The Changing, but over half of humanity died over a period of years. I didn't want you to be affected by what was going on, so your father and I agreed to find somewhere safe to raise you, away from what was happening. We found this island and have lived here ever since. That is why you cannot leave the island, it's not safe for our kind on the mainland."

I remain quiet, allowing her words to sink in. It wasn't what I was expecting at all. A million thoughts are running through my head, and I begin to feel sick. I thought perhaps we were on the run from other people - not that the mainland isn't safe, this changes everything.

"Is this why I can't go to school?" I ask slowly, my head trying to get to grips with the bombshell.

"There are no schools. Not like in books and movies, things like that don't exist anymore. They haven't for years now," she adds sadly.

"Can I ask questions or is there more?" What Mum has revealed makes sense, but there's so much I still want to know.

"There's a lot more, but I can't tell you everything. I'm going to tell you more, but I don't know how to without this becoming too confusing. Bear with me and you can ask questions when I've finished, is that okay?" she reaches over and squeezes my hand reassuringly.

I stay quiet while she processes her thoughts and tries to process my own. What on earth happened? Half of humanity died. What could kill that many people? Aliens? No that's crazy talk. A disease maybe? If it's a plague, why isn't this island affected? Is that who we send the healing supplies to? Why does no one else come to the island if it's safe here? And what about everything Joe said about a change coming? I don't understand why Mum won't tell me everything, what could be worse than half the people on the planet dying?

"Peri, aside from what I've just told you, the world is different in other ways too," she avoids eye contact and looks out the window, "some in ways I promise you will learn in time, but others in ways you need to learn now. I don't want to overwhelm you with too much, too soon, so I'm going to give you the basics, and then as time goes on and I can see you're ready I'll tell you more. Is that fair?"

I've just been told half the world died, so I kind of understand what she's saying and simply nod again.

"As you know, we come from a long line of healers, but there are other special traits certain people acquire too. As you saw tonight, Joe is a Seer, which means he can sense certain aspects of the past, present and future when he tries to. I'm sure you've noticed that Ann has a very calming effect on us, she's what's called an Empath. Her ability allows her to affect emotions. Others can do many wonderous things..." she stops to look up at me, "we normally come of age on our thirteenth birthday and our traits start to leak out as it were from then onwards. I wanted to sit down and show you all of this properly yesterday, but we had the break-in. You are one of a few gifted people left in the world Peridot. You are like me, and a few, extremely rare, incredibly special people left in existence. You are born of magick. An Elemental." She stops, looking square in my eyes, holding my gaze.

I feel numb. Not bad numb. Not good numb. Just numb. How are you meant to feel when you learn half the world's dead and you're a rare person with hidden abilities? I thought magick was only in books and movies. What the heck was an Elemental? And how could I be one? I'm just a kid.

"Would you like a cup of tea?" Mum asks, sensing my increasing anxiety. I nod, still numb, the shock of these last few days and this conversation has left me completely speechless. She places a cup of chamomile tea with a sprig of mint in my hands gently. I breathe in the musky aroma as a welcoming sense of clarity washes over me. I start to feel a sense of calm. I understand now why we live alone. Why I can't leave the island. All the odd things Mum, Joe and Ann have said or done over the years were to do with their abilities, which I didn't understand at the time. My life all made sense now. I look around expecting to see Ann responsible for the change in my mood, but it's just us in the kitchen still.

"The tea helps, doesn't it?" Mum smiles, "chamomile for calming and mint for clarity. Ann and I will start teaching you soon, you can learn for yourself, now you're of age."

We sit in comfortable silence for a moment while we sip our tea, I let the effects of the herbs sink in.

"Can I ask my questions now?"

"Yes, but please don't be cross if there are certain things I won't answer. You have been thirteen less than a day. When you're older if you want to face what's out there then I will tell you."

"What is out there?" I ask, "Is it a plague?"

"I'm sorry Dot, that's the one thing I won't burden you with yet. In time I promise, when your sixteen perhaps, but not now."

This annoys me, but I don't argue, I know she won't budge. I pick another of my growing list of questions.

"What's an Elemental?"

"An Elemental is a person who has the ability to work with the elements of nature. They are all that make life possible, namely, earth, air, fire, water, and spirit. There's a lot more to it than that and I promise you will learn everything in your schooling, now you're of magickal age."

"Why are we safe here on the island if it's only us that live here? If it's so dangerous out there, why haven't others come to live here too?"

"Not everyone has the abilities that we do. I performed certain rituals and practices to ensure no-one wanting to cause harm, can get within distance of the island."

"So, people could come and go if they wanted to? Providing they're not dangerous?"

"Perhaps. But only a handful of beings know about the island, so other than when our remedies are needed urgently, or an animal is sick, we don't get visitors."

"Don't you want to help people? We could make this place a sanctuary?"

"I care too much about your safety to jeopardise what we have here. We have the sanctuary, but it is for animals only. Humans aren't welcome here for a reason."

"What reason?" I ask perplexed.

"Many humans don't know about our gifts Peri; people fear that which they do not understand. Given your age, you would be in great danger if the wrong people were to learn of your potential abilities. A young Elemental would be a prized possession on the mainland, that can't ever happen."

I gasp in shock.

"Don't worry, you're perfectly safe on the island, no one uninvited has ever come in the years we've been here."

"But what about Euan?"

Mum pauses for a moment.

"I've been wondering that myself. The swim alone from the mainland should have killed him, given his condition. He is just a boy, and a severely hurt boy in need of a lot of healing, we needn't fear him. We'll patch him up and then he can be on his way."

"No! You can't make him leave, he's just a kid like me, he could get hurt again, if you send him back out there - he said he was in captivity!"

Mum thinks for a minute.

"Providing he doesn't become a negative impact on our home or cause any disruption to your schooling, we will ask him if he'd like to stay. We can home school you together perhaps. How would you feel about that?"

I nearly jump for joy, spilling my tea by accident as I wrap my arms around Mum in a hug, "I'd love that more than anything!" I squeal. Mum hugs me back, when she pulls away, I see genuine happiness in her eyes.

"Well, I can honestly say this isn't how I expected tonight to turn out after our chat. I was expecting you to follow out after Joe," she grimaces, looking out the window towards their barn. Their lights are still on.

"Peri, do you mind if we call it a night? I need to patch things up with Joseph. Go get some rest and you can help me with Euan in the morning. I think he'll respond better to someone his own age."

"There are still questions I want to ask though."

"I know, I wouldn't expect any less. There's a lot of unanswered questions, I understand that."

A frustrated sigh escapes my lips without meaning to, I can't help it. There's still so much I don't know or that doesn't make sense. There are a million questions I want to ask but if I do, I know Mum will shut down and I won't get anything more out of her. I wait quietly while Mum battles it out in her head. I can see her arguing with herself mentally on what she should do, and I see the exact moment that she decides resolutely that tonight won't be the night.

"I promise that from tomorrow, you can ask anything you like about our craft and being an Elemental, but any more questions about the mainland are off-limits until you're older. I'm sorry Peridot, but that's how it must be for now. One day you'll understand why."

I don't want to, but I shrug out a yes. I know more now than I ever have, I potentially have a friend at last and I'll not have to put up with constant riddles and feeling lost around the adults anymore, especially when they talk about our craft. I know not to push my luck any further, so I agree.

Mum gives me another hug, "Okay off to bed, you can sleep in tomorrow. Make sure to pop amethyst under your pillow, so you sleep well."

I yawn in response and head up the stairs, my mind still reeling from the events of tonight. Popping my head into the spare room as I pass, I watch Euan sleeping peacefully with Phoenix at the foot of the bed. As I clamber into my bed, I can't help but feel grateful that he came along. With an overwhelming sense of knowing, I can feel that the skinny boy covered in dirt is going to change my life forever.

THE LOST BOY

The next few days are an adjustment I wasn't expecting. I was so desperate for friends my age, but Euan is hard work. Like really hard work. I don't know what he went through on the mainland, but he doesn't trust anyone. Especially not my mother, and because I left him alone with her after he begged me not to, he no longer trusts me either. The only time Euan speaks is when Phoenix is in the room, which makes zero sense. He'll have a full-on one-sided conversation with our family dog, but not utter more than a grunt to me. I've tried everything to break the silence, bringing him food, making jokes, offering to show him around, but nothing. He's just not interested.

He's warming towards Joe and starting to get comfortable around Ann, so I'm hoping he'll come back round to me in time. My current tactic is giving him space which has given me one saving grace, I now have lots of time to learn about being an Elemental. It still hasn't sunk in that now I'm thirteen I'll develop abilities. I haven't noticed any changes yet, so I'm spending as much time studying and learning as I can. I'm knee-deep in books on my bedroom floor when I hear Phoenix pad past with Euan, he doesn't even glance in my direction and natters away to Phoenix animatedly.

Rolling my eyes, I return to my book, The Histories of Herbalism. There seems to be a natural remedy for almost every ailment. From cuts and scrapes to diseases - even broken bones. I'm a long way from knowing which plant does which, but I jot down the ones that stand out to me; A tonic of blessed thistle for a headache, a balm of blackberry leaves for itches and scratches, a sprig of lavender to help you sleep, a tea of lemon and turmeric for cold and flu symptoms, I keep listing the different herbs and their uses until my wrist aches and I can't write anymore. I wish Mum would let me use the computer unsupervised, that would make this so much easier. Sliding a bookmark into the thick handwoven volume, I make my way downstairs.

"Peri, you're up," greets Ann, "Can I get you some lunch? I'm teaching Euan how to make bread and jam if you fancy joining us?"

"Sure, that sounds nice," I glance at Euan, but he turns his back to me, continuing to pummel a bowl of berries into a compote with his hands.

"Do you want a cup of tea, I'll put the kettle on?" I ask, trying a different tactic. Euan doesn't answer and continues to squish away in his bowl. Ann smiles at me encouragingly, she's convinced he'll come around in time.

"That'd be lovely, how's the studying going?" she tries to keep the atmosphere light.

"It's a lot to take in, but I'm getting there, would be a lot easier if Mum would let me use the computer though," I sigh, filling the kettle to the brim.

Euan startles, his bowl crashing to the ground, berry particles fly everywhere, "You have computers here?" he asks.

"Yeah," I reply, shocked he's finally speaking to me,

"You can use it with me if you like, I just have to ask Mum first though..." I trail off, Mum's a taboo subject around Euan, he remains wary of her.

"Can we go now? After I've tidied up my mess," he adds, not wanting to get in trouble for the berry medley plastered all over the kitchen.

"I don't see why not," answers Ann, "but you need to eat first - you've got to get your strength up. I'll go find Val while you two clean up and we can all have lunch together."

Euan busies himself picking up the broken bowl pieces as Ann leaves the room. I'm dumbfounded. He hasn't spoken to me since his first night and now he's acting like everything's okay.

"What on earth was that all about?" I confront him.

"Huh?"

"You haven't spoken to me in days! Now out of nowhere, everything's okay just because we have a computer?"

"Pretty much," he shrugs.

I gape in response. I want to be friends with him and I'm glad the barrier's back down, but boys are weird.

"Fine. Will you at least explain why you've ignored me the last three days?" I grumble, crouching down to help him clean up the mess.

"Coz you're like her."

"What do you mean?" my voice rises.

"You're going to be like her. Can see it in your eye's sometimes."

"That didn't seem to bother you when you knocked on my window the other night."

"I had to get out of the cold. It was worth the risk. I didn't think you'd use your powers on me."

"I don't have any powers yet," I grumble, "besides, why would any of us want to hurt you? I've been trying to be your friend since you got here."

"I don't need a friend. I need to get back to the mainland. You might be a white witch in the making or

73

whatever but your mum's a dark user if ever I saw one. Soon as I'm better, I'm out of here."

"Why are you so funny around my mum?" I exclaim, "she does not use dark magick, for your information she's a healer, she saved your life!"

"This is why I don't speak to you, she's your mum, I knew you wouldn't believe me. Just drop it okay."

"I will not drop it – you're making out like my mum's evil or something!" my voice lowers to an irritated whisper as approaching footsteps echo down the hall.

How dare he! Mum may be hard work, no one can argue with that, but she's not a bad person.

"I hear the two of you would like permission to use the computer," Mum enters the room, "the answer is yes, but only for studying purposes. Agreed?"

"Agreed!" I beam, this is perfect, now I have a way to keep Euan speaking to me, even if he is super annoying. Plus, I can study without my arm feeling like it's going to fall off.

"Can we use it after lunch?" Euan asks Mum.

"I don't see why not, although you need to remember your manners if you want to use it too," she replies sternly. Euan looks away in response as Ann nudges Mum, ushering her past us, whispering in her ear as they go.

"I don't care if he doesn't know his please and thank you's, he had better learn quick," Mum whispers back in exasperation, loud enough that we can hear.

"And speaking of which, Euan?" she turns back to the table, "if you're to stay here with us, then you will be homeschooled with Peridot. No if's, no buts. Peri has a lot to learn this year and we can't have anything getting in the way of her schooling. Should you wish to, you can learn too. All I ask in return is that you help around the sanctuary and don't cause any trouble. And that you learn to say you're please and thank you," she adds, "I simply won't abide bad manners." She takes a tray of freshly baked granary bread out of the oven, placing it on the table as she sits down, "Well, would you like to stay here with us?"

He shrugs in response and looks away.

"I'll give you to the end of the week to decide. You can either stay, and learn our ways, or we can get you patched up and send you back to the mainland. It's one or the other, you either stay, or you go."

Euan takes a seat at the table and nods solemnly.

"I'll think about it."

Mum gives him the look and raises her eyebrow in warning.

"Thank you," he adds begrudgingly.

"That's better. See, you're learning already," she smiles smugly. Ann and I take a seat and hand out plates whilst Mum and Euan stare daggers at each other across the table. You could cut the tension in the room with a knife. Thankfully, Joe stomps into the room at that moment, Phoenix at his heels, "Hello gang, what's for grub?"

Euan visibly relaxes as he notices Phoenix who pads around the table to give him a nudge with his head before sitting next to me. I ruffle behind his ears making a fuss of him. I've barely seen him since Euan arrived.

"How are you boy?" I ask.

"You shouldn't talk to him like that," observes Euan, "he's older than you, he's not a boy."

I gape at him, lost for words, "how do you know how old he is? He's a dog for earth's sake!"

"Peridot do not curse," scolds Mum, "ignore the boy he's trying to wind you up. They do that a lot so get used to it, your father used to drive me potty with his wind-ups."

Euan glares at Mum again but stays silent, Joe starts laughing to himself as Ann brings over the resurrected jam compote.

"This is going to be a fun ride isn't it!" he guffaws to the table. Joe's laugh is infectious, and I can't help but snigger out loud as he begins to shovel heaps of jam onto a slice of bread and chomp away, mouth wide open for all to see. Euan can't keep a straight face either and before you know it, we're both laughing hysterically in unison. Mum tuts, rolling her eyes and heads to the sink in disgust. I offer Euan a sheepish grin and tuck into my bread and jam. For his first attempt, it's surprisingly good.

"Good jam lad, I think you'll fit in just fine," approves Joe as he also gets up from the table. I notice him go to ruffle Euan's hair, then think better of it at the last minute, picking up his plate instead to take to the kitchen sink.

I'm glad it's not just me that isn't quite sure how to act around Euan, he's a strange addition to our home, but I hope he decides to stay. If I can just get him to trust us and be comfortable around Mum, then everything will be okay. I finish up my serving and pop an extra slice onto my plate for Phoenix.

"Can we head to the office now please Mum?" I join her at the sink to help with the washing up.

"Yes, that's fine, but any nonsense from the boy and you call for one of us straight away."

"Nonsense?" I ask confused.

"Yes Peri, nonsense. Teenage boys are full of it, you'll see what I mean."

She finishes drying her dish and leaves the kitchen, eyeing Euan as she goes. Getting him to warm to her is going to be harder than I thought, I'll have my work cut out for me, one's as judgmental as the other. Oh well, it's a small price to pay to have a friend at last, so I'm up for the challenge.

"Are you coming?"

Euan nods and leaves the table, then turns, remembering his plate and washes it up at the sink. I think he knows his manners already - he's just trying to test Mum. As we head to the office, I take note of his appearance as we walk down the corridor towards the back room, the dull greyness of his skin from before has warmed up and he now has a healthy glow. He's gained weight in the few days he's been here, no longer looking gaunt. His dark brown hair now clean from dirt is long and wavy, a few freckles are dotted here and there.

"Why are you staring?" he looks uncomfortable as I flush crimson and avert my gaze,

"You look healthier that's all," I shrug, "do you feel any better?"

"I guess, not sure how much of that is natural and how much is magic though."

"Magic's not real, don't be silly."

"Of course it is, what do you think your powers are?" he snaps rolling his eyes. "Considering you grew up with two witches and a warlock, you don't know much, do you?"

"My Mum said I'm an Elemental, not a witch," I snap back irritably, "and I'm of *magick*, not magic like in cartoons, it's not the same."

Euan stops dead in his tracks.

"Your mum said you're an Elemental?"

"You know I'm an Elemental, you said about me using powers yourself! Why are you so confusing?!"

"I thought you were an ordinary witch, I didn't realise you were an Elemental, that's completely different."

I'm silent while I digest this. This is all so confusing. Taking a few breaths and trying to remain calm, I ask,

"Why is it different?"

"Huh?"

"Why is an Elemental different to a witch?"

"You're more powerful. A lot more powerful. Or at least you will be. When your mum stops lying to you."

"She's not lying to me she's just not told me everything yet. She says it's for my safety..." I trail off embarrassed.

Euan rolls his eyes. I choose to ignore it as we head into the back room, that's a mix of an office and a study. Bookshelves line the walls overflowing with large dusty volumes and parchment, our computer sits on a large ornate desk near the window. I plonk myself down on the chair lost in thought. How can this boy know more about me than I do? I understand that one day I'll have abilities, but I never thought of them as magic like in films. Now he's pointed it out, I can see the similarities. It doesn't make sense anymore. It did yesterday when Mum explained it, but now I'm confused again. Everything I thought I knew a few days ago is different, yet everything's the same. Magic or magick, witches, warlocks, and Elementals – it's like something I'd read in a book, not real life.

"Are you going to turn on the computer, or shall I?" Euan distracts me from my thoughts. I don't reply, turning on the computer in silence. I don't feel much like studying anymore. What's the point? I can read every book in this room and still not know the thing I really want to know.

"Euan?'"

He looks up at me, I've not used his name before.

"Will you tell me what's out there?"

"What do you mean?"

"Outside of this island. Why my mum won't let me leave. What's out there?"

"You really don't know do you?"

"I've never left before," I admit, looking away embarrassed.

"You've never left the island?" he looks incredulous.

"No, I'm not allowed. Mum says it's to keep me safe."

"But you're an Elemental, couldn't you just use your powers to stay safe?"

"I don't think I have any powers. Not yet anyway. I only found out I was an Elemental the night you arrived, and you seem to know more about me than I do."

I look out the window feeling tears come to my eyes, I don't want to look childish in front of Euan. I blink a few times, then look back at him,

"Well?"

"Well, what?"

"Will you tell me what's out there?! For the love of earth, will someone please tell me the truth for once?"

"Sure," he shrugs nonchalantly, not at all bothered by my dramatic outburst, "what do you want to know?"

"Is everyone really dead?"

"No," he laughs, "Is that what she told you?"

My heart quickens and I feel my pulse racing, why would Mum tell me everyone was dead if they weren't?

"She said something bad happened killing half of humanity, she refused to tell me what until I'm older though. Is that not true?"

"Oh. Okay yes, that's true. But we're not all dead. Lots of us survived. And now we're slaves. And food."

I stare at him perplexed. That's a weird thing to say.

"What do you mean, we're food?"

"For the animals."

"That doesn't make any sense, why would we be food for animals? Who are we slaves to?"

"Erm, the animals? Why don't you just ask Phoenix he'll tell you?"

I'm flummoxed. The boy has lost the plot. Or he's taking the mick out of me. Whichever it is, I'm done trying to make sense of him either way. Mum's right, boys are full of nonsense. I want him to be my friend, but I'll leave the serious stuff to the adults to tell me, even if it does take forever, at least it will make sense. What Euan says is just downright gobbledygook. I sigh, standing up.

"Computers yours, I'm going for a walk."

"Suit yourself," he shrugs, "What's the password?"

"Lucien. In capitals."

"Lucien?" He asks surprised.

"Yeah, do you need me to spell it for you?" I ask. I forget I know nothing about him, maybe he can't read or write properly.

"No, it's just strange that name is your password," he answers cryptically.

"It was my dad's name, why would that be strange?"

He opens his mouth to say something; then thinks better of it, "Don't worry you wouldn't believe me if I told you, you already think I'm crazy."

"Hey! That's not fair - I don't think you're crazy I just think you say some weird things that don't make sense. Maybe you hit your head or something," I trail off awkwardly.

"Do me a favour, *Dot*," he glowers, "stop questioning what I say and start questioning whatever it is that your mum's been telling you. There's a whole world out there you know nothing about, and you need to know if you ever plan on leaving this island. You'll get eaten up out there, you wouldn't last a day."

With that, he turns around and focuses on the computer. I'm speechless. And I can't argue, he's right. I know nothing of the world outside of this island. I leave the room. Tears flowing freely this time. I need to know more. Mum won't tell me. Asking Euan is like banging my head against a brick wall. The two of them are as infuriating as the other, no wonder they don't like each other. No point asking Ann, she will just tell me to speak to Mum. I pop my wellies on, the only chance I have of learning the truth, is Joe.

I find him in the main barn with Roland, Amy and a few of the pigs scrummaging in hay bales.

"Will you stop bickering for earth's sake? You're worse than the frogging rabbits when it comes to hay!" he exclaims, bending down to separate hay into even mounds between them all. I try to muffle a giggle, but it slips out.

"Oh - hey kiddo! Didn't see you there," he greets, wiping his brow with his forearm. "Had enough of teenage boys already I take it?"

"Kind of. He's okay, just weird. What he says doesn't make any sense, he accused me of thinking he's crazy."

"Do you?"

"What do you mean?"

"Do you think he's crazy?"

"It's hard not to. Anytime I ask him anything serious he says something weird. He just told me to ask Phoenix if he's telling the truth," I shrug, "what am I supposed to think?"

"Ay lass, that would be hard to understand given your upbringing. If I remember correctly, you used to think I was the crazy one," he muses.

"Not crazy, a bit out there that's all. Anyway, what does he mean? Should I ask Phoenix if he's telling the truth?" I joke.

"No, sadly, in your case it would do no good."

"See! This is what I mean, riddles, riddles, and more riddles! Why can't anyone just give me a straight answer? I don't know who I am, what I am, what the world is. Nothing! Everything is a big riddle to me!" I throw my hands up in exasperation and start to stomp off.

"Peridot," Joe grabs my hand, gently pulling me back, "I'm sorry lass, you're right. You're completely right. I wish I could be the one to tell you everything, but I can't."

"But why can't you?" I sob, tears flowing again.

He wipes a tear from my cheek, "Now, now, less of that, chin up. All I will say is this; learn from the boy. Don't dismiss everything he says as crazy."

"Yeah right," I scoff.

"Hey, you want to know what's out there, right?"

I nod.

"Well, he came from out there. Alright yes, he's knocked up around the head a little and got a temper on him like your frogging mother, but he's got a good heart. Can see it. Can feel it. Just spend some time with him, teach him our ways and learn some of his. He'll be able to tell you things that we can't. Not without betraying your mother's wishes anyway. And, as much as she makes me want to bang my head against a bean pole, I owe her my life and won't go behind her back when it comes to your upbringing. I may not agree with it, but I understand why she's doing it this way, she's been through a lot your mother. Most women would've broken. Not Val though. Tough as old boots she is. What will be will be."

"Can you see what will be?" I ask, thinking about his powers, "with your abilities I mean. Euan called you a warlock?"

"Ay, see. Not as mad as you think he is. And this is one thing I can talk to you about freely at long last!" He beams, "I am indeed a warlock. Not many of us left, unfortunately. T'was always more women born of the craft than men."

"And they're called witches? Why am I different, why am I an Elemental?"

"Anyone with powers, or abilities as you prefer to call them, is a witch if they're female, a warlock if they're male. Most have a significant trait that they stick to, mine is a Seer. I can sense what has past, and what is yet to be. I have other powers too, I'm not too bad at healing, nothing like your mother of course, but not too shabby, handy in a fix as it were anyway."

"And an Elemental?" I press.

"An Elemental is someone born of the original family of the first witches. A descendant. Almost always female, very rarely born males. Elementals, it is foretold, can tap into all powers with unfathomable force. Everything is born of the elements. Earth, air, fire, water, and spirit. Legend says a true Elemental can wield them all."

"That can't be me. I'm just … me."

"And that's what makes you so special, most Elementals shout to the high heavens about their powers. That was what got most of them killed. Not your mother though, and not you. You're going to do great things one day Peridot, I've seen it."

"You've seen it?"

He taps his nose secretly, "First trait of a good Seer - keep your sights to yourself. Just trust that even though things are uncertain now, they will all work out in the end. I know it. You will know it soon too. I promise."

"You're not just saying that to cheer me up?"

"Course I'm trying to cheer you up woman! But I'm also telling the truth. Scouts honour."

"What's a scout?"

"Never mind, you've no hope. Don't even know what a scout is!" he guffaws, slapping his leg in mirth. I have no clue what he's laughing about, but as always, his laugh is infectious, and I start to feel a little better.

"I'll go find Euan and try to make friends again," I rise.

"That's it, good girl, maybe leave the heavy stuff a while and get to know him first, ay? He's been through it that kid, he could do with a friend just as much as you could."

I nod and give him a hug.

"Thanks Joe."

"Anytime kiddo, anytime."

Heading back towards the house I glance back, Joe's chiding away at the pigs again already. Martha, one of the mother sows is heavily pregnant and refusing to move out of Joe's way, he stamps his foot, cursing wildly and I chuckle to myself. Mum would have a fit if she heard him. Closing the door behind me as I re-enter the house, I make my way towards the office, determined to give it another try with Euan.

"Hey," I sit beside him, "did you find what you were looking for?"

Euan looks up in surprise, "I didn't think you'd come back."

"Just needed some air that's all." I shrug, heeding Joe's advice and leaving the heavy stuff. Yes, I want to ask questions, but I want a friend more, and maybe once we're friends, I'll be able to take some of what he says a little more seriously, instead of getting cross with him.

"What did you need the computer for?" I change the subject.

"The internet, but you don't have it."

"The internet?" I ask confused.

"Yeah, it's a kind of system where people can contact each other. I was hoping to find help for my mum."

"Oh, sorry I've not heard of it before. You know, if you weren't so off with her, I'm sure my mum would help you if she can."

"No one can help my mum," he mumbles sadly.

"Why not?"

"She's a slave at one of the A.I stations. No one gets in or out. Until I did anyway."

I go to ask what an A.I station is, then think better of it. Joe said he's been through hell and he's right; Euan needs a friend more than I need my curiosity sated.

"If you managed to escape, maybe your mum will too," I placate instead, trying to comfort him.

"It's not that simple. Mum's useful to them so they guard her. All women they do. It's different if you're male, I was just another boy in line to be disposed of. You're no good to them unless you're super-strong, if you're normal like me, your chicken feed."

"Chicken feed?"

"Yeah."

I stay silent. I don't know how to respond to that. They – whoever they are – obviously don't feed young boys to chickens, so I have no idea what he can mean. The silence becomes a little awkward. Euan sighs and gets up to leave.

"Do you want to do something?" I ask, not wanting him to go.

"Like what?"

"We could watch a film if you like? You can pick which one, I've seen them all before, we don't have a wide selection."

"Sure, I've never seen a film before," he perks up.

"Great!" I squeal, a little over-excited, "I'll make some popcorn while you choose a film," linking his arm I steer him towards the television room. He's stiff at first, uncomfortable with the contact, but I natter on about my favourite films to ease the tension and he slowly relaxes.

"This house is really big," his eyes take in his surroundings as we enter the tv room.

Unlinking his arm, I open the video cabinet, "I don't know any different, it's the only house I've ever been in - except Joe and Ann's, but that was a barn for the horses originally, so doesn't really count."

"I like them - Joe and Ann I mean. Joe's funny and Ann's kind."

"They're pretty great," I agree, "do you like me?" The words slip out without my meaning to, I feel my cheeks flush beet red, mortified I voiced the question out loud.

"Yeah, you're alright," he grins, "frustrating though."

"Likewise," I grin back a little sheepishly, and he laughs. He has a good laugh. Hearty and deep, I laugh back beginning to feel comfortable around him for the first time since he arrived.

"Pick a film, I'll get some snacks," I instruct, returning moments later with a tray of goodies. Cucumber sandwiches, popcorn, dark chocolate slabs and two tall strawberry and lime waters.

"What did you choose?" I set down the tray, offering him a sandwich. He takes it gratefully, passing me one of my all-time favourite movies as he does.

"Good choice," I beam, sliding Toy Story into the VCR, "prepare to laugh your socks off."

"Don't think I'll ever get used to this," he chomps between a mouthful of sandwich.

"How'd you mean?"

"The food. It's so nice not being hungry all the time. And the things you eat are so good, I could spend all day eating."

"I'll teach you how to cook if you like, I can show you all sorts," I suggest, sitting cross-legged next to him on the sofa.

"I'm starting to think you're bribing me into staying."

"Maybe. I do want you to stay."

"I'm coming around to the idea," he admits.

"Good, after you've watched this, you'll never want to leave," I beam, throwing a blanket over our feet and pressing play. It's hard to believe that earlier on I could've throttled Euan. Now, I don't want him to leave.

Half an hour into the movie Phoenix pads in, jumping on the sofa to settle in the middle, he gives Euan a sniff then rests his head on my lap. Sneaking a sideways glance at my new friend, he's laughing at something Buzz Lightyear just said. Ruffling Phoenix's ears, I get back to the movie and laugh heartily alongside him. I have a feeling he's going to stay.

THE CRAFT

Three months pass, and for the first time in what feels like forever, I'm genuinely happy. The sun beams brightly, it's a typical June afternoon and we're getting ready to celebrate Summer Solstice with a garden party. I'm knee-deep in the soil, picking fallen petals from the fields when Phoenix shoots past me, tongue out gleefully.

"Get your furry butt back here!" Euan sprints after him.

I roll my eyes and get back to gathering. Euan has well and truly settled here on the farm with us, those two are always up to mischief. I'd normally be messing around with them, but this is my first solstice celebration as an Elemental and I'm taking my duties seriously. I'll be leading the celebrations as we give thanks under the Strawberry Moon, and I want my first solstice to go without any hiccups.

Mum's been teaching me the craft every day as she promised. We've covered a lot in a short space of time, but I find our heritage fascinating. From studying the wheel of the year to learning the importance of lunar activity and the placement of the stars, each topic is as enthralling as the next. Euan's been learning with me in some lessons, histories of the craft, crystal healing, herbal lore and so on. Not Elemental studies though, Mum says our rituals are ancient knowledge that only those of magick should know.

Euan seemed to understand and has been learning how to plant and tend to the crops with Joe when I'm in my Elemental lessons. He's still wary of Mum but has learnt a lot during our lessons and is finally letting his guard down around her.

"Get that daft dog back here!" Joe thunders after them.

I turn to see what all the commotion's about, realising Phoenix has a basket of crops in his mouth. I can't help but laugh. Euan's still learning, you never leave food on the floor around Phoenix. I watch them chasing unsuccessfully after him, tail wagging furiously, he thinks it's a game. I decide now would be the opportune moment to trial my abilities like Mum's taught me and give the lads a hand.

Sliding off my shoes, I sink my feet into the earth to ground myself, as we do before our lessons. Breathing in deeply, I take my time, feeling the earth under my feet, the grass rustling in between my toes, pausing to breathe in the smells around me. Pollen is in the air, the trees smell of dew from last night's shower of rain. I can sense energy all around me. Closing my eyes, I call upon the elements, earth, air, fire, water, and spirit. I focus my intent on earth and air, willing the trees to create a breeze around Phoenix. My spine tingles as warmth spreads into my hands. I picture the basket rising high and floating towards me. I can't help but feel excited as I sense the ritual working and imagine the basket landing close beside me.

WHACK!

"Ouch!" I cry, opening my eyes in shock.

The basket and its contents are sprawled upon the floor and my head feels like a brick just hit it.

"What happened?" Euan rushes over.

"Supposedly magick, Mum would most likely call it a mistake," I grumble, holding my head.

I can feel a bump forming already. Euan bursts into laughter, as I take my hand away.

"Hey! It's not funny, I was trying to save your blooming basket," I gripe, wishing I hadn't bothered.

"Thanks for trying," he grins, "he'd have brought it back though, we were playing a prank on Joe."

"Please tell me you're joking?"

"Afraid not... turns out jokes on you too huh?"

Rolling my eyes, I attempt to get up, blood rushes to my head and I fall back on my behind, crying out loudly as I do. Great now I'll have a bruised butt too.

"Take this as a sign from Mother Nature that you might need to work on your spells more," Euan jokes.

I roll my eyes again and attempt to get up again, I hate when Euan refers to rituals as spells, it makes the craft sound like child's play.

"Take no notice of the joker over here, doesn't know what he just witnessed," tuts Joe, flicking Euan behind the ear as he reaches us, "your magick's fine, it's your catching skills you need to work on."

"You think so?" I grimace, "I felt like I was doing it right, but I had my eyes closed, so I couldn't see what I was doing."

"Aye lass, you did well, work on keeping your eyes open next time though. Takes most of us years to be able to do what you just did in a matter of weeks. Val will be proud."

I doubt that once she sees the state of my face for the garden party, but I keep that thought to myself.

"Quite a bump you've got there, do you want to try to fix it, or shall I give you the once over?"

"Would you Joe? I've tried enough practical magick for today, dread to think how bad my healing abilities will be."

"Don't be daft woman. Too hard on yourself you are. Powers' so strong you nearly knocked yourself clean out with it – quite an achievement if you ask me."

I don't believe him but smile despite myself. Joe kneels beside me, sprouting a leaf from the ground. He places it between his fingers and murmurs something softly before applying it with pressure to my head. The leaf feels warm and soothes my pounding headache.

"I can't wait to be able to do our craft properly, that feels better already," I smile gratefully.

"Well kiddo, I've got a few years on you don't forget; you'll get there in no time. I couldn't summon things until I was in ma twenties - you just did it with your eyes closed," he helps me up, managing to stay on two feet this time. I feel my head, the bumps smaller already and no longer sore to touch. I love magick.

"Do you want a hand with the gathering for tonight?" Euan approaches sheepishly,

"Sure, I was hoping to have everything ready early so I can take my time getting ready."

"No worries, I feel bad about your head, what are we looking for?"

"Fresh berries, would be great if you can find some."

"On it," he mock-salutes before jogging off towards the woodland, passing Phoenix as he goes.

"Woah there don't expect any attention from me that was your fault too," I grumble, as he pads over. His ears go flat, solemnly sitting beside me as I get back to collecting my offerings for tonight. An hour later and I have a good mix of petals, seeds and hopefully if Euan's had a good haul, a good selection of berries too. I head back to the house, Phoenix in tow. It's hard to stay mad at him, he has one of those faces you just want to make a fuss of.

"Peri wait up!" Euan catches up to us, his arms full of twigs and berries.

"Wow! Where'd you find them? There are loads!"

"Trick is to look up not down, lots of thorns though," he frowns, arms covered in scratches.

"Some of those look mean," I observe sympathetically, "you didn't have to go to all that trouble but thank you."

"Only fair, you tried to help me and got hurt, now we're even," he shrugs.

"That's true, I didn't look at it like that."

"I'm going to find Joe and get patched up, Ann said she'd made me a top for tonight, I don't want to get blood on it."

"Okay, see you in a bit," he heads in the other direction as I enter the house, placing my gatherings on the kitchen side.

"Well done – that's a lot of offerings!" Ann appraises, rolling dough onto a sideboard.

"Hope Mum will be pleased, although I can't take all the credit, Euan helped. Well, kind of," I laugh, leaving out the headbanging incident.

Ann nods absentmindedly, focusing on kneading the dough with her fingers. It smells amazing already.

"I hear you tried your first solo ritual this afternoon," Mum's voice finds me as she enters the kitchen, "Joe said it was quite a spectacle."

"You could say that" I flush, "what I was summoning kind of hit me in the face."

"Nearly knocked you senseless I hear. Must've been a strong summoning spell. Remember to keep your eyes open next time," she waggles a finger in my direction.

I look away embarrassed, beginning to sort through my basket of gatherings. Mum joins me, sorting the goods into piles, discarding any thorns and the berries that aren't to her standard, "Be careful storing them next time Peridot, there's a lot gone to waste," she chides.

I stand back disappointed - I'd been expecting her to praise how much I'd brought in.

"Do you want some poppy seeds for your loaf?" I ask Ann, trying to disguise my disappointment and not wanting any of my haul to go to waste.

"Sure," Ann nods, "any cranberries in there going spare, I can make some sweet shortbreads with them?"

I pass her the cranberries Mum had disregarded as unworthy, then go to throw the remaining berries in the compost heap.

"Leave those dear," Ann takes my hand relieving me of them, "I'll get some apples from the tree and make a pie, run along and get cleaned up, none will go to waste," she rubs my back as I leave the room, trying to lift my mood but it doesn't work. I was hoping Mum would've been impressed.

I take my time getting ready, trying hard to get back in a good mood. A steaming shower helps. Stepping out, I pick out the dress Ann made for me earlier this week and do a twirl in the mirror. My dress is a soft pale green, a fitted camisole top leads into a floor-length skirt that trails behind me. I wear my necklace from Mum and Dad and apply some lip balm. Checking my reflection, I feel quite pretty, heading downstairs with a smile back upon my face.

"What a beauty," whistles Joe, as I enter the kitchen, he nudges Euan in my direction.

"Come on you, we need to change too," Ann ushers him out of the room.

"So," begins Euan, not making eye contact, "tonight's kind of a big deal, huh?"

"What makes you say that?"

"I've never seen you look like this before."

"How'd you mean?" embarrassed I grab a cardigan off one of the stools to cover up.

"No - I didn't mean it like that, I mean you look nice. Really nice."

"Oh," I blush, "so do you. Is that the top Ann made you?"

I avert the focus onto him, not comfortable with compliments coming from someone other than Mum, Ann, or Joe.

"Yeah, I love it, she's good at everything Ann, wonder if that's an Empath thing?" he muses.

"Perhaps," I reply, taking a moment to take him in, he looks happy. There's a warmth to him I've not noticed before and his clothes suit him well, his new top's the same colour green as mine.

"Do you think she meant to match our outfits?" I wonder out loud.

"Don't talk to me about matching frigging outfits!" curses Joe re-entering the kitchen, also sporting an Ann special, a deep mustard yellow gown. Ann enters wearing the same, but with pretty flowers dotted on the hem.

"Oh, will you shush your whining Joseph, you look handsome?"

"I don't doubt that woman, it's the codswalloping colour that's the problem!"

"It's a solstice celebration, so we are in summer colours, what did you expect?!"

"A green would've worked just as well, I look like a giant sunflower!" he exclaims, arms in the air.

I turn away to stop myself from laughing, he does look quite ridiculous.

"Let's make our way down to the gathering area shall we, Val's already down there doing the finishing touches," Ann ignores Joe's blustering about dodging bumblebees as we head out the door.

I don't want to hurt Ann's feelings, so resist the urge to tease Joe, Euan isn't quite as tactful and makes buzzing noises behind him all the way down to the fields, earning a zap from a not impressed Joseph. I can already see the solstice area as we approach, it looks beautiful.

The outer fields are wild with blooming meadow flowers and a large grass circle stands out in the middle, the foliage trimmed short by the various grazing animals that live with us. Mum's set out the gatherings that we'll use as offerings for tonight. Apparently, the adults have done this every year since they came of witching age, I hate that I've missed out on it up until now. I feel like ancient senses have awakened within me that I didn't have before - it feels natural to give thanks for the seasons and celebrate the changes each solstice offers us. I've been studying the wheel of the year and as I understand it, today is the last day of Beltane, so we say goodbye to spring and give thanks for all this season has blessed us with, the seeds sprouting and flowers coming into bloom. Then tomorrow will be the first day of Litha, the summer solstice, so tonight we welcome back the sun and give offerings for abundance and a fruitful crop to follow.

Euan's taken everything in his stride. I was worried he'd think we're crazy dressing up and throwing flowers about, but he looks just as excited as I am. I'm assuming this is his first-ever magickal celebration, so I want to make it special for him too.

"You look lovely Peri," Mum surprises me, approaching with flower garlands, she pops one over my head and hands the other to Euan, who does the same.

"You're starting to look like one of us," she appraises before heading over to help Ann with the food.

"I think she's trying to be nice to me," Euan observes bemused.

"Mum is nice to you - you just don't notice it," I reply, sitting down on the grass. Mum's still a touchy subject between the two of us, although I will admit, she's as bad as him for snide comments, but he's so standoffish around her,

I'm surprised she's kept her cool all the months he's been with us.

"So, what do we do now?"

"I think we wait until the sun starts to set, then we say goodbye and thanks to Beltane, then feast and give offerings to welcome Litha when the moon rises."

"This is like something out of a dream, I still can't believe I'm here."

"Neither can I, it was pretty boring until you came along."

"How can all this be boring? There's so much you can do. I'm used to a dark room, cramped with other kids being made to do stuff I don't want to do all day. This place is heaven in comparison."

I go silent, rarely approaching the subject of the outside world for fear of clashing again, "does that mean you're going to stay?" I ask instead.

Mum told him he had to decide months ago, but it's not been brought up since. I think she'd been letting him try to enjoy it here, so he'd be more likely to decide to stay.

"I do want to. But I want to save my mum too. I can't do that here. I've been putting off deciding if I'm honest."

"I understand. I'd want to help my mum too, maybe we can help her from here somehow. If our powers are strong enough, maybe we could magick her out or something."

"Are your powers that strong?"

"I have no idea. Still don't have a clue what I'm doing, but from what I've read, anything is possible, so maybe one day I will be. If you help me get better at magick, I'll try. I promise."

"Your mum would have a fit."

"What she doesn't know won't hurt her," I shrug, "besides, what's the worst that could happen? It'll either work and your mum can live here with us, or it won't work, and everything stays the same, she doesn't have to know."

"You'd really go behind her back for me?"

"Euan, you're my friend, I'd do anything for you."

He looks abashed for a moment, then gives me an awkward hug. Smiling I hug him back,

"So, you'll stay?"

"Yeah," he grins, "I'll help you with your magick and we'll try to get Mum back."

"It's a deal."

"What's a deal?" Ann takes a seat on Euan's other side.

"Euan's decided to stay here with us!" I announce excitedly.

"Oh, how wonderful," she beams before calling to Joe.

"I'm not doing anything!!" He exclaims, jumping nearly two feet in the air. I notice the bottom of his gown changing from deep green back to yellow and nudge Euan who laughs.

"Poppycock, I've been watching you try to turn that gown green since we got here," she rolls her eyes, "that can wait. We have a double celebration on our hands tonight."

"Oh really, and what would that be?"

"Euan has decided to stay with us."

Joe looks at Euan a little surprised, "You're sure that's what you want to do?"

"Yeah, it's what my mum would've wanted," he concedes.

"Ay lad, I reckon she would too. VAL!" he booms, making us all jump, "double celebrations – boyos staying indefinitely!"

"Double celebrations it is," Mum joins us, "we'd best get a move on before the sun starts to set."

She ushers us up and we head onto the circle area. Mum gets out what I used to think was a gnarled wooden stick, back when I thought she was crazy, but what I now know to be a wand, and begins to draw up energy from the earth. It's amazing to see her work, even Euan is speechless, as she draws forth more energy, until there's a shimmering orb at the tip of her wand. Ann takes Joe's hand in one of hers, Euan's in the other and motions for him to do the same, he holds his hand out to me and I take it as Mum takes my other, bringing me forward as she chants.

"I call upon the elements of this plane,
Earth, air, fire, water - protect this area in our name,
I call upon spirit for each in hand,
Bless all upon this land,
As above, so it is below,
United together, let it be so."

With that she paces in a wide circle, clockwise, all of us in tow, once the circle is complete, she draws us into the centre closing the circle by taking Joe's hand. The adults look up and then below, Euan and I watch and follow suit. I feel a little daft, but it's exciting, I can feel the magick in the air around us, everything hums with pent up energy.

I take a moment to ground myself, closing my eyes and breathing through my nose, it smells of flowers, warm bread, and Euan, I can smell Euan. His smell is of earth, cloves, and something I'm unsure of, but it draws me to him. As I open my eyes, I realise everyone has unlinked their hands except for us. His eyes remain closed as I let go of his hand, he rocks slightly then opens his eyes too.

"By my decree, our coven adheres to the following creed," Mum announces, "if it harms none, so mote it be."

"Mote it be," Joseph, Ann and I repeat back in acceptance.

"It is now safe to move freely within the circle," Mum nods her head approvingly, "Peri, would you like to be the first to give thanks?"

I step forward, feeling a little nervous with everyone's eyes on me, but I know what I want to say. Making my way to the centre of our circle I look up to the sky.

"To the God of the sun and the Goddess of the moon,

I give thanks, for making my birthday wish come true..." I taper off feeling my cheeks flush, embarrassed to go on, but continue regardless, "I've wanted a friend for longer than I can remember. I wished for a friend as I blew out my birthday candles, and later that night, Euan tapped on my window. I couldn't believe my wish had come true. I am eternally grateful and give thanks that you brought him here to us."

My cheeks continue to flush crimson, but I mean it, I'm so glad to have Euan as my friend. As annoying as he was at first, we've become close the months he's been with us, I couldn't imagine my life without him now. I step back to re-join the circle and look up to find Euan grinning at me. I bashfully grin back, as Ann begins her thanks, then Joe, followed by Mum who then turns to Euan.

"Is there anything you'd like to give thanks for?"

"Okay," he shifts uncomfortably before taking his turn to step forward, hesitates, then looks up at the sky.

"Thank you, God, Goddess or whoever you are. I don't know how I survived the journey here, but I know you had something to do with it. I could feel myself drifting here, even when my arms gave out and I couldn't swim anymore. I begged someone to save me, and you did." He looks at Mum nervously as he continues, "I didn't understand why of all places you would bring me here, I was scared when I saw their magick, I wanted to get off the island as quick as possible. But then, I saw Peri that night by the pond and I wasn't scared anymore..." he looks up at me shyly, "I knew I could trust you from the moment I first laid eyes on you, I could just tell." He looks back up at the sky, "so, thank you, whoever you are. I'm grateful you brought me here." Then, turning to look at Mum, Joe, and Ann, "and thank you to all of you, for accepting me into your home. I'd like to stay for as long as you'll have me."

Mum nods her head in approval.

"You are welcome Euan. Should you truly wish to join our coven, I shall allow you to be an extended member of this circle. You would be bound to us, as we would be to you, by circumstance albeit, not by blood, but from this solstice forward, you would be one of us. Should you wish to be?"

Euan thinks long and hard, then nods slowly.

"I do. Does it matter that I'm not of magick?"

"I had some trouble getting used to that at first, but no, it does not matter. All I ask of you is to live by our ways and to keep the existence of our coven to yourself, the mainland can never know that there are people of magick on this island, especially Elementals. You understand why don't you?" She gives a meaningful look in my direction as she presses this, their eyes meet fleetingly in agreement.

"Secrets safe with me, I promise," he agrees without hesitance.

Mum steps forward, taking Euan's hand in hers, murmuring, as a singular orb of white light circles over their wrists, "we have an accord then," Mum nods, "welcome Euan. You are now one of us. As of this moment forth, you are to be a member of this coven."

"Thank you for accepting me into your family," he nods gratefully.

"You're welcome," Mum motions to the rest of our circle, "we are an independent family, with no interaction from outsiders. We live with each other – for each other. Under the moon, the sun, the stars. We are all mere children of the earth, and we live as such. As the strongest person of magick in the family, it is my role to protect our coven, I do what is in our best interest, always; even when you cannot see it for yourself." Mum turns to me, "Peri this applies to you too. Euan may not be of magick, but you are, you hold powers that you are yet to fully comprehend. You must both promise to trust me to do what is best for this family. To be part of this coven my word is law, do you both agree?"

Euan looks at her with doubt in his eyes. I can see the cogs ticking. He likes it here and wants to stay. But he's about to promise my mum that he will trust her always, when he doesn't, not yet anyway. He surprises me by replying first.

"I agree." It shocks Mum too, but she holds her tongue, looking at me expectantly.

"Oh! Of course I do Mum," I take her hand and give it a reassuring squeeze. "I didn't think I'd need to answer that."

"Well, I wasn't sure if you would agree Peri. This applies to the outside world also. I promised to teach you all I know of our craft and being an Elemental and I'm doing so, but of the outside world, I can't reveal all to you until you are older. I need you to trust that this is for your own good. I've thought long and hard about it, but I won't budge on this. I don't want to speak of it again, not until you are old enough, and this would mean that Euan, while you're here you can't tell Peridot certain things about the outside world. I need you both to agree to this."

Woah. I wasn't expecting that.

I feel a little bombarded put on the spot in front of everyone. I don't want to agree to this, but I don't want to ruin the evening.

"I don't think it's very fair if everyone here knows what's out there, except me Mum," I begin tentatively.

"Be that as it may," she interrupts curtly, "that is my condition. No if's, no but's. When you are older you can know, but not yet. It may seem harsh, but you'll understand one day why it had to be this way."

I don't understand, this isn't fair. But if I say no, Euan will too, and then Mum will cast him out. I know she will.

"When is older?" Euan asks.

"What do you mean?"

"I understand why you're hiding certain things from Peri, I didn't at first, but I kind of get it now." He catches my eye discretely, willing me to be quiet, just at the right moment as I feel like screaming at them for talking about me like I'm not there, "so, I'll agree," he continues, "but when can we talk about it freely?"

"When Peridot is eighteen." Mum states.

"Eighteen?!" I exclaim, "you can't be serious?"

"Eighteen is a little extreme Val," Joe intervenes, "you can't expect her to wait that long, fifteen would be fairer don't you think?"

Mum stares daggers at Joseph, but he stands his ground, "you know what I'm saying Val, you'll just end up pushing her away."

"Fine! I'll compromise at sixteen, but that's it. We either all agree, or we don't, and you know what happens if we can't agree on this," she crosses her arms obstinately.

"Wait, what happens if we don't agree?" My voice rises.

Everyone's deciding what's best for me and as always, it's completely out of my hands. My head spins, as irritation turns to anger in the pit of my stomach. My hands subconsciously wring together, as my thoughts begin to spiral into a frenzy of pent-up fury. I can't help it, I'm so mad at her for doing this on my first solstice celebration, she's ruining everything. Before I realise what I'm doing, I've taken a step forward.

The earth around my feet begins to rise. Rocks and stones begin to encircle my feet as energy surges from my body in the direction of Mother. She looks in my direction momentarily shocked, then affronted. Her eyes flash purple in warning, but I don't budge. I'm angry, I'm not a little girl that can't handle the real world. She needs to see that. We both stand in defiance of the other, I can see the disbelief in her face, and she the anger in mine.

"Dot, calm down sweetie you don't want to do this," Ann stands in between us, palms raised. I've never seen her do that before. Her hands are glowing, and she looks afraid.

I can feel the Empath try to settle my anger, but this infuriates me more. Everyone having a say in what I should and shouldn't know, how I should and shouldn't feel. I'm sick of it. Even Ann whom I love dearly, is trying to control me right now.

Stupid Empath. I'm an Elemental. She can't control me.

No one can.

Except perhaps my mother. And I can't have that anymore. I won't have that anymore. Something stirs within and I know what must be done. Mother thinks she's the strongest person of magick within our coven, but she's wrong. I am. It's time to show her.

Stepping forward, I will Ann aside with my mind. I hear a thud but pay it no bother. Joe rushes forward to step between Mother and me but I will him away too. Another thud. Louder this time. Something inside yearns to go to them, but that goes dormant when I set eyes on the older Elemental.

Her eyes now shine a deep purple, bright orbs encircle both hands, her wand lies discarded upon the floor, hair standing on end. She levitates from the ground, magick radiating from her; "Peridot, calm down! You must control it, this isn't you!"

I turn my head quizzically at her.

"Goodbye Mother."

I call upon the elements, earth, air, fire, water, and spirit, willing them to show the lesser Elemental my true power. A part of me knows it's too soon, but I can't draw it back, my power wants to be free. I scream. I scream loud and I scream hard. Every moment of frustration and infuriation from the past thirteen years is on the brink of release. You can't keep a creature caged. It makes us wild. I surge my power towards the older Elemental, willing her to bow down.

"Peri - no!"

A boy jumps in front of me. A beautiful boy at that. His hair a chestnut brown, eyes a deep ocean blue. They're swirling. Strange. He's not of magick, I sense no power from him. Yet those eyes. They draw me in. He's afraid, I can feel it in his soul. But not of me. He's afraid for someone else. He misses them terribly. I see his soul torn from within.

Years of torment and sadness beat through his heart in waves, cascading into his veins and pulsing through his body. This poor soul, to have endured such pain.

It hits me. Deep. Like a bag of bricks to the stomach.

It hurts to see, to feel.

I feel all he has felt, all his pain, his helplessness.

I cry out, no longer screams of rage, but cries of sadness. I weep for him, dropping to my knees as I do so.

He rushes forward, holding me in his arms, allowing me to breathe him in. His strength grounds me. To have been through so much yet still be here, alive and breathing. My feelings are trivial in comparison. It confuses me. I can feel my Elemental trying to hold on, but she slips away as my will to understand this boy and what he's been through battles through stronger.

Closing my eyes, I breathe in the boy once more. He smells of home. Silently, I ask his permission to see what he has seen, to feel what he has felt. He nods freely, understanding my silent request. Closing my eyes, I go forth.

I find myself in a large, dark room. A barn of some sort. There's a small opening allowing a little light to shine through, but not enough to see clearly. There are young children everywhere, crying, shivering, some in tatters of material, others with bare skin. They're cold. They're scared. And they want their mothers. I can feel this with every fibre of my being. Their pure desperation and need for their mother's warmth.

The youngest have strange metal rings through their noses with a spike attached, they look in pain. The barn door opens suddenly, distracting me as someone I can't quite make out enters with a booming voice, "Herd one, approach the gate!"

I watch in horror as the eldest of the group within the paddock move forward, the younger children cry out and scream, they don't want them to go. Those that don't move forward are struck by what appears to be lightning. There must be other magick dwellers here. I must help them. I stand to help the boy whose just been struck to the floor with a bolt of light. He writhes in pain. I look up to see the attacker and what I see makes me sick to my stomach.

The barn is in two sections. Mothers on one side, children in a separate enclosure with me. The mothers are bare skin, many wounded and appear to be attached to a machine of some sort by their chests. Some cry tears freely. Others look dead in their eyes. One looks directly at me and cries out in fear. "Euan get back, get back now!"

I don't see in time, but I feel it, a thousand volts of pure energy strike my chest, I scream in agony. Then everything goes black.

GONE

My body feels like lead as I attempt to lift my pounding head from my pillow. The sun shines down bright, the first day of Litha upon us. I reminisce on the night before; the solstice is a blur. Making my way into the bathroom, I try to remember what happened after giving thanks. I vaguely remember feasting after our offerings, I think I tried some wine sneakily with Euan, after that, the rest is gone. So that's why you need to be an adult to drink alcohol – all I had was a sip!

After a brief hot shower, I head downstairs, the scent of fresh cinnamon buns wafting through the house making my mouth salivate. I'm surprisingly hungry given how much food was at the feast last night. I go to enter the kitchen, only to stop short before opening the door upon hearing whispered voices, I know I shouldn't, but I eavesdrop.

"She's a creature of magick the same as you Val, she craves freedom and knowledge. The more we keep from her, the more likely that is going to happen again."

"It's a risk I'm willing to take, she's too young to handle the emotions that will follow once she knows the truth. The Elemental in her will take over, she needs to be an adult to control that side of herself, hence I said eighteen!"

"I understand your logic, but last night proved it's not that simple, and the boy's connection to her can't be overlooked," sighs Joe, "mark my words, twill happen again or worse, longer it's kept from her."

"What will happen again?" I ask entering the kitchen.

"Morning Dot," greets Ann, avoiding my gaze to busy herself around the stove.

"Is everything okay?"

"Let's not get into this now Peri," asserts Mum looking irritable, "wake Euan for breakfast please."

"But – "

"Listen to Val please kiddo, emotions ran high between you Elementals last night, the rest of us could do with a break from it all there's a good lass?" Joe looks at me pleadingly and I can't refuse.

I head upstairs anxious to get to the bottom of their cryptic conversation - what on earth happened last night? What did I say to make everyone so on edge? Rushing into Euan's room I find him wide awake, looking troubled.

"Oh no! Not you too, what happened last night, what did I do?"

"Hmm?" he replies groggily.

"What happened last night, everyone's being weird?"

"I don't remember," he looks up confused, "I think I got drunk you know? Won't be doing that again, I feel like dung."

"Me too! Mum looks furious with me though, Joe and Ann said we had a row, but I can't remember a thing."

I sit down beside him trying desperately to remember.

"Holy cow!" Euan startles me, "I remember, we were celebrating the solstice and Joe offered me some of his wine to toast my deciding to stay. Your mum snapped at me when I went to pour you some too, she said you were too young. You pointed out you're older than me and then the two of you just started shouting at each other. You called her out on everything. I think you even called her a curse word."

"For earth's sake why did I do that?" I grimace, holding my head in my hands, "no wonder Mum's mad at me."

"Don't be so hard on yourself. Everyone keeps all these secrets from you, I'd have lost my temper way before now."

"Thanks," I answer ruefully getting up to leave, grateful for his reassurance, but it doesn't quell the anxious feeling in my tummy.

"Some good news though – I'm officially part of your witchy circle thing now," he makes silly hand gestures, trying successfully, to lighten the mood. I grin, launching a pillow in his direction, which narrowly misses his face.

"Looks like you need to practice your throwing as well as your catching," he tosses it back at me, hitting me square in the face. I launch myself at him and he bowls over laughing, "hey, experiencing my first hangover here!"

"Wimp," I laugh clambering off him. It's very tempting to pummel him right now, but my head throbs too, so I let him be. My tummy no longer feels as squirmy, but I need to make things right with Mum. I can't believe I swore at her.

"We are both never to drink again, agreed?"

"Most definitely," he nods, attempting to get out of bed and failing miserably. Lending him a helping hand, I pull him to his feet. The sheet drops to reveal his upper torso and I can't help but stare at the various scars and markings he's covered in. One stands out, a circular welt in his chest. For some reason, I can't tear my eyes away.

"Like what you see?" he asks uncomfortably.

"Sorry, I didn't mean to stare, I hate that someone did this to you," I reply earnestly, wishing I could take his pain away.

"This is nothing compared to some of the others," he shrugs.

"Why did they hurt you?" I ask.

"You wouldn't believe me if I told you."

I don't pry further, we've tried to speak a few times about his life before he came here, but it always ends awkwardly, as he makes up bizarre stories instead of telling me the truth. He'll tell me when he's ready.

"What shall we do today?" I change the subject.

He looks annoyed, but refrains from saying what he wants to, "I might go for a walk, clear my head a while. Or can Joe heal me? Does magick work on hangovers?"

"I hope so, I want my head to stop banging."

"Okay, give me a minute to get washed and I'll come down, we can ask him together."

"Good idea, I'm going to find Phoenix."

Closing the door behind me I make my way out the back of the house, Amy, and Roland whinny as I approach, Phoenix running circles around my legs. I sit down and pat Phoenix's head absentmindedly. I cannot believe I argued with Mum on my first solstice, I feel dreadful. I really should make it up to her. It's the grown-up thing to do and I want to prove to everyone that I'm a responsible person, not a whiney teenager feeling sorry for myself all the time.

I have Euan and I have my magick, I'm happier now than I think I ever have been, the quicker I can prove I'm responsible, the quicker they'll fill me in on everything else and I can truly be content. In the meantime, I want to be good at magick, so that can be my main priority, that and helping Euan's mum so he can be content here too.

Phoenix pads along with me, as we stroll back to the house, Roland and Amy in tow. They must be able to smell the cinnamon buns. The smell hits my nostrils, making my tummy rumble loudly.

"Hungry, are we?" Euan teases, as I take a seat at the table.

"Famished, I feel like I've not eaten for a day."

"Same, definitely staying away from alcohol from now on, I feel like I've been hit by a horse," he groans.

Mum, Joe, and Ann all look at their plates in awkward silence. I'm assuming they want to reprimand us for having wine in the first place, but they don't want it to cause an outburst again. Ann looks especially troubled. I don't think my apology can wait until tonight - I need to fix this now.

"Um, everyone, I'm sorry about last night."

The table goes deadly quiet except for Euan and only Mum meets my gaze.

"Why are you sorry?" She asks curtly.

"Last night's a bit of a blur, but I think I over-reacted and said some stuff I didn't mean. Everyone put such an effort into making our first solstice special and I feel like I ruined it," I rush out, looking down at my hands.

The table remains quiet, Mum the first to speak.

"Thank you for apologising Peri. All is forgiven," she waves her hand dismissively, causing me to look up from my hands surprised. That was a lot easier than I expected it to be. The table breathes a collective sigh of relief as we all begin to eat, the tension no longer unbearable.

"However," she continues, oh great here it comes - I knew that was too easy I think to myself, "there is an unsettled arrangement we didn't get to finalise last night, that we need to settle now."

"Val don't –" starts Joe.

"It's okay," I intervene, "by the way everyone's acting I must've reacted bad last night, I want to make it right, what is it Mum?"

She nods brusquely then continues, "it was agreed that Euan is welcome to join our coven, however, the bonding process was initiated, but not sealed. To seal the bond, I need you both to agree to trust me as your elder and the strongest person of magick within our family. My word is law, and this must be agreed if Euan is to remain as one of us. Can you both agree to this?"

That I was not expecting. I understand now why I may have lost my temper last night. But I want Euan to stay, and I always end up doing what Mum says eventually, so fine. So be it.

"Okay, I agree," I look to Euan who nods uncertainly but follows suit.

"Okay, I agree too."

"Excellent. That was much less stressful," snipes Mum, "if we can all head to the solstice area, I will seal the bonds."

She gets up from the table, Ann following suit, myself and Euan go to follow, but Joe remains seated.

"Joseph?" Mum prompts.

He reluctantly gets up from the table, not making eye contact, as we trail behind Mum leading the way back to the solstice area. Just as we're about to enter, Joe hurriedly pulls Euan back, putting his fingers to his lips and putting something in Euan's pocket before joining the circle. We stop short before following, confusion on both of our faces.

"Come along now, the bonding won't take a moment," Mum chides.

Uncertainly, I take Euan's hand and we enter together. I take Mum's outstretched hand as she chants and makes the circle. Once it's safe to move freely she lets go, as do the others but Euan holds tight. I assume he's nervous and give him a reassuring squeeze that everything is alright. Mum steps into the centre of the clearing, her eyes shining a brilliant purple, as she begins to chant:

"I call upon the Goddess of old,
Unite this coven for years untold,
For each and all present here,

I am thy leader, to follow and adhere,
As above so it is below – bound together as one,
Let it be so."

A glow radiates from her chest, gradually glowing brighter, it shoots forth to the rest of us, encircling us together. I step forward as the circle gets smaller, huddling our bodies together until we are all touching. Mum continues to chant incoherently, as the light encircles us, rising above our heads until a brilliant bolt of lightning strikes the sky. The strike reverberates across the land, a deep rumbling echo that stretches on for what feels like forever. Eventually, the air clears, and the heavy feeling is gone. I look up at Euan to check he's okay, just as a sting hits my wrist, we jump apart, my skin tingling.

"What on earth was that?"

"You've both received our covens mark," Mum answers, taking our hands to face them skywards, in the sunlight we both have a small star on our wrist, enclosed in a circle.

"Why a star?" Asks Euan.

"It's the sign of the elements," I explain, reciting from my lessons, "it's called a pentacle. Each point of the star represents one of the five elements, earth, air, fire, water, and spirit. The circle unites them all. And now us too, I guess," I smile. I'm so glad he's one of us, even if he can't do magick, I throw my arms around him and give him a hug. He holds me back laughing at my unexpected show of affection.

"Does this mean I can do voodoo now too?" he grins.

"I wouldn't mock the craft young man," Mum tuts, "I have a friend in a jungle tribe many seas away, who is fluent in voodoo and not a witch to be messed with."

"Wow really?" he asks awed, "are all the types of magick I've heard of real?"

"Most likely yes, all stories start somewhere, the truth tends to get a little warbled along the way. We can add

Voodoo to one of the lessons perhaps, history of all magickal practices is something you'll both be fluent in soon."

I grin at Euan, who looks abashed for a moment.

"What's wrong?" My grin falters momentarily.

"I thought voodoo was dark magick. Well, I thought you were all dark magick users if I'm being honest. Especially you," he looks at Mum awkwardly, "now I'm one of you. I guess it's just a lot to take in."

"Where there is light, there is dark Euan, you will learn this as you grow," she replies matter-of-factly, "no one is all good, or all bad. I'd like to think there's more of the light in us than the dark, but if the time arises where dark magick must be used, then so mote it be. That time, thankfully, is not now though, so you can both take the afternoon off."

"Thanks Mum," I give her a timid smile before yanking Euan away with me. We run towards the barn, ducking into Amy and Roland's stable. It's warm inside and smells of straw and newly cut grass, we take a seat on a freshly cut bale.

"So, that was intense, how do you feel?"

Euan looks dazed. "I think that stone Joe gave me stopped your mum's magick from doing something. I could feel its energy pushing hers away. It's like I was in a bubble."

"What did he give you?"

Euan pulls out a piece of shiny black stone. Obsidian.

"I don't understand," I gasp.

"What is it?"

"Obsidian is a crystal of protection. What was he trying to protect you from? You just joined our circle - you weren't in any danger."

"Joe didn't seem to think so…"

I go quiet. I don't want to row with Euan. But he's wrong. Mum wouldn't hurt him. I know she wouldn't. But why would Joe give him obsidian, the strongest protection crystal, just as he's about to be initiated into our coven? Maybe, it's because he's not from magick, he may have needed it? But that doesn't explain why he was shifty at the table, or why he gave it to Euan when Mum wasn't looking. Something's not right and I don't like it. "Let's go find Joe. I think we should just ask him."

"Yeah, me too. I don't like not knowing what's going on, it makes me feel on edge."

I nod in agreement.

"Sorry," he grimaces.

"What have you got to be sorry for, you haven't done anything?"

"This must be how you feel all the time. Left in the dark questioning everything."

His reply leaves me stumped for a moment, "I guess I'm used to it," I eventually shrug, "Joe wants to tell me things, he just won't as Mum said I've got to be older. Doesn't mean he won't tell you though."

"He speaks to me about the outside world sometimes. It helps. He understands. That's why he was surprised I decided to stay. He caught me trying to leave once and convinced me not to go."

"You were going to leave and not say goodbye?"

"I left you a letter," he looks down uncomfortably, "I knew if I told you, you'd try and come with me. Your mum would kill me. I reckon her magick's strong enough to cross onto the mainland."

"Maybe mine will be too, I could've stopped her."

"Perhaps, but I didn't want to be responsible for you leaving. I understand why she protects you so much, you have it good here. It's any kids dream from the mainland.

Not even just kids. Adults too. This place is heaven, it's how it must've used to have been. Before everything changed."

I can't help myself. But I need to ask. I want to know so badly, "what happened out there, truthfully?"

"Truthfully. No-one knows. One day everything was just different. I was only young the day The Changing happened, I don't remember what life was like before."

"You don't remember anything?"

"Not properly, it must've been how it is here, only the other way round."

"I don't understand," I feel myself getting agitated like I often do when I try to talk to him about his life, but hold it back, he's trying to explain, I just don't understand what he means.

"You won't understand lass, not now anyway. Val's seen to that once and for all," Joe walks in, looking serene.

"What did she do?" Euan looks up.

"She knew if you stayed you two would eventually talk about the outside world. How can you not? Well, now you can't. You're bound by our coven not to do so. Until Peridot is sixteen, none of us from within the circle can speak freely of the outside world around her." Joe sighs.

"I'm sorry Dot. There's nothing I could do. Val's word is the law."

"But how could she have done that without us knowing about it? That's not fair, we didn't know what we were agreeing to!"

"I know, I know, it was sly. But she's done what she thinks is in your best interest, who are we to argue? She is your mother."

"Is that what the stone was for?" interrupts Euan.

"I couldn't interfere with Peri's side of the spell, but I could with yours. Val wanted your memories of the outside world to be 'put on hold' whilst you're here with us."

"She doesn't have the right to decide that!"

"Ay, lad I agree. So, I intervened. That stone there should've kept your memories intact. But you won't be able to speak to Peri about them. I'm sorry. It was the best I could do."

The barn falls silent.

Amy and Roland trot in, whinnying as they approach.

"This is why she can't hear them isn't it?" Euan asks exasperated, "It's part of the spell. Why she doesn't understand them?"

"Afraid so. Until Peri is sixteen, anything relating to what's out there is 'muted' as Val calls it," he sighs heavily again, "she thinks it's what's best for you. I don't. But I'm not your mother. I really am sorry."

I don't know what to say. I feel swindled. I should feel angry. But I don't. I feel hollow if anything. Almost like I expected this to happen. And as per usual I have no clue what they're talking about. It is as it's always been once again.

"There's nothing you could do Joe. I'm glad Euan still has his memories."

"You're taking this better than I thought you would," Joe rubs my back as he stands up to leave, "well – I best get back to my duties, farm won't run itself."

"Do you want a hand?" I ask.

"Not today, you two explore or something, do what kids are meant to do. Have fun."

He shuffles out of the barn, looking troubled. An awkward silence follows.

"You're allowed to be mad Euan, I think I am too. I'm just so used to all of this – it's normal for me."

"I get that she's doing what she thinks is best for you, but she goes the wrong way about it! She hides everything from you and it's not protecting you from anything! You'd be the least protected of all of us if anyone came here, you wouldn't have a clue what was going on!"

He continues ranting, but it's just a blur of sound. I gape lost for words.

"I can't understand what you're saying."

"Huh?" He looks up quizzically mid-rant.

"I can see you speaking, but I can't understand a word of it. It's just noise. And your mouths out of focus, I can't make out the words."

He throws his hands up in exasperation.

"This isn't right!"

He kicks the bale of hay in frustration. I want to lash out too, but what's the point? Mum's word as always, is final.

"Do you want to get out of here for a bit?" I ask, needing to think about something, anything else.

"Where?"

"There's somewhere I went on my birthday I think you'd like," he follows me outside to where Roland and Amy are laying, basking in the sun, "have you ridden before?"

"Ridden?"

"Yeah, it's quite far, Amy and Roland will have to take us."

"They let you ride them?" He asks shocked.

"Sure, you can see how tame they are."

"Yeah, but -," his voice goes muffled and out of focus again.

"This is going to be so annoying; I don't understand what you're saying again," I grimace.

"Figures," he rolls his eyes in exasperation, "now I get why you want to leave so bad. You're in a whole different version of captivity here." He goes on to say something else, but I can't understand him.

"Euan!" I snap.

"Sorry," he huffs, "I didn't use to say anything as I didn't want you thinking I was crazy, now I think you'd finally believe me, and you can't understand me."

"Nothing we can do about it now, so drop it, please. It's exhausting," I sigh.

"Okay," he grabs my hand and gives it a squeeze. I squeeze back before letting go and walk over to Amy, lifting myself easily onto her back.

"Your turn," I motion Euan towards Roland.

"Ha! As if I'm doing that, he'll have me for dinner!"

I laugh at his choice of words, "don't be ridiculous, Roland wouldn't hurt a fly."

Euan looks uneasy and goes to the black stallion warily, "I'll get on you while you're sitting down, okay Roland? Then you get up slowly and I'll try to stay on... no kicking me, this is her idea, not mine."

I can't help but giggle, he talks to animals how Joe does. I hold back titters while Euan wobbles all over the place as Roland rises to all fours trotting over to me and Amy.

"Never thought I'd ride a horse," he sounds awed, running his hands through Roland's thick, shiny mane.

"Wait until we get up to a gallop," I grin, "It's the best feeling, you're going to love it. You need to trust Roland though, follow his movements, don't be stiff or you'll fall straight off. He's got you don't worry, you'll be fine."

He looks nervous for a moment and then the look is gone, "let's do this!"

We head off. Trotting until Euan is riding comfortably, then increasing to a slow gallop. He looks up at me, smiling from ear to ear.

"This is amazing!" He exclaims, "I wish the kids from back home were here they'd −" the rest of his sentence is hidden from me, his face once again out of focus, but I say nothing, not wanting to ruin this moment for him. He's not doing it on purpose, if anything it's nice that he wants to talk to me freely at last. I just wish I could understand him.

Roland looks back at Amy whinnying loudly, she picks up the pace and my thoughts are forgotten as we gallop across fields and meadows in full bloom. Bright colours flash past, vibrant yellows, purples, pinks, and greens, with a clear blue sky above us, it feels like we're racing through a rainbow. Emptying my mind, I lose myself in the moment and howl into the wind, Euan laughs wildly and howls back, both horses now gallop freely as we hurtle towards the end of our land.

Roland and Amy begin to slow down as we approach the cliff, the ocean carries on forever in front of us, sparkling like diamonds in a sea of blue. Coming to a halt, it's silent other than the crash of waves cascading below us. Euan looks elated. It's hard not to be. It's so beautiful. I wish I came here more often. Breathing in deep I can taste the ocean on my tongue, salty and sweet.

"Now this, is a view," Euan breaks the silence.

"I thought you'd like it."

"I've never seen anything like it. This place is a paradise."

"It has its moments."

"I'll say," he looks lost for a moment, "it's hard to stay mad at her when this is all she wants for you. Your mum I mean. I guess she wants me to have that too while I'm here. Maybe, that's why she tried to take away my memories?"

I remain quiet. After years of trying to understand my Mum's reasoning, I don't want to elaborate. It'll only ruin my mood.

"Wish my mum were here," he says sadly.

"Me too, I'd like to meet her."

It must be hard for him to be here all alone with his family stuck in whatever his life was before he came here.

"What was she like?" I ask.

"Brave. Stubborn. Beautiful. A bit like your mum in a way - just not as scary," he shrugs. "And no magick, obviously."

"Do you wish you had magick?"

"I didn't until I met you. We're taught that magick's evil back home. Now I've experienced it, it's not quite so black and white."

"Why do they think magick's evil?" I ask shocked.

His reply is as before, a blurb of noise without words or meaning. I sigh frustrated. I'd forgotten for a moment.

"You didn't understand any of that, did you?"

I shake my head.

We sit in silence again. Both wanting to rant, but not wanting to ruin the moment.

"Tell me more about your mum," I suggest instead, dismounting from Amy, walking round to help him clamber off Roland. They wander off a little to graze as we sit down on the grass overlooking the cliff.

"What do you want to know?" he asks.

"Well, I meant what I said, I will try and bring her here for you somehow, so I guess it'll help to know a bit about her. Could even practice a ritual while we're here if you like?"

He visibly perks up again.

"Okay. Well, her name is Louise, she's fair-skinned like me, with mousey brown hair and a huge smile. Her mouth looks a bit too big for her face when she smiles," he reminisces, "not seen her smile since I was little though." He trails off, but the rest of the sentence is concealed from me.

"For this to work we need to focus on only your mum, when you speak about her, I can hear everything, but soon as you talk about anything else, it's hidden."

He nods, "Okay I'll try. She's skinny, like when I arrived, and she'll be dirty. Don't picture her smiling, she'll be a mess now I've gone. She'll be so worried because she's not seen me," tears fill his eyes as he looks away, seeming helpless.

I feel like the night he first came to my window - I just want to help him. I decide resolutely there and then that no matter what I must do, I will reunite him with his mum.

"How are we going to get her back Peri?" he sniffs.

"I'm not sure," I admit, "I don't know how, or when, but I swear by the Goddess I will unite you with your mum, no matter what it takes," I promise.

He nods as a tear escapes his eyes. I don't shy away like before, we weren't close the first time I saw him cry, but now he is my best friend. I lean over and hold him fiercely. He holds me back. His pain dripping from him like a leaky teapot. I can feel it.

It hurts.

Mother of earth it hurts so much.

How he wakes up each day with this weight on his shoulders I'll never know.

Part of me understands why Mum wanted to take this away from him, the other part of me is furious at her for trying. He needs his memories, not to forget them. He'd have forgotten all about his mother and earth knows what could happen to her if she gets left behind where Euan came from. How could she do such a thing?

No matter how good her intentions were, she has no right to try to control him like that. To control me like that! All of this is to delay my knowledge of the outside world. I finally have a friend and I can't even hold a normal conversation with him without Mum controlling it. It makes me so angry! With each beat of my heart, I feel anger pulsing through my veins, slowly spiralling into a frenzy.

"Peri," Euan pulls back to look at me, "Are you okay?"

I can't answer.

I want to, but it's like something has hold of my words and they won't come out.

I feel numb.

I want to help him, but I can't without being able to speak freely. It's so frustrating! I can see in my mind-eye Euan being reunited with his mother and the joy it would bring him. I wish so desperately that I could make it happen for him.

"PERI!"

I look up to find Euan surrounded by a bright white glow. It encircles him brightly, swallowing him whole.

Then just as quick as it came, the light is gone.

And so is Euan.

EUAN

I land facedown with a thud.

Ouch. That hurt. A lot.

Slowly, I roll onto my back, taking a moment to regain my bearings, everything's out of focus. I appear to be in one of the barns. I have no idea how Peri did that. Blimey, her magick's strong. When she can control it, she's going to be able to move mountains. She must've projected me at least a mile and she didn't even do a ritual. She'll be looking high and low for me. I chuckle to myself picturing her having one of her Peri fits trying to find me, then dust myself off.

Attempting to sit up, an unfamiliar noise startles me.

Hang on. Something's not right.

I hear murmured voices, but not voices I recognise.

"Herds! Back to your paddocks, roaming time's over!"

No! No! No!

It can't be. I can't be back. That's impossible.

I watch in horror as the room comes into focus.

I am in a barn. Back at the A.I station.

CHANGES

I've been an Elemental for nearly three years now. So far, all I've accomplished is bashing myself in the head with a basket of vegetables. Oh. And making my best friend vanish. If there was an award for the worst Elemental, I think I'd win hands down. I looked everywhere for Euan, searched every nook and crevice of the entire island. As did Joe, Ann, Phoenix, Roland, Amy, even Mum. All to no avail. Euan was gone. And has been gone ever since.

Everything changed after that. Mum and I barely speak outside of lessons. She refuses to go and search for Euan on the mainland, even though I'm certain where I sent him. She still won't tell me the truth about what's out there, and we clash anytime I try to bring it up. It's infuriating. I wish Euan were still here and miss him terribly.

I've lost count of the nights I've spent wide awake until gone midnight, willing with all my might to bring him back, but it never works. I've lost touch with magick since then. The one ritual I want to work, won't. And the previous two didn't go to plan either. I'm apprehensive to try any other magickal practices in case I accidentally set the island on fire or something.

I've managed to keep myself busy learning about the history of witchcraft and focusing on practices that are still our nature but don't rely as heavily on the magickal side of the craft. Mostly healing, which I'm confident in now, I tend to the animals where needed and even help with Joe's cancer treatment.

Joe misses Euan as much as I do, I think he bonded with him more than he lets on. I've mentioned to him where I think I sent Euan - to the A.I station he spoke of once, where his mum was kept. I was focusing so hard on reuniting them, I must've sent him over there, instead of bringing her here. I didn't even realise I was doing magick at the time, I hadn't said any incantations, grounded myself or anything. It just happened. I'm so angry with myself.

Although I'm angrier with Mum. If she hadn't cast that spell on us, then it could've gone differently. Euan would still be with us, and his mum would probably be here too. If I'm strong enough to get him there without trying, then I must be strong enough to bring her here when I do try. Well, I'd like to think so. But perhaps not, seeing as I've not managed to magick them back. And I've been trying for nearly three years.

My only hope of ever finding Euan is going to the mainland, finding the A.I Station and rescuing him and his mum myself. I've been planning it for the past few months now. My bags are all packed and ready to go. I just need to get as good at healing as I can before I leave. And ideally to learn what's out there. I've tried to make sense of the snippets I got from Euan, back when I thought he was crazy. I think maybe there was a disease that killed everyone, making the remaining humans unsafe to be around and allowing wild animals to roam the land. That's the only thing I can think of that explains his comments about humans being food for animals and that would explain why so many people died. I'll find out the truth soon enough.

I'm sixteen in a few days, so Mum will have to tell me. The ritual was that the outside world must remain hidden from me until I turn sixteen. So, from that day onwards they will have to answer my questions finally. I'm nervous, excited and scared to know the truth. It's been made into this big thing where it's been kept from me for so long. No matter what it is, I will not abandon Euan. I am going to find him whether Mum allows it or not. I would much rather have her permission, and her help if I'm being honest, but I'm doubtful I'll get it.

The sun begins to set making the sky an inky blue, setting to purple in the evening sky. It's been a long day today, lessons all morning, then tending to the crops all afternoon. I'm covered head to toe in mud and grime, earth embedded under my fingernails.

"Shall we call it a day?" Joe trudges over, his wellies caked in mud too.

Nodding in agreement, I wipe the sweat from my brow.

"Same again tomorrow?"

"I reckon so, then we're all set for April showers next month. Should see another good crop this year."

Together, we head back towards the main house, parting ways as I head upstairs to get cleaned up. After a thorough shower making sure to rid myself of all traces of dirt and grime, I take a seat at my dresser. I take my time drying off, running a towel through my hair. What was once a short cut, has grown long and wavy past my shoulders. My once dark hair is now a shade lighter and serious blue eyes look back at me, my previous green shade no longer visible. My eyes changed to blue soon after Euan disappeared.

"Peridot?"

Mum enters distracting me, she looks the same as always. She doesn't seem to age, not physically anyway. Unlike her personality, that gets more serene by the day.

"Peridot, are you listening?"

"Yes Mother," I sigh.

"Peridot, you know I hate being called mother."

Rolling my eyes, I turn my attention back to drying my hair, "what is it *Mum*?"

She gives me the eye but ignores my retort.

"Family chat at the table in ten minutes, we need to discuss your birthday plans."

"I didn't realise there were any birthday plans," I look up surprised.

"Sixteen is a big one, we'll do something to celebrate, something magickal if you like?"

I look away again. Mum knows I'm dubious of my magickal capabilities since the incident. She's not forced me to do any rituals since, which surprises me. It's almost like she's glad I'm not practising the practical side of our craft.

"Sure, hopefully, nothing goes wrong this time."

"You must be confident in your abilities Peridot. Intent is everything. If the will isn't truly there – then how can you expect it to work?"

I know she's right, but say nothing, returning to my hair in the mirror. She lingers a moment; goes to say something, then thinks better of it and heads downstairs. I used to feel bad about our lack of closeness, but her refusal to leave the island to find Euan makes me resent her. She's right though. My magick's not been working properly because I don't believe it can. I'll have to work on my intent.

Leaving my hair wavy, I change into a loose t-shirt that hides my newly acquired curves, I'm as uncomfortable with my body right now as I am my magick, not used to my 'lady areas', as Mother refers to them. Heading downstairs, Ann's chopping away at the sideboard, and I grab an apron to help.

"What are we cooking today?" I ask, selecting a carving knife from the counter.

"Butternut squash stew for tea and apple pie for dessert," she beams, handing me the cooking apples.

My mouth salivates at the mention of pie, and I get slicing and dicing, my fingers deftly cutting the large apples into bite-sized chunks. Ann rolls out a thick layer of pastry and generously sprinkles cinnamon on top, before placing it into a deep baking dish. I pop in the apples with brown sugar, golden syrup, and extra cinnamon before placing the top layer of pastry on top and carving a pretty flower design into the crust.

"Turning into quite the cook I see," Mother enters nodding her head in approval. I make the effort to smile in response, placing the baking dish in the oven, while Ann ladles out hearty servings of stew for everyone.

"Smells good love," Joe gives Ann a peck on the cheek before taking a seat at the table. I tuck into dinner along with everyone else, eating in silence, partly because the food is delicious, but mostly as Mother and I are in the same room. Any attempt at normal chatter always ends in an argument, so I rarely attempt to start a conversation unless she's out of the room. For months Joe and Ann would make idle chit chat to ease the tension, but there's no need anymore, it's become the norm and no longer feels awkward. It's just how it is now. I'm first to finish and take my plate to the sink to wash up, before checking in on desert.

"Ten more minutes should do it," I inhale the aroma that wafts from the oven, then take one of my workbooks from the side and sit back down at the table.

The volume I'm currently studying is on old English witchcraft. Or to be more precise – the lack of it. People with the craft were persecuted for their abilities by the church, purging Pagans from the land and converting society to Christianity. Anyone that had any association with magick from healers, herbalists, seers, empaths, even relatives or friends with no magickal ability were being killed in the most awful of ways. Women mostly. But some men too. I think I understand Mother's comment about people fearing what they don't understand. Thousands upon thousands of people were slaughtered. It was a massacre. Since then, witchcraft was only spoken of in hushed whispers for fear of being tortured, drowned, or in the worst case, burned alive. I visibly shudder at the thought.

"Grim, isn't it?" Joe notices my trepidation.

I nod in response. "I don't understand how people could be so cruel."

"Humans have been cruel since the dawn of time, it's in their nature," asserts Mother, "they do as their leader does, and unfortunately, humans had a habit of putting bad people in positions of power."

Normally, I'd ask more questions, but no doubt we'll disagree on something, and it'll end in a row. I'm not missing out on apple pie for a pointless argument that won't result in my favour. Placing a bookmark into the thick volume, I leave the table to retrieve the pie from the oven.

"Smells good, dish up, will you? I'm dribbling over here," Joe nudges me, close to drooling.

Grinning, I dish out four generous servings, hesitating as I go to pop a fifth, slightly smaller serving in a bowl.

"Where's Phoenix?" I ask.

He's not around as often as normal. No idea where he goes but he's often gone for days. I've not seen him in over a week, this is the longest he's been gone before. The table goes quiet. Joe eyes Mother, while Ann busies herself eating her pie.

"What's wrong, what's happened to Phoenix?" my voice wavers, fearing something's happened to him.

"He's okay, don't worry," Mum sighs. "I wanted us to have a nice family dinner before trying to approach this, but I guess I can't put it off any longer."

"What do you mean, what's happened to Phoenix?"

"Nothing, Phoenix is fine. He'll be back in time for your birthday, he's just running some errands for me."

"Huh?" I reply, perplexed. How can Phoenix run errands?

"Earth, how do we explain this?" Mum grips the table anxiously.

"I'll make us some tea," Ann heads to the stove.

"No, Ann, I need you at the table for this. Joe, do you mind making the tea, please?"

"No problem but give kiddo something she looks like she's swallowed a golf ball," he pats my back on his way to the kettle. "Everything's fine lass, you're just about to get all your answers at long last."

I drop my spoon in shock, apple pie splattering everywhere. "But I'm not sixteen yet?"

"I want you to have a nice birthday Peridot," Mum sighs, "Ann suggested it might be better to explain now so that you can try and enjoy your sixteenth properly."

"Really?" I exclaim excitedly, "you mean it? You're really going to tell me?"

"I wanted to wait until after your birthday celebrations, but Joe, ever so tactfully pointed out, that if we didn't tell you on the day, there would be nothing to celebrate as you'd be sulking all afternoon - so yes. I will tell you everything now."

My mouth goes dry. I've been wanting to know the truth for so long that part of me thought I'd never find out. Now I'm about to, I feel overwhelmed with anxiety.

"Ann, take Peri's hand, will you?"

Ann scoots over and takes both of my hands in hers. I try to ground myself like I've been taught in my lessons, Ann's hands glow a gentle yellow.

"Focus on the light dear," Ann soothes, letting her Empath abilities calm my rising nerves. It works a little, but my heart continues to race. Joe places a tray down with four mugs of tea. A mix of aromas fills the room as he hands us each a mug, I notice each has a different scent. Mum's eyebrows raise as she takes hers, eyeing Joe questioningly.

"Just sip it woman!" He exasperates, "you'll thank me afterwards, trust me."

Nodding towards me, he takes a seat at the table, sliding my mug into my grasp. I breathe in the rising steam, inhaling deeply whilst trying to focus on staying calm.

"Dot?" I look up, he rarely if ever calls me that. "What you're about to hear is going to sound downright crazy. It's going to be a lot to take in. Even after we've told you, it most likely won't make a lot of sense, but know you are safe, and everything will be okay."

Nodding numbly, I turn to face Mum. She looks scared. I feel bad for referring to her as 'Mother' for the past how-ever many months. Her fear, oddly, calms me. I feel like I need to be calm for her to be able to do this. I release Ann's hands and take Mum's in my own.

"Mum. It's okay. Just tell me. Please."

She gapes for a moment, turning to Joe haplessly.

"Vallaeartha, it has to be you that tells her."

She nods. "Okay. Here goes nothing," her lids brim with tears and with a shaky breath, she offloads at long last. Her lips move quickly, as she rushes to get it all out. Or at least, she tries to, only, I can't hear a word of it. Just like it was back when Euan tried to tell me things. Her face goes out of focus, her words completely distorted like a swarm of bees buzzing past me.

"I don't understand," I interrupt.

"I know it's hard, but please let me finish -"

"No, I mean I physically cannot understand a word that's coming out of your mouth. It's still distorted," I explain in angst.

"The spell," she gripes, head in her hands.

"Codswallop Val, it's your frogging spell, you must be able to undo it!" Joe throws his arms up in exasperation.

"I – I already did..." she stammers in frustration, "last night after we spoke about it. I don't understand."

"I do."

Mum looks up at me, apprehension in her eyes.

"It's like you told me this morning. Intent is everything. How can your will work if the will is not there to begin with? You don't genuinely want me to know yet. So, the spell won't break. Not until you genuinely want this for me or until the spells complete."

The table goes quiet. Everyone knows I'm right. The silence stretches out between us, no one wanting to break the peace.

"It's okay." I sigh.

Joe snorts. Then covers his mouth like he didn't mean to out loud.

"I mean it, it's fine. I was prepared to find out on my next birthday. I've waited five thousand, eight hundred and thirty-six days so far," I calculate the math in my head, "four more will be a doddle."

Finishing the last of my tea, which I think is responsible for my taking this so well, I rise from the table.

"When you put it like that..." Joe slumps forward in his seat.

"You're more worked up about it than I am," I observe.

"I was excited about being able to talk freely at last, but like you say. Four more days after eighty-nine billion, or whatever the number was, can't hurt, can it?"

Mum gets up and leaves the table.

"Val," Ann calls out, going after her. Joe Sighs.

"Sorry. I've gone along with her wishes for so long now, can't wait for it all to be over, it's been hard on all of us," he sips his tea, "made sense when you were a littlun, let you grow up free from it all. Soon as you came into magick I'd have told you though. You need to be prepared."

"Prepared for what though?"

"Well, I can't blooming tell you now, can I? When I do tell you, you probably won't believe me. You'll go back to thinking I'm crazy," he nudges me gently in the ribs.

I force myself to smile. "He was telling the truth, wasn't he?"

"What, boyo? Ay, lass, he was telling the truth. Every weird sentence he ever uttered, all true."

That hits me hard. I feel awful for not listening to him when he first arrived. It was so long ago, none of it makes sense to me now. Why didn't I just listen to him? Four days I think to myself. Four days and I'll know and then I can go and, bring him back.

"You'll need help," Joe interrupts my thoughts. I look at him quizzically. "When you go to find him." He continues, awaiting my response.

I stay quiet not knowing whether to admit my plan or try to deny it. I'm not sure if it's a coincidence he said that or if he read my thoughts.

"Listen to me Peridot and listen well. There's so much out there you aren't familiar with. Your magick will get you so far, but you cannot use it out in the open. You'll have to keep your true nature hidden if you want to survive out there. Only unleash it when completely necessary. Do you understand?"

I nod. Yes, I understand and no I don't. It doesn't surprise me that he knows what I'm planning. I'm grateful he speaks so plainly with me. He always has done.

"Do they know?"

"Ann suspects. We haven't told Val though. Your freedom belongs to you. You're not a child anymore. You hold more power than all of us combined. When you get through this block and learn how to embrace it properly, you'll do amazing things." He smiles warmly at my look of disbelief.

"That's what makes you so special Dot, you have no idea the abilities you hold. But you need to get boyo before you do any of that. Your magick won't work properly while your intent's set so desperately on finding him."

"Is that why my magick's not working?"

"I think so yes," he agrees.

"I've been trying to ritual him back for so long and nothing works, what if my magick's just not powerful enough?"

"It is," he assures me, "the spell Val meant to protect you is backfiring on your other capabilities. How can you bring someone back from somewhere you've never been? Somewhere you've never seen. Somewhere we can't even talk to you about. It's impossible. Especially at the age of fifteen Peri. Your magick is fine, your knowledge just needs filling in. Once you know, it might work. And if it doesn't. Well, your plan B is a secret safe with me."

"Scouts honour?"

"Ha! Quite right lass, scouts honour indeed." He chuckles doing a weird salute with his fingers.

"Thanks Joe," I lean into him for a hug.

"Least I can do kiddo, least I can do. Wish I could do more. When the time comes I will. But that's a talk for another day." He gets up from the table taking the leftover mugs of tea with him. Four days I think to myself. Four Days.

My birthday has finally arrived. Four days felt like a thousand, I thought this day would never come. I can't explain it, but I feel different. My senses feel heightened, more alert. Everything seems a little less morbid, I no longer feel weighed down by the burden of Euan's disappearance, and what may, or may not, be out there.

I'm awake early, it's barely five in the morning, but I'm eager to get the talk out of the way, so I can make my plan of action. Looking outside my bedroom window everything is clearer, sharper, I feel grateful to be alive, less confused about my future. I hope this feeling stays when I'm finally filled in on the outside world. I need to wake everyone up and get this out of the way.

A knock on my door averts my attention.

"Come in," I greet sleepily.

"Good morning birthday girl," Ann enters bearing a tray laden with food, "thought you might enjoy breakfast in bed to gather your thoughts before things get too heavy later."

"Thanks Ann," I smile gratefully, "this looks delicious."

Sitting up, I slather a generous dollop of raspberry jam across a sweet sugary croissant. Each bite is heavenly, I'm going to miss Ann's cooking when I leave. The thought hangs in my mind for a moment, like a cloud about to shower down a torrent of rain. I'm leaving. I'm really doing this.

I think I've known for a while that I would leave as soon as the spell broke. It's the only way to bring Euan back. Mum will not allow me to leave the island if I ask, and I can't risk her using magick to keep me here longer. I need to leave. And I should probably leave before she wakes up. I have an idea, but I don't know how I can ask it of them. Or that they'll even say yes.

"Of course we will," Ann whispers.

I glance up in surprise.

"I didn't mean to pry, your aura is loud and clear for all to read, there's no hiding what your plan is Dot. Wait a moment while I summon Joe."

I chew quietly on my second croissant as Ann closes her eyes murmuring faintly. Joe appears at the door within minutes, knocking before sitting himself down on the bed.

"So, it is time, are you sure you're ready for this?"

I nod. There are no words for me to say. They know as well as I do that Mum will not let me find Euan. If I can't hide my plan from Ann and Joe, there is no way on earth I will be able to hide it from Mum. If I'm going. I'll have to go now.

Joe takes a deep breath nodding to himself, squeezes Ann's hand, then looks at me serenely.

"I want to come with you, as does Ann, but for reasons I can't explain, we cannot. I've seen your path, and this is something you must do alone."

I nod again. I already knew that too. There was never any version of this where we all went together to get Euan. It always had to be me.

"Well, kind of alone," Joe turns to the door just as a golden nose pokes its way around the corner.

"Phoenix!" I exclaim softly.

He pads round to my side of the bed and places his head on my lap, I give it a vigorous patting and kiss him on the nose.

"I've missed you so much boy, where have you been?"

Joe looks at Ann, then shrugs looking at Phoenix.

"What is it, where has he been?"

"I think we'll let Phoenix tell you himself," Ann smiles warmly at him, "Joe and I will soundproof the room, so it doesn't wake Val. Meet us outside when you're ready to go, I'll get supplies ready for you."

I look at them both in utter bewilderment.

Joe smiles a toothy grin and leaves the room.

What on earth are they on about? How can Phoenix tell me himself? They've gone off their rockers, it must be the shock about me leaving. Maybe I should stay if this is what it's doing to them. I move the covers and go to stand.

"I think it'd be better if you sat down for this Peri," suggests a low, earthy voice I don't recognise. I jump back looking around. No one is in the room. And Phoenix isn't growling for an intruder. What on earth...

"Happy birthday Peridot."

I look down. The voice. It's Phoenix's.

The Truth

Phoenix can talk. Phoenix can talk. Phoenix can talk?!

I fall back upon the bed. How is that even possible? Magick? It must be magick! Maybe it's my birthday present? I don't want to hurt Joe and Ann's feelings, but I don't want a talking dog, I want Phoenix back the way he was.

"Joe! Ann!" I whisper-yell, "Come back in!"

"Don't be scared Peridot, it's me."

Phoenix hops up on the bed and sits next to me at eye level. I glance into those golden marbles of his and try to calm down.

"I've always spoken to you, it's only now that you can hear me properly," he leans into my face, our noses touching.

Running my hand up to his neck I fiddle with his ears as I often do when I'm nervous, letting the motion calm me.

"You've always spoken?"

"Always. You used to hear me, back when you were little. But, as you got older, you started asking questions... it was decided it would be better to hide our voices from you. Until you were older."

"Our voices?"

"Yes, all animals speak, not just me. That's the reason we've been muted from you for so long. Myself, Roland and Amy can be trusted to not speak of certain things, but some of the other animals, they had a habit of talking about things that a five-year-old girl doesn't need to hear about."

I rise absently in a daze. Attempting to take it in, whilst at the same time trying not to completely freak out. I understand what Ann meant by soundproofing the room. How I've not screamed my head off, is beyond me. My dog is talking to me, and not just a few words, a full-blown conversation. Suddenly something clicks - Euan!

"Euan could hear you, couldn't he?"

"Yes, we spoke often. That's where I've been. Looking for him."

"You've been looking for Euan still?" I stammer, "but we looked everywhere on the island, there's nowhere else he could be."

"I've not been looking on the island Peri, I've been on the mainland. And I think I've found him."

"You've been to the mainland? How?"

"By boat. Sometimes Joe takes me, sometimes Vallaeartha. I look for a few days, then they come back for me. Vallaeartha got me last night, but it was a rough ride back, it took a lot out of her. We must go now if you wish to leave."

My mouth feels like sandpaper and my tummy is in knots. All clarity from earlier this morning is well and truly out the window. Talking animals, I was not prepared for.

"Phoenix, what's out there?" I whisper anxiously.

"I can explain on the way, but if you want to go, we really must go now. If Vallaeartha wakes whilst you're still on this island, she will be able to prevent us from going. Once we leave, it'll be your choice when you want to come back."

"Why are you helping me do this?"

"It is the right thing to do," he replies solemnly, "I care for the boy also - he should not be where he is. Nobody should be. We must break him free."

I breathe in and try to ground myself. I'm no longer facing this alone. I have support. Support with exceptionally large teeth I might add. That reassures me. I can do this with Phoenix with me. It is decided.

"Let's go."

Changing as quickly and quietly as I can, I make sure to grab my pre-packed bag and place the necklace from my parents safely in my top drawer for safekeeping. I feel naked taking it off, but I can't risk losing it on our journey, I'll wear it on my return. Taking one last glance at my bedroom, realisation hits that this will be the first time in my entire life that I won't be sleeping in this room tonight. The thought both exhilarates and petrifies me.

"Goodbye room," I whisper, closing the door gently behind me. The motion has a feeling of finality to it. I'm really doing this. We hurriedly exit via the kitchen, treading as carefully as we can. Joe and Ann await at the edge of their barn, Roland and Amy next to them. It feels so strange not to hear them whinnying a greeting to me.

"Happy birthday Peridot," Roland's voice startles me. It's scratchy and gravelly and if I'm being honest, a little creepy. Not at all what I'd expect him to sound like.

"Th... thanks," I stammer.

A soft glittery laugh shimmers from Amy,

"Stop horsing around will you, this is no time for jokes," exasperates Joe, giving them both a stern gaze.

"Quite right Joseph, quite right, my apologies Peridot. My apologies," says Roland, in what I can only describe as the poshest British accent I have ever heard.

I grin up at him. That's more like it. If I were ever to imagine Roland speaking, this is what he'd sound like.

"So, that's why Phoenix is always after you is it," I run my hand up and down his mane, "a fellow prankster."

"One of many reasons," giggles Amy in her light, airy voice.

This is amazing. I've changed my mind. Talking animals are the best. I could listen to them all day.

"I can't believe you could talk all this time," I gush.

"We wished you could understand us, we truly did. But perhaps, given the circumstances, it was meant to be this way. Vallaeartha only wants what's best for you. I'm sure we'll be the same when our little one is born," she nuzzles into Roland.

"You're pregnant?" I beam at them, "how exciting, I can't believe I'm leaving when you're having a foal."

"Don't worry, you'll meet him or her when you return. We're sorry we're not coming with you, it is the only reason we're staying," Amy looks worriedly to Phoenix, "you will be extra careful not to be seen, won't you?"

"Yes, of course, don't worry, she's safe with me. Besides, it'd be harder to hide if you came along. Two giant horses are a little more conspicuous than a dog and a human."

"I guess you're right," she concedes, "oh, but I'm so worried! Peridot, are you sure you must go?"

"Now-now, darling now-now. Peri is of witching age, and we must let her be free to make her own choices my dear," says Roland in his regal voice.

It makes me chuckle. Genuinely chuckle. How could Mum have hidden this from me for all these years? So much I've missed out on, all the fun I could've had.

"I'll be back as soon as I can, I promise," I soothe, seeing Amy tear up, "I can't leave Euan, it's my fault he's where he is. I must bring him back."

"I understand. Ignore me it's the hormones, pregnancy you know," she jitters trying to lighten the mood.

"Dot, I'm sorry, but we really must head off if you're to go before Val wakes up," Ann worries looking over her shoulder.

"Quite right, quite right," agrees Roland, bending down so Joe and Ann can mount him. Amy bends for me too, I hesitate, not comfortable riding whilst she's pregnant.

"Don't worry, it's only a short ride and you weigh next to nothing, hop on," she says.

I mount her extra carefully, trying to shift my weight evenly as we head off towards the shoreline. We go a different way to the route I know, and after a short ride we end up at the base of the cliffs. A rocky shoreline greets us, no beach or sand, just stone. I wonder where the boat is hidden.

"This is where we must part ways," Roland looks to me serenely. I dismount Amy slowly, tears brimming my eyes as I give them a fierce hug. They hold me close with their manes.

"Travel safe my girl," whispers Ann.

"Farewell for now young Elemental," salutes Roland.

"I'll see you and your foal when I get back, look after each other," I wipe my eyes. They whinny in response which now feels odd after hearing them speak.

Leaving them at the base of the cliffs, I follow Joe, Ann and Phoenix across the rocky shoreline, coming to an abrupt halt as the rocks end sharply. There's a gap of approximately five meters from the rock we're currently on to the next. In between is a gravelly area with a small boat nestled into the rocks.

"Well. I guess this is us," sniffs Ann. She grabs me into an emotional hug, I can feel her holding back sobs.

"Don't worry Ann, I'll be back soon I promise," I comfort her, tears once again falling free from my eyes.

"It's going to be strange you not being here," she cries, tears falling from her eyes also. "Listen to Phoenix whilst you're out there, it's not the same as this island. If Phoenix tells you to do something, don't question it, please just trust and do as he says. And do not tell anyone, and I mean anyone, that you're an Elemental."

"I promise. Listen to Phoenix and pretend to be human. That I can do," I assure her.

"I've packed some food for the journey," she hands me a bag laden with food. "You go, get Euan and bring him home. And don't worry about any of us we'll be fine, we can handle Val's temper."

"You can read minds, can't you?" I ask bemused.

"Yes. And when the time comes – you will be able to too. Oh gosh, she's up, she's awake!" Ann looks positively petrified. "You must go, right this second!"

I grab Ann hurriedly in a final embrace then amble across the rocks, trying and failing not to slip everywhere. Phoenix leaps directly into the boat in one giant bound, landing perfectly. I somehow manage to clamber on board.

"Wait! I don't know how to drive a boat!" I exclaim.

"No worries lassie I'm right behind you," Joe thuds into the boat behind me. "I'll be coming straight back mind, Ann can stall Val until I get back and then we'll endure her wrath together," he noticeably grimaces.

I feel awful. They're going through so much trouble to help me get off the island, Mum will be positively furious, she'll know I had help. I watch Joe untying ropes and fiddling with the starter motor to get us going.

"Are you sure you want to do this?"

"I've bonded to the boy just as much as you have - get him back safe and sound."

"But Mum – "

"Don't be daft woman, I've dealt with your mum's frogging temper for years, I can handle her, don't you worry."

"Thanks Joe."

"Nothing to thank me for," he shrugs, "it's the right thing to do."

Anxiously I take a seat, feeling a little better about leaving, but unable to quell the nervousness rising in my tummy. I jump at a sudden whirring noise - the starter motor roars to life and our boat chugs its way out of the rocks and into the open sea. Looking back, Ann waves a last goodbye atop of Roland. The stallion rises, up on his hind legs, Amy following suit in farewell, I wave back, tears in my eyes. I can't believe I'm really doing this. Leaving my home for the first time, behind Mum's back, going into earth knows what on the mainland. My tummy continues to swirl anxiously, but I'm not backing out, I need to rescue Euan. I just have no idea how I'm going to do it. I'm so glad Phoenix is coming with me. Sitting down next to him, I begin to fiddle with his ears.

"Sorry," I take my hand back, "does it bother you?"

"Not at all, not as good as a belly rub mind you, but it'll suffice," he leans into me.

Facing the stern of the boat, we watch our island get smaller behind us. It's strange to see home from a distance, I didn't realise just how little it was.

The early morning sun is hidden by clouds, and I shiver slightly, leaning further into Phoenix for warmth. I take a moment to try and ground myself, breathing in the sea air, its light, salty and oddly refreshing. In through my nose and out through my mouth. Focusing on my breathing, I say goodbye to our island and recite it in my mind repeatedly, "I embrace my journey and leave my doubts behind me".

After a few minutes, it's done the trick. My tummy no longer swirls and I'm ready to face whatever it is that's out there. Turning back to face the front of the boat, I prepare to ask the question I'm dreading the answer to. I wasn't prepared for talking animals in the slightest and a niggling feeling tells me my presumption about the mainland is going to be way off.

"Phoenix?"

"Hmm," he turns to look at me.

"I need to know what's out there, I don't think I can wait any longer."

He nods in understanding, "I'm sad that it will be me that unveils the horrors of our world to you. Once you know, you will never be able to return to your old way of life. It will change everything Peridot. There is a reason Vallaeartha kept this from you for so long."

"I need to know Phoenix. I'm not a child anymore, I'm ready."

"I know you are young Witchling, I know."

He looks away for a moment towards Joe who nods solemnly, "it is time," he agrees.

I remain seated, my hands clammy, balled into fists. I try to relax them, but I can't, I'm on edge again, the anxiety creeping its way back in. I just want to get this over with. Phoenix turns back to face me, for a moment I think I see a flash of purple in his eyes, but then they are deep, golden amber again. It must've been the light.

"Peridot. I don't know how to explain this to you, so, I'm just going to come out with it and then you can ask the questions that help it make sense, okay?"

"Okay." I hold my breath, knowing the next sentence will change everything.

"Peridot, humans are enslaved... by animals."

"Huh?" That, I most definitely was not expecting.

"Well," he continues, "certain types of animals. Not all of us agree with what's happening, but those that do, treat humans in the worst ways imaginable. The place where Euan is held is one of those places."

I'm speechless. Physically lost for words. I gape at Phoenix, with no idea how to respond or what questions to ask.

"Do you believe what I am saying is true?" he prompts after minutes pass without a response from me. It takes a while to find my voice.

"If I was back home, and someone else was telling me, then I wouldn't believe it. But I'm here. With you. And you can talk." I pause and let that sink in for a minute. "Yes, I believe you."

"Okay," he pads round to face me again, "what else would you like to know?"

"What do you mean by enslaved?"

"Most humans are kept in farming facilities and bred in vast numbers for food, which is distributed between the carnivores. The herbivores use humans to grow, pick and prepare the food. The remaining humans that do not serve a purpose, either as food or a worker, are used for entertainment purposes."

"Entertainment purposes?"

"Yes, racing, fighting, sports and so on."

"That's absurd," I stutter, struggling to get my head around what he's saying.

"Absurd, but true I'm afraid kiddo," Joe takes a seat beside me. He looks out across the open sea, and I follow his gaze. The three of us lost in thought for a moment as the boat continues forward across the choppy waves and towards the mass of land ahead of us. We're still a way back from the shore, but the land appears bigger by the minute, it won't be long until we're there. Soon I'll be stepping foot into a world where humans are kept as slaves.

"How can this be possible? It's worse than any scenario I'd imagined." I utter, lost for words.

"It's why Vallaeartha was so insistent on you not knowing," explains Joe, rubbing my back gently. The motion helps, but I still feel sick. Talking animals was a shock, but humanity enslaved by animals? I'm completely dumbfounded.

"But we're of magick, we can help surely?" I suggest.

"We may be able to help, but in doing so, you'd be putting yourself in dangers you couldn't even comprehend. Val doesn't want that for you. Heck, I don't want that for you. But, as you say, if anyone can make a difference to this awful way of life, it's people of magick."

"Then why don't we at least try? We can't let people suffer if there's a way to stop it?"

"It's not that simple kiddo when you see it for yourself, you'll understand. There are billions of them and so few of us left. Well, that isn't enslaved anyway," he looks away sadly, "and even fewer of us of magick."

"Why are there so few people of magick in the world?"

"Many went into hiding after The Changing, those that hadn't already been killed by our own kind mind. Like Vallaeartha says, people fear that which they don't understand. Knows a lot your mum does. For now, let's just focus on getting Euan back safe and sound, ay? He's our main priority."

Numbly I try to get to grips with what he's saying. The idea of animals talking was bizarre enough, but for there to be an entirely different way of life out on the mainland, the world run by animals with humanity enslaved. I shiver inwardly. Partly because of the cold, and partly out of fear. I understand now what Euan meant about me getting eaten up on the mainland, he was being literal.

"If we see animals, what do we do?" I ask suddenly.

"Trust your instincts," replies Joe, "they'll see you right. When the time comes, you'll know what to do. If it feels right and it harms none, then just do it."

"But everyone's warned me not to be seen doing magick, how can I avoid doing magick if I need to protect us?" my voice rises unexpectedly.

"I can't explain it, but just trust me that you'll be okay Peri."

His certainty quells my rising panic, "You've seen things, haven't you?"

"Aye lass, I've seen a lot of things. I need you to believe that you'll be okay, no matter how dark the things you see, how horrid the feelings you experience, just remember this moment. I am promising you Peridot. It's all going to work out, just follow your heart. Can you promise me that you'll try to do that?"

"I'll try Joe, I promise."

"Then all is not lost," he smiles, giving my back one last pat before heading back to steer the boat.

I continue to look ahead, the mainland now scarily close, I'm eternally grateful that I am not doing this alone. Leaning back into Phoenix I feel a little of my fear dissipate in his stance. He feels sturdy, safe, strong. And smells like home. Oh, the irony; I've wanted to leave for so long, now I've finally left, a large part of me is tempted to go back.

"You don't have to come with me, if you're not ready," Phoenix's earthy voice lifts me from my thoughts of home.

"I need to get Euan. I won't leave him. I'm coming." I say resolutely. The certainty in my voice installs a little much-needed confidence within me.

"In that case, prepare yourself Peridot. We are nearly there," he nods his head towards the skyline, the shore now a stone's throw from us. My tummy doubles over in knots. I cannot shake the anxiety of going through with this, but I refuse to let cowardice take over. I am going to save my friend. Standing, I shakily make my way over to Joe, gaining sureness with every footstep. He pops his arm around my shoulder, one hand keeping the boat steady, the other steadying me.

"It's going to be quiet back home without you," he squeezes me tightly.

"You'll give my love to everyone I didn't get to say goodbye to, won't you?"

"Of course," he nods, "it's a good thing you didn't get to say your goodbyes properly. Pigs probably wouldn't have let you leave, and don't even get me started on the raving rabbits."

"They're feisty, I take it?"

"Oh, you think my language is bad, you have no idea. Those rabbits can curse like nobody's business," he shakes his head, steering our little boat towards a cove in the rocky shoreline. The mainland looks on as far as I can see, vast in comparison to our island. Looking back, home is but a dot in my peripheral, making the journey ahead even more daunting. I am very aware that I am going into completely new territory.

"Are you ready?" Phoenix joins us, standing tall.

"As ready as I'll ever be."

"You'll be fine, don't worry. Phoenix knows the land better than most, you're going to be alright Dot. Scouts honour," Joe salutes with his fingers.

I somehow manage to salute back before throwing my arms around him in a hug, "I love you Joe, thank you for everything."

"Love you too kiddo, what are family for ay?" he kisses the top of my head then looks up, "be careful Phoenix, good luck."

"Peri won't leave my sight," he leaps from the boat, landing effortlessly on the rocky shore.

"Your turn," Joe picks me up to help me over the side. Before placing me onto the rocks, he whispers hurriedly, "when in doubt, follow your heart Peridot. Always follow your heart."

I look back at him, confused as to why he didn't say that in front of Phoenix.

"See you both soon," he averts his gaze, manoeuvring the boat back around towards home. I wave him goodbye, still wondering what he meant by follow your heart. Phoenix pads over to join me and stays silent as we watch Joe leave. The little boat chugs further and further into the distance and I feel both sad and nervous, excited, and hopeful. I'm going to get my friend back. No matter what it takes.

The Mainland

We travel in silence, which feels strange knowing that Phoenix can talk. I repeatedly bite my tongue to prevent myself from asking questions every other minute. So far, we've travelled without interference from other animals, but that doesn't mean we're safe. Phoenix is on high alert, ambling forward stealthily, looking to the sides and behind constantly to check we're not being followed. His actions make me feel both safe and nervous, I feel like we could be ambushed at any moment, by who knows what?

The terrain is green on all sides, various wildflowers sprout through the undergrowth with trees as far as my eyes can see. It's not at all what I was expecting, it's beautiful. I find it hard to resist stopping, the inner healer in me wants to inspect every new variation of shrub and berry. There's foliage I've only seen in Mum's books back home. Phoenix continues to move ahead of me, coming back around, then moving forward again, until we reach a forest. He stops and I follow suit, in awe of the mass of trees in front of us, it goes on forever, starting in light shadow and ending in pitch blackness.

"Woah," I whisper.

"We'll travel through the trees, it'll be safer undercover, less likely to be spotted by poachers. We're a walking target out in the open."

"Poachers?" I ask alarmed.

"Yes, mainly foxes and badgers. They roam the land in search of wild humans. Any they find, they bring back to the farms for reward. Luckily for us, quietness isn't their strongest attribute, we'll hear them coming from a mile away."

He nudges me forward with his snout as I numbly begin to find my way through the trees. This feels surreal. The more I learn of the mainland, the more bizarre it seems. Hiding in a forest in fear of being caught by talking badgers and foxes. It's utter madness. A bemused giggle escapes my lips without meaning to, causing me to cover my mouth hurriedly.

"We can talk freely in the forest - the trees hide us from any potential listeners."

I exhale in relief. "This doesn't feel real."

"I understand, was the same for me the day it all changed."

"Where were you when it happened?"

"I lived in kennels with other dogs."

"Kennels?"

"Yes," he nods, "my breed was banned by the humans."

"Banned?"

"Humans deemed my kind dangerous. They would keep us in kennels and test us for signs of aggression, if we passed, we were permitted to live with the humans providing we wore a muzzle."

"What's a muzzle?"

"A device that prevented us from opening our mouths."

I gasp in shock causing Phoenix to chuckle grimly.

"They feared we would bite them," he explains, "when animals found their voices, the humans freed other breeds, but refused to free our type out of fear. A mob tried to burn down the kennels we were imprisoned in. It was your mother that saved us. I'd have died had she not intervened."

"I'm so sorry that happened to you," I go quiet, wondering what he means by his type, he looks no different to any other kind of dog.

"What do you mean by humans feared your type?"

"Dogs have different types caused by breeding patterns they created. My breed was named a Pitbull Terrier. Our type was raised, many years ago to fight. Not all of us, but enough of us for humans to fear the entire breed. Any dog that looked like a potential Pitbull would be killed on sight or put in kennels to be tested."

"Like the witch trials," I gasp.

"Yes precisely. Breed Specific Legislation they called it, the terminology seemed to make it acceptable to most. I think that's why your mum saved us. Well, one of the reasons, she saw the injustice of it. We bonded and have stayed together ever since."

"She's going to be so mad at me," I'd been so engrossed in our conversation, I'd forgotten about back home for a while, "I bet Joe and Ann are getting it in the neck," I grimace.

"Most likely, but Vallaeartha will come around. If we had not taken you, you would have come alone and most likely have been caught and sent to a farm already. This way, you are safe. She will forgive us."

"You really think so?"

"She will be mad at first, but yes, in the end, she will understand, this is the way it had to be."

"Thanks for taking me Phoenix."

He tilts his head, "Like I would leave my favourite human."

"I'm your favourite? Really?"

"Just don't tell your mother," he chuckles, the sound making me smile. He has a good laugh.

We continue in comfortable silence, both lost in our thoughts. I have no idea where I'm going and am so grateful to have Phoenix with me. He's right, there is no way I could've done this by myself. The forest goes on for miles, it's a wonder he knows where he's going, let alone someone that's never been here before. Or anywhere before for that matter. I still can't believe I'm here. My tummy grumbles loudly and I wonder how long we've been travelling.

"Let's stop here for a while, we still have a day or so's travel until we reach the A.I station. We'll take it slow and reserve our energy."

Gratefully I sit down, taking my shoes off as I do. My toes feel squished from walking in boots for so long, I wiggle my toes to relieve the sensation. Opening the bag of food from Ann, my mouth salivates instantly. I pull out two spiced bean and wild leaf wraps, inhaling the scent gratefully.

"Shall we try to spread the food out until we get home?" I ask, passing him a wrap.

"Don't worry about me, you eat your fill, I'll be able to get my own food on the mainland."

"Really? What will you eat?" I unwrap a tortilla, my mouth salivating at the homely scent of Ann's cooking wafting through my nostrils.

"Squirrel mainly, perhaps a rabbit or two."

My wrap drops to the floor, contents spilling everywhere.

"You're joking?"

"I have big teeth for a reason Peridot. I am a carnivore. Well, an omnivore. I eat both meat and earth-grown food."

My tummy feels squeamish.

"But, at home, you ate with us?"

"Yes, I enjoy your earth-grown food, but what we have will not suffice to get us both back home. Whilst we are on the mainland I will need to hunt. Does this make you uncomfortable?"

"A little," I admit.

"Would you rather I eat later?"

"No, you need to eat, but can you not just eat with me? I'll find us other food, so you don't have to kill anything."

"It is the circle of life Peridot; animals have always been predator and prey."

"I know that, it just didn't cross my mind," I go quiet, "we had rabbits back home, would you have eaten them?"

"Those rabbits were my friends, rest assured the rabbits here will not be allies. They will be spies. If any see you, they will report back to the farms and scouts will be sent out to bring you to them. Tonight, I shall eat with you to ease your comfort, but if we see any scouts, I will hunt and feed on them. Both for my hunger and your safety."

He pads over, eating the contents of my fallen wrap as I unwrap a fresh one, I nibble away uncomfortably, my appetite lost. The thought of Phoenix hunting makes me feel physically sick. The reality of life outside our island is beginning to sink in with even more clarity than before. It is a completely different world out here.

"Worry not Witchling, I won't hunt in front of you."

"It's not that," I sigh, "this didn't feel real to start with, now it seems too real. And we're not even at the A.I station yet, I dread to think what that will be like."

"Would you like to know before we arrive, so it's not as much of a shock?"

"Yes and no," I shrug, "I need to know, but I don't want to. It's going to be awful, isn't it?"

"I won't lie to you Peridot; it is one of the worst places a human can end up."

"What do they do there?"

"A.I Stations are Artificial Insemination Stations. They are where animals create milk."

I look at him confused, "That doesn't sound so bad?" I question, my mouth full of spiced beans, rocket, and watercress.

"Apologies I didn't word it properly. It's where animals make human milk."

I choke on a bean in surprise. "What do animals need human milk for?"

"They don't. Not really. Many like the taste. Haven't tried it myself, can't bring myself to after being inside one of the facilities, it's not a nice place to be."

"I don't understand?" I question, beginning to feel uneasy, I don't like the sound of where this is going.

"At A.I stations animals harvest human milk. The females are caught by poachers, then used for the rest of their life cycle to produce milk for animals to drink."

I stop eating my wrap, my appetite now lost.

"Animals drink humans' milk?"

"Not all, but many, yes."

I feel sick to my stomach. Poor Euan, no wonder he wanted to free his mum so desperately.

"Why is Euan there, he's not female?"

"Euan would have been a milking mother's child. They separate the child when it's born, so the mother's milk can be harvested. Although, males are normally sent off as meat when they are big enough. The females they keep for artificial insemination and used for milk like their mothers."

"Artificial insemination?"

"I'd rather not explain that procedure - it's probably best if you see for yourself when we get there."

He looks away uncomfortably.

"Why was Euan so thin if he was being raised for meat?" I ask, thinking back to when I first met him, he was so underfed, he could barely stand.

"The children aren't allowed to stay with their mothers, they would inevitably drink their milk – which is forbidden. The infants are separated and fed a formula made with basic vitamins they need to grow. Not all drink it, many end up malnourished like Euan was."

"Why don't they make milk as we do back home, from oats?"

"Some do. But not enough to stop the A.I stations from running. They enjoy the taste of human milk too much."

"But human milk is for humans, it makes no sense."

"I agree, as do most of my kind. The other species, not so much. It is the law. After The Changing, animals agreed not to eat each other, and to feed on humans instead. Humans don't have enough flesh on them to feed many carnivores, so they're mass bred in farms and A.I Stations by the herbivores. It's not nice, but it is just the way it is." He shifts position to scratch behind his ear, by instinct I go to scratch it for him, he leans into my fingertips gratefully, his hind leg twitching as I hit the spot.

"I think we've had enough for our first day, let's find some cover and get some rest. It's a lot for you to take in," he rests his head momentarily against my brow, "at least this way you're prepared for what you may see tomorrow."

I lean my head into his, once again grateful for him being with me. I think I'd have had a heart attack if I'd have seen all of this for myself first-hand without any warning. Standing unsteadily, we head a little further into the undergrowth, after another ten minutes or so, we come to a stream, thick with bushes and turned over trees.

"This will do nicely," he approves, gathering fallen branches in his jaw. I follow suit and soon we have a good pile of timber which I place strategically atop a large bark, making a covering of sorts that we can lay under.

"Are you cold, shall I make a fire?"

"Too risky. I'll be fine, we'll rest together for warmth," he replies, turning around in circles, twice one way, twice the other, then back around again until finally, he lays down.

"I've always wanted to know, why do you do that?"

"Hmm?" He replies, closing his eyes.

"The turning around thing before you lie down."

"Good question, it must be a dog thing," he yawns, tail wagging slightly. I feel comforted by the motion and lay down next to him, grabbing the cloak Mum made me from my bag and draping over us. Phoenix moves his head onto my chest letting me fiddle with his ears, as I try to quieten the busy thoughts flowing through my head. Awful images of humans and animals fighting and trying to take bites out of each other. I shudder involuntarily. I glance down to find Phoenix watching me, he holds my gaze. As always, I find myself getting lost in the golden swirls of his eyes and somehow, even after the chaotic madness of the day, I manage to fall asleep.

I wake hours later, a cold draft on my side where Phoenix once lay, making me sit bolt upright. It's pitch-black outside, a crescent moon waxes in the night sky, offering a dim light amongst a dot to dot of stars, trying to shine through the thick cloud gathering above. It feels eerily quiet. Something's not right.

"Phoenix?" I whisper.

I wait a moment, but he doesn't answer. Everything in my body is telling me to move, but I won't leave without him. Hurriedly, I shove my cloak back in my bag and as quietly as I can, creep out from the covering.

"Phoenix!" I call louder this time. Still nothing. I can't help but start to panic. My head orders me to stay calm, but my body itches to get out of here. Pacing back and forth, I wish inwards for Phoenix to come back soon.

"Peridot!" he bounds over to me out of no-where, making me jump,

"Phoenix! Thank earth you're okay!" I hold him tight, relieved he's alright.

"Peridot, you must listen to me. I need you to hide, do you understand?"

"Hide? Who from, who's coming?"

"We must've been seen, there's a pack of foxes heading this way, they'll be here in under a minute. You must go. Now!"

"But what about you? I won't leave you!"

"Peridot you promised before we left that no matter what, you would do as I command. You must run and hide, Peri. Find a tree with plenty of branches, climb as high as you can, and do not move until you are certain it is safe. No matter what you hear. Do not come back for me, do you understand?"

"Phoenix no!" I cry, "I won't leave you!"

"I'll be fine Peri, I am a dog, I can be out here, you're a human, you cannot! Peridot you promised me you'd listen now run – *now*!"

He ushers me away with his snout forcefully, I don't want to, but I do as he says. I run. I run as fast as my legs can carry me. Adrenalin pumps through my veins urging me forward, my legs ache and my chest burns, making my eyes water. I try to make out a tree I can climb, but I'm too panicked to focus properly, everything looks the same. I hear snarls in the distance behind me and begin to slow down. I know I shouldn't, that I promised Phoenix I'd do as he said, but another promise I made stands out more. Joe said that everything would work out fine, providing I follow my heart. Right now, my heart is telling me to help Phoenix. More snarls assault my ears from afar, this time with ferocious snaps thrown in and a yelp for good measure. That decides it. I won't leave him.

I turn abruptly, stumbling as I do. My legs are on fire as I backtrack, trying desperately to retrace my steps. The sound of dogs fighting gets louder, angry snaps and growls echoing through the trees. I pray to the Goddess that Phoenix is alright. I'll never forgive myself if he's hurt, I should never have left. A strangled yelp reverberates through the forest around me, and I urge my legs to keep going despite their protest. I can make out the stream in front of me. I have no idea how, but it seems I've run in a circle, ending back where I started. I can just make out a flash of tails amongst trees ahead of me. With no idea what I intend to do, I quickly, quietly hide behind the largest bark.

Peeking out, I can't believe my eyes. An array of foxes lay wounded, scattered across the ground. Phoenix looks like a warrior, hurt but standing his ground. He growls deeply in warning to any others that try to take him down. Two foxes' approach from his rear, I go to warn him, but the outburst is wasted. In a flash Phoenix swiftly turns, taking one down with his teeth, the other with his hind legs, the kicked fox gets back up for another try, as two more circle him from the front. Phoenix has taken out at least half a dozen, but there are so many, there's no way he can fight through them all.

I don't know what to do. Everyone's told me not to use my magick, but if I don't, Phoenix will be captured or killed. I need to help him. If I can just distract them without being seen, but, how? Foxes are everywhere, I can't subdue them in one go, it'd have to be individually, and they'll notice me eventually. I don't even know if my magick will work, it's been dormant for so long. A yelp brings me back to the ongoing fight in front of me.

Phoenix now struggles to hold his ground, his hind legs falter, a wound flowing freely from one side. One of the larger of the group lunges at his front, while another sneaks out from behind, taking another swipe at his injured leg, Phoenix goes down hard on that side, an angry cry escaping him as he falls. They don't miss their opportunity, in seconds, the skulk is upon him, pouncing from all sides, Phoenix grunts in pain as they snap, scratch and tear away at him.

"Get away from him!!" I scream, jumping out from my hiding place.

"A human!" one cries.

"Fresh meat!" cackles another.

The majority keep Phoenix pinned, while the two largest circle me, snapping, tittering, barely controlling their glee. I am very aware that they want to eat me.

"We'll take her back to the A.I station," asserts the female.

"Why bother? To be paid in tampered human bones with no meat on. Look at this one, she's fresh and unscathed – I say we eat her raw!" argues the other.

"Don't be stupid – that's breaking the law!"

"Who would know!? She's not been tagged or branded, look - no one is missing her! We haven't had fresh unfarmed meat in years."

"Human," the female approaches, her bushy red tail swishing back and forth, pointed snout baring small razor-sharp teeth, "who owns you?"

"Nobody owns me," the words slip from my mouth before I can stop them.

"See! A wildling! Let's eat her Cleo!!" The male leaps towards me, only to be blocked by who I'm assuming is Cleo.

"You dare take the first bite?" She snarls, looking me up and down, debating whether I am worth the risk to eat.

"No. It is not worth the comeuppance. We have a good deal with the cows, I'm not risking it for one meal. We take her back with us." Cleo advances towards me.

"Human - sit!" she commands.

I look at her in defiance. Sit? Sit?! Something inside stirs. A fire of sorts. It burns. Flaring wildly to break free.

"I said *sit!*" she snaps. Her teeth clamp down painfully on my ankle making me cry out.

My ankle stings from her sharp teeth, blood flowing from the bite marks.

"Sit down human. You do not want another one."

The fire inside me burns brighter. I battle to keep it down, but something within me shifts.

"Silly vixen," I look at the female fox with pity.

She gasps, realising her mistake too late. Her ears go back as she notices my hands begin to glow.

"I'm not human," I whisper.

I let the fire free.

EARTHLINGS

"Peri!"

"Peri, wake up, we must go, now!"

Ouch. My head. I feel like I've run headfirst into a tree. My eyes slowly open, I'm on my back and the air stings my eyes, I'm forced to squint to keep them open. It smells of charcoal and burning.

"Peri! Peri, are you alright?"

Phoenix stands above me, his fur darkened by soot, dried blood stains his jaw and chest. He looks like a soldier fresh from battle.

"What happened?"

"You happened little Witchling," he grimaces, sitting awkwardly at an angle. I notice his back leg, a large gash taken from his hind.

"Phoenix! You're hurt, let me heal you," I move to get up, head spinning as I do.

"We don't have time, we must go quickly, this blaze would have been seen for miles, more scouts will be on their way, and I won't be able to fight them off. You mustn't use your powers yet, it's too dangerous."

"I did this?" I gape shocked.

"Yes, you nearly set the entire forest ablaze."

Looking around I see what he means. The trees are charred as far as my eyes can see, the smell of burning wood, floating ash, destruction everywhere.

"But w - why?" I stammer, "why did I do this?"

It flashes back to me then. The foxes. Phoenix pinned down. The one that bit me.

"Phoenix! The foxes!" I exclaim, jumping up expecting an ambush.

It's then that I notice the other smell in the air. Not just wood burning. But bodies. The smell assaults my nose making me wretch, there are remains scattered around us, some bare bone, others with flesh still scorched and charred. I wretch again, this time heaving onto the floor.

"What did I do?!" I cry.

"Peri, I'm sorry, but we must leave, more are coming. If they find us, they will know you are of magick - no human could have done this. We need to get out of here, now!"

He limps forward as best he can, I notice a lump of tissue missing from his leg, he's hurt badly.

"Phoenix you can barely walk, let me heal you."

"We don't have time, if we stay, we'll be captured."

"Okay then, let me carry you," I exasperate.

He goes to protest,

"Phoenix, we won't get far with you limping and I will not leave you behind no matter what you say, get across my shoulders, I can carry you!"

Before he can protest further, I bend down and scoop him up and over my shoulders. He yelps loudly, then his body falls limp. He must've passed out from the pain.

"Sorry boy," I stroke his head, "My turn to look after you for a change."

I begin to walk forward. Slowly, one foot at a time, making sure not to bump his leg or trip on any fallen timbers. I pass another body still a flame, the smell is putrid, bile rises in my throat. I can't believe I did this. All those animals, dead, because of me. I manage to keep down the sea of tears that threatens to escape, I will mourn my mistakes later. Right now, I need to get Phoenix to safety.

Losing Euan was my fault, I will not be responsible for losing Phoenix too.

I continue forward as best I can, staggering uneasily under his weight. This would be much simpler if I could heal him. I may have zero belief in my capabilities as an Elemental, but I'm a darn good healer. I know I can get him back to health if I can find a safe place to hide us away. The smoke makes it hard to see which is both a blessing and a curse. It'll make it harder for us to be spotted but trying to find cover is going to take a while. The surrounding woodland is burnt to a crisp.

It troubles me. To have done something so cataclysmic, yet, I have no idea how I made it come to pass. How can I have these magickal abilities, and not know how to yield them properly? It's like a baby having hold of a blade – disaster is bound to happen. I should have spent more time learning how to use the elements instead of being angry with Mum. She'd know exactly what to do right now. She could probably fly us out of here on one of the fallen branches and heal Phoenix mid-flight. I roll my eyes at myself. Don't be daft Peridot.

My foot catches on broken timber causing me to fall forward, nearly losing hold of Phoenix as I do. This isn't going to work, he's too heavy. I need to heal him so we can travel on foot. As carefully as I can, I crouch down, allowing Phoenix to fall heavily to the floor. He lands with a thud, but does not stir, I'm glad I stopped, he's wounded badly, this can't wait. Blood pours from the open gash in his leg, causing a puddle to form upon the ground.

I stifle back a sob of worry and get to work, removing my supplies from my backpack. I sort through the various tonics, lotions, and ointments until I find the supplies I'm looking for. Mugwort and a large quartz. With the wand I received for my birthday, I bind the two together, supercharging the herb with the crystals power. I watch the herb glow bright until it warms my hand, then place it upon the open wound, murmuring an incantation that Mum taught me in lessons as I do.

The effect is instant, the blood slows, then stops dripping completely. I watch in awe as Phoenix's leg begins to regenerate, replacing the missing tissue and re-growing skin over the top. It takes only a moment, other than a bald patch showing the pink flesh of his newly grown skin, his leg is completely healed. I breathe a sigh of relief. Now to replenish his blood loss and get his energy back. Phoenix begins to stir, eyes opening slowly.

"Stubborn Witchling," he utters with a hint of annoyance, "that's twice you've disobeyed me." He sits up swaying slightly and looking cross.

"I'm not saving myself at the expense of losing you," I sit down beside him to steady his balance, "Phoenix, I'll trust you always, I promise - but not if it means putting my safety before yours. We're in this together." I ruffle behind his ears in an attempt to get him to forgive me.

"This is bigger than me Peridot. I am a dog. You are an Elemental. You can't risk your life repeatedly to save me. We'll get into fixes worse than this on our journey. Next time I tell you to go and not come back, you need to do just that."

"Phoenix you'd have died!" I exclaim. I was expecting him to be grateful that I'd healed him.

"Have more faith in me than that Peri, did it not occur to you that I fell so that you could get away?"

"I – oh." I look away. I hadn't thought of that.

"But your leg Phoenix, you'd have bled out eventually."

He looks down at his newly healed leg.

"Perhaps."

"Now who's being stubborn?" I raise my eyebrows irritably muttering to myself as I retrieve my healing supplies. That's the thanks I get for saving his life – twice? I know I'm an Elemental, but that doesn't make my life any more important than his. Angrily, I begin repacking my bag.

"Calm down Peri, you'll start a blaze again." He eyes my hands which unbeknown to me had begun to glow again.

"How do I do that?" I gasp out loud in shock.

"You lose control when you're feeling overly emotional, fire appears when you are angry."

"How can I summon fire and not know I'm doing it?"

"It is common amongst Elementals. When Vallaeartha first came into her powers, she struggled to control her abilities too. Sometimes, they would take control of her."

I think back to the feeling of something desperately trying to get out of me, back when the fox bit my ankle. My ankle! I was so busy focusing on Phoenix, I completely forgot I'd been bitten myself. Rolling my trousers up, I apply a thick layer of ointment to my leg, incanting until it heals.

"How did she learn to control it?" I ask absentmindedly, wishing I could do other magick as well as I could heal.

"That I do not know. Your mother is very secretive about her abilities."

"I wish she'd given me an inkling something like this might happen, when I came into my powers too," I huff.

"In Vallaeartha's defence," Phoenix wobbles over towards me, "by bringing you up away from the truth, she was hoping to prevent what happened to her, from happening to you."

I can't help but feel resentful, in trying to protect me, Mum just made the thing she didn't want to happen – happen. The irony in that seems so unfair.

"Peri, we must move on, scouts will be upon the land soon."

"Can you walk?"

"Yes, I think so," he puts his weight onto all four legs evenly without wobbling. "Thank you. Stubborn Witchling," he nudges me affectionately as he passes.

"There was never a moment in this scenario where I would have left you Phoenix. Just like you wouldn't leave me. We're family."

He goes to say something, then thinks better of it and begins our journey out of the charred woodland. I follow behind letting him set the pace, his leg may be healed, but he lost a lot of blood. He will need food soon.

"Phoenix," I whisper.

"Hmm," he replies, glancing back, to the sides then ahead of us, it's a wonder he's not dizzy.

"Do you need to hunt?"

"I am hungry. I don't want to make you uncomfortable though."

"You need to eat - I'll look the other way."

"Are you sure?"

"Yes," I attempt to convince myself as my tummy goes funny, "but where will you find food, I think I've scared everything off?"

"The blaze would've reached more than our attackers. I'll pop my head down a rabbit hole, do you want to wait here?"

"You mean, my fire would've killed them?"

"Yes," he nods, "nothing could withstand that blaze.

"How did you survive it?"

"You protected me. I was in the fire, yet it did not burn. Just tingled from what I can remember. Your mother would be proud, it was beautiful magick. Terrifying. But beautiful. Wait here I won't be long."

He pads off as I take a seat, the numbness returning. Joe said to follow my heart providing it harmed none. Yet I harmed many. More than harmed. Killed. I feel queasy as the contents of my stomach threaten to upheave upon the floor. I swallow heavily to keep it down. I need to learn to control my abilities. Once again, I wish Mum were with us. We'd probably have Euan and be on our way back by now, unseen, unscathed and all those animals that died in my fire would still be alive. I shake my head to get the thoughts out. Phoenix returns a little while later, looking replenished and his normal self, except for the bloodstains and soot embedded in his golden fur.

"Don't feel bad," he consoles sensing my mood, "some may have perished in your flames, but in doing so, the next wildling that may have crossed their path shall now roam free. It is eat-or-be-eaten on this land. Your flame killed some but saved others in the process. Put it from your mind young Witchling."

"Why do you call me that?" I change the subject, "Witchling? Does that make you a dogling?"

"Dogling?" he chuckles, "Not quite. I am an Earthling."

"An Earthling?"

"Every creature that inhabits the earth is an Earthling," he continues as we amble across the undergrowth, "except for magick folk that is. You were born of the stars, so the legends say. Every other being from the tiny ant to the human or elephant, we are all Earthlings."

"Surely, I am an Earthling also, this is my world too?"

"That is true. Yet, you can do things we Earthlings cannot, that makes you a little different to the rest of us."

"I'm more like a human than you are, you have four legs and a tail. Humans have two legs and no tail. You don't see yourself as the same as humans, do you?"

"Yes and no. We have similar souls. We breathe, we feel, we procreate, live our lives, and eventually, we die. In that sense we are equal. I should have no more priority on this planet than any other animal, including the humans. Elementals, Witches, Warlocks ... you are of magick. That makes you different."

"I guess," I ponder out loud, "that shouldn't mean I am more important than another being though."

"And that," he smiles, "is what makes you special."

"We'll agree to disagree on that," I shake my head.

Phoenix chuckles softly shaking his head also. We continue onwards in silence after that, both lost in our thoughts. We finally clear the last of the charred woodland, it went on for miles, my legs ache, and my tummy rumbles. I'm hungry, but I don't want to stop to eat until we're clear of this area. Taking a wrap from my pack I nibble as we walk, offering some to Phoenix before finishing the last bite.

"Do you really think we came from the stars?" I muse, it seems so far-fetched, yet here I am having a conversation with my dog, after just having shot flames from my fingers, so I guess anything is possible.

"In some sense we all did," he replies, "the earth we walk upon was once stardust itself. It is said that magick folk were the first to roam earth though, then followed the remaining species."

"How do you know we came first?"

"No one knows for sure. Some believe that. Others do not. Humans think they came first. They have books dedicated to it. Some believe that a God created the earth in seven days, then created man in his image. Some believe the earth evolved over time to create life. Magick folk believe in the powers of the universe and that we descended from the Gods and Goddesses of old. Nobody can agree on one version, humans fought many wars over the subject."

"What do you believe?"

"I believe in what my eyes can see. And I can see you are capable of magick beyond any I have ever witnessed. It gives me hope."

"Hope?"

"Yes Witchling, that things won't always be like this."

"Do you think I should try to help the humans?"

"I think you will do what you think is best, no matter what anyone else thinks, and earth have mercy on any that stand in your way."

I chew thoughtfully on his last remark. My powers are strong. There's no denying that. But I have no idea how I use them.

"Are we likely to come across any other people of magick?"

"It's unlikely, there are other lands where magick folk roam freely, but not here. This land is farmland. We shall come across livestock mainly, A.I stations and slaughterhouses."

"Slaughterhouses?!" I reel.

"Where they make meat," he explains uncomfortably.

"But you don't make meat – you kill it!"

"I assume that's where the phrase comes from, to slaughter is to kill in vast numbers. The terminology makes sense. As unpleasant as it may sound."

"Who does the slaughtering?" I press horrified.

"The animals that are in power now. Chickens and cows mainly. Before The Changing, it was the other way around, humans bred their kind for food, so extensively that they took up most of the grasslands. After The Changing, the herbivores had the numbers to revolt. There are trillions of chickens, billions of cows... hence they're the ones in power. Carnivores may be stronger, but they don't have the numbers to rule."

"Why are there so few carnivores?"

"They're still repopulating. Bears, wolves and wild cats haven't lived on these lands in centuries, perhaps, overseas, they may be rulers once more."

"There isn't any left over here?"

"Not since the medieval period," he shakes his head, "they were hunted for pelts and food. Humans would wear their fur and eat the remains."

I stop dead in my tracks, lost for words.

"Th – they… what?"

Phoenix continues forward, not having noticed my reaction. How can he be so non-phased by all of this? It's as if the realities of the mainland are normality and I'm strange to be so horrified by it. He ambles on, the strength now fully returned to his step. Ahead lies a steep climb as the terrain becomes a mass of hills jutting upwards. His paws thud heavily into the ground as we ascend the first of many gravelly dirt paths woven into the grass. Taking a moment to look back, the acres of destruction I caused lies hidden amongst endless leafy green. I trudge upwards as guilt threatens to resurface, it builds in my stomach as we continue upwards, causing me to grit my teeth to rid the rumblings that won't cease. When we finally reach the top, I'm out of breath. Phoenix pants freely beside me, his tongue lolling from his mouth, serious eyes looking forward. I follow his gaze and see it. We made it. We're at the A.I station.

THE A.I STATION

It's not what I expected. From the outside, I'd even go as far as to say, it looks nice. A quaint farm in the middle of the countryside. Meadows flourish with blooming wildflowers on either side, cows graze in lush fields of green, just past the barns and surrounding buildings. The only thing out of place is the noise. Not continuous, but now and then a strangled female cry assaults my ears, making me feel sick to the pit of my stomach.

"What's happening down there?"

"You don't want to know," Phoenix replies not meeting my gaze.

"I do."

"Later," he shakes his head firmly, "it'll make you angry and you'll lose control. Trust me, it makes me angry and it's not even my kind. For now, we'll stay hidden while we come up with a plan to get Euan out of there."

I sigh in frustration, but he's right. I can't control my emotions. My hands are clammy already and we're still a kilometre from the area itself. I need to prepare for what's down there before I see or hear about it. Begrudgingly, I head back towards the shadow of the trees. The sun is blanketed by clouds making the air chilly, I pull my cloak on while Phoenix scouts the area to check it's safe.

"How are we going to get Euan out of there?" I ask, trying not to feel defeated before we've started. There were at least a hundred cows down there, we don't stand a chance if we're seen.

"I have a plan," Phoenix senses my worry, "but it requires you to control one of the elements to do it."

"Which element?" I hope it's not air or fire after my last two attempts.

"Water."

I'm Pisces, so by nature water should be my strongest element, I perk up a little trying to feel determined.

"What's the plan?"

"I need you to create a diversion so that I can break the children free."

"The children? We're freeing them all?"

"We may as well try whilst we're here. Whilst the cows are trying to get their livestock back to the barns, I should be able to get Euan out un-noticed."

"Livestock?"

"Sorry, that's what they call the children."

I don't allow myself to dwell on the terminology that makes my tummy rumble with anger, "how do I create a diversion?"

"There's a river running past the A.I station, I need you to create a flood with it. The cows won't be able to stop the water and they'll let the children out of their pens, whilst they're distracted, I'll find Euan."

It's not the masterful plan I was hoping for, but I don't have anything better, it'll have to do.

"I'll need to practice with water first," I look around.

"There's a brook down the hill that leads into the river, we'll await nightfall then head down there. Try to get some rest, for now, I'll keep watch."

I'm surprisingly tired from the healing and the hiking, so I don't argue and lay my head down on the ground, pulling my cloak around tightly. Quicker than expected, sleep finds me. I wake groggily a few hours later to darkness, looking up, there's no sight of the moon, just the odd star peeking out from behind a sea of clouds.

"Are you ready?" Phoenix sits beside me, sniffing the air. A strong wind blows in from the east, bringing with it cinders of ash we'd left behind.

"Let's do this," I'm itching to get Euan out of there.

The A.I station no longer looks quaint in the darkness, it now appears out of place amongst all the greenery surrounding it. Slowly we make our way downhill, Phoenix on high alert for any signs of interference. The night is eerily still, we aren't disturbed. As we approach the brook, I allow the tinkling of water to soothe my increasing anxiety. I feel like we're being watched.

"Phoenix," I whisper, "do you smell anything?"

"It's hard to tell," he whispers back, "the ash from the forest is masking any scent, do you sense something?"

"Maybe. It's too quiet."

"Let's make this a quick practice then find shelter," he agrees, sitting down beside the water's edge.

I join him hurriedly, taking off my boots, rolling up my trousers and paddling out to ankle depth. The coolness of the water calms my mind as I try to push away the foreignness of the night. Closing my eyes, I imagine I'm back home, in my favourite spot, under the tree by the pond. I can picture the aged bark towering over me, the bramble bushes, the stillness of the water, the occasional whinny from Roland and Amy. I smile despite myself and begin to relax. My shoulders once tight and scrunched up in anticipation, loosen as my arms sway freely.

Knowing what I need to do, I imagine water rising, gallons rapidly flowing from the distant sea, to the river, overflowing into the brook where I now stand. A cold splash to my front makes my eyes open.

"Phoenix look!" I exclaim softly.

He grins up at me toothily.

"I imagined more water flowing from the sea and it came to me," I beam, slightly in awe of myself.

"Well done Peri, your mum and the others would be proud."

"I wish they were here," I sigh, "we'd probably have Euan free by now and be back home."

"Perhaps, perhaps not. This is our adventure Peridot, we're going to get our friend back don't worry."

I go to say something else when sudden screams echo out across the night making me jump.

"What was that?"

"I'm not sure, it's too late for the slaughter collections to be down there. Stay here I'm going to look," he goes to head back down the hill.

"No!" I startle alarmed, "something doesn't feel right Phoenix, I'm coming with you."

He goes to argue then changes his mind, "Peri you must stay in control of your powers, no matter what you see down there, do you understand?"

I nod hurriedly, scrambling to get to the top of the hill as the screams become wilder, the sound makes me put my hands over my ears, I want it to stop. The wind from the east appears to be picking up, the cinders that once swayed softly now billow past us, causing me to squint.

"Peri you must calm down, we can't help them while you're not in control!" he runs in front of me, forcing me to look into his eyes. I'm not sure if it's the light, but his golden marbles have a hint of purple behind them, it confuses me for a moment and the winds begin to falter.

Voices from below now ring out clearly.

"It's an ambush! Kill them all!"

"It's the N.A – stand your ground!"

Then screams. Screams of panic. Screams of pain. Growling, snapping and snarling, and in amongst it all, children crying in fear amid wails of distress.

"Phoenix what's happening down there?" I cry in angst.

"It's The Resistance," he replies alarmed, "Peri, I must find Euan - breakouts like this never go to plan, there will be casualties on both sides. The cows will kill them out of spite rather than let them go free."

"I'm coming with you!"

"Can you promise you won't let anger take over? You cannot let your fire free again."

"Yes, I promise! We can't let anything happen to Euan!"

Before he has time to answer I'm running down the hill, my feet carrying me as fast as they can, all I can think of is Euan, I must get to him. Phoenix charges along beside me and we're at the foot of the hill and across the field in less than a minute.

My steps begin to falter as a sea of what I think are children rush towards us. They're human, but they don't look right. They appear deformed, struggling as best they can to get away from the looming building of terror behind them. Some are mere skin and bones shackled together by metal cuffs on their ankles, others hobble along solo, so large they're unable to run, weighed down by rolls of fat and excess weight, others are mere toddlers, unshackled, but with metal spikes through their noses. I manage to hold back the screams of rage that want to spew out, what has been done to these poor children? My hands glow fiercely despite my promise to Phoenix, I set eyes on the cows far behind, the fire inside me desperate to burn them all.

"Peri no!" he barges my legs with brute force, making me fall to my knees.

"You'll kill them, you're not a murderer!" he pleads, his amber eyes glowing brightly in the night.

Once again, I notice a line of purple enclosing his irises and I feel the fire within me dissipate slightly. He's right, I know he's right. I'm not a violent person, I do not want to do to these cows what I did to the foxes, I must control the Elemental within.

I think of water. Cool. Calming. Gently flowing water. The glow from my hands changes from orange to an almost transparent blue. The burning fizzles out and I look to Phoenix gratefully. The sound of hooves is now upon us as he leaps atop a vast body of black and white, taking it down by the neck. It came out of nowhere. I look up to find a herd of cows charging towards us.

"Get the livestock back! We can't lose all this meat!" one bellows, charging right at us.

I don't hesitate, I call upon the earth instinctively. Minerals from deep below rise from the ground and hurtle towards the charging cow. She doesn't see it coming, going down by the head as a mound of earth clashes with her skull. Others are approaching rapidly, unaware as I will forth rocks and minerals of old, hurtling them wildly at the rest of the herd. Loud clumps sound through the night, cows thudding heavily to the ground around us as the earth makes impact. I'm stunned at how quickly they fall.

"You got them all?" Phoenix joins me breathlessly.

I stumble from exertion looking around in disbelief, my powers worked! And I didn't hurt anyone! Well. I didn't kill anyone. The cows certainly felt the force of my magick, but it was non-fatal this time, thankfully. They surround us, large masses of black and white, dotted across a dark sea of green. They almost appear to be sleeping, chests rising and falling with each breath. How could something so gentle, be so cruel to have done what we witnessed to those children? I look behind to see if any of the children remain, but they're long gone. I hope they're alright.

"Follow behind me," Phoenix's voice cuts through my thoughts, "only use your powers if necessary, we can't draw any attention to your magick. We'll find Euan and get out of here."

Shakily I run behind him, fear threatening to take over the adrenalin coursing through my veins. I come to a halt as we finally approach the eerie building that is the A.I station. The barns are all but empty, their doors open wide for all to see. The smell makes my stomach turn. The distinct smell of urine and faeces is pungent, it reminds me of that first night when Euan clambered through my window a bag of bones. It really wasn't dirt in his hair. Within the barn are small paddocks with thick wooden crates lining the gates, inside the crates lie a variety of restraints. Heavy metal rods lean up against the walls alongside a variety of different sized ropes and nooses. I dread to think about what they're used for.

We move quickly and quietly from barn to barn, the smell getting worse by the moment. Each barn appears empty until we reach the largest, there are no children to be seen, but women remain, chained and unable to move. I know we must hurry and find Euan, but I can't leave them behind.

"Phoenix wait – we have to help them," I cry.

He looks back and his eyes land upon the women, they're in nothing but their skin. Cuts show clearly on their flesh alongside bruises and other wounds, many sway in exhaustion, struggling to remain upright. What horrifies me more, is that many are visibly pregnant, bellies protruding with their infant within. Phoenix must share in my horror, as he immediately U-turns inside their barn without argument.

"Can you unshackle them?" he asks hurriedly as we approach the first of the women chained. She flinches away in fear.

"Please don't be scared, we're going to help you I promise," I try to comfort her, looking over her restraints as

I do. I can't get them off without her seeing my magick. The woman whimpers in fear.

"It's okay, I promise," I stroke her hand and gain eye contact. "Close your eyes, everything's going to be alright."

I will her to close her eyes and she complies, no fight left within her. Using my mind, I urge the remaining females to do the same, I can feel my magick working, my spine tingles delightfully, but I have no time to revel in the pleasure of my powers, I must help these poor women. When I'm certain none other than Phoenix can see, I envision the shackles breaking free. They don't budge. Frustration builds as I'm aware every second here, is a second lost finding Euan. I will them open more forcefully, gritting my teeth with exertion. I feel them bending to my will but holding tight and scream, as I urge every ounce of my might for them to break. The sound of clatters and heavy clangs bring my eyes open, the restraints all falling to the ground. I gasp in a lungful of air, unaware I'd forgotten to breathe whilst trying to break them free. My head thuds, my vision a blur, as I try to get to my feet.

"Peri! Are you okay?" Phoenix tries to help me find my balance as I lose my footing and fall to the floor.

"I'll be fine, we have to keep going," I try to get up again, falling short for a second time.

"Phoenix what are we going to do?" I panic, how can we find Euan if I can barely stand, the cows won't stay down forever.

"I'll help you stand," an older woman comes forward to help me up, I avert my eyes bashfully as her nakedness comes into full view. With her help, I manage to stand, the other women walk slowly towards us.

"How did you do that?" One asks in awe.

"She didn't, I did," Phoenix stands tall, the women cower back in fear and don't question any further.

"It's okay he won't hurt you, he's my friend."

"A pet?" one asks, an irritated growl vibrates from Phoenix's chest, and she stumbles backwards.

"What's a pet?" I'm thwarted by yet another odd wording.

"We don't have time for this Peri, we need to find Euan and get out of here," Phoenix hurries.

"Did you say Euan?" the lady holding me upright asks.

"Yes, do you know him, do you know where he'd be kept?" I ask urgently.

"They took him," she looks away sadly.

"Who took him?" I cry, "took him where?"

"The ones like him," a lady glances in Phoenix's direction, "they took the strong boys first, then left the rest to fend for themselves."

"I don't understand," I try to make sense of what they're saying, "you mean dogs broke the children free?"

"Yes, a massive pack, largest I've ever seen," she continues, looking at Phoenix with fear in her eyes, "they broke into the older boys barn and took them. Then they broke the younger children free and told them to run, the cows chased after the young ones and the foxes went after the dogs. They left us behind."

I gape lost for words, "Phoenix what does this mean? How will we get him back?"

He sits down defeated, "We're back at square one. The pack will have covered their tracks if they're with The Resistance, it'll take us days, weeks, maybe even months to find them."

I can't believe it. All of this for nothing. We came so close. If we'd got here but moments earlier, we'd have found him. Tears escape my lids as I cry freely.

"You're her, aren't you?" The woman holding me asks.

I sniff loudly, looking up in confusion.

"You're the girl he spoke of," she continues, "Peri he called you is that correct?"

"Yes," I sniff again, wiping my nose, "who are you?"

"My name is Louise," she smiles.

I can't believe it. The naked woman in front of me. It's Euan's mum.

Captured

Louise isn't what I expected. Euan described her as like my mum, but not as scary - I think it's the other way around. This woman is fierce. She all but hauled me out of the barn, ordering one of the other women to take my other side and half dragged, half carried me out of the A.I Station, back up the hill and down to the brook where we began earlier that night. Much to the relief of Phoenix, who realistically would've struggled to get me under cover before the cows came back around.

We passed them on our way back, they remained knocked out cold. A few of the women gave them an extra kick for good measure – not that I can blame them after what they've been put through. Many of the women's chests are engorged, milk overflowing painfully with every step. Those that bear children are helped to walk by the others, the rest of us a barrier between them and the cows. I empathise with these women wholeheartedly to the point I can feel their pain, even though I have no idea what their bodies have been through. Louise appears to be the leader of the group, checking in on the others and paying extra attention to those that struggle to walk. We are a large group of almost forty in total, including Phoenix and myself. He keeps watch should any animals come our way, but so far, the night remains still.

The women take turns to bathe in the brook, when none look my way, I summon fresh water to run through with my magick, swirling the blood, dirt and grime away back down the river. It's not much, but it's the least I can do to give them clean water to bathe with. Many of the women had never seen fresh water before and squealed with joy. The majority were born on neighbouring A.I stations by milking mothers, then moved to this one to become a milking mother themselves. My heart breaks for them.

"Quite a gift you have," Louise takes a seat beside me.

I stay quiet, unsure whether she means my magick or something else.

"It's okay, your secrets safe with me, I won't tell a soul. Although many of the others suspect."

I look up startled.

"They're not daft Peridot, locks do not break free by themselves, just as a herd of cows do not fall by themselves either. If you wish to keep your gift a secret, perhaps use it a little less often. You needn't worry though, you saved us. Many would've kept going. We'll take your secret to the grave."

Another of the group sitting close by makes eye contact and gives me a grateful smile. She is one of the pregnant women. She shivers from the cold now that she has been washed clean, yet that isn't what troubles me. Now the dirt is no longer visible, the extent of her injuries laid bare for all to see, even in the twilight. She is covered in bruises, from top to toe. Lacerations cover her chest and personal areas, her bump stretches her skin-tight.

Making my way slowly to her I take her hand, fighting back my tears, whilst hers fall freely. I don't ask questions, I don't want to know how this happened to her, the image of metal prods and wooden crates with restraints remain cemented in my mind. These women have been brutalised to their limit and then some. I don't care if I risk my identity,

I want to heal them. What's the point of being born of the stars with magickal abilities, if I don't use them to help those that need it? I close my eyes and begin to heal her.

No supplies are needed, I focus all my attention on nurturing her broken body back to health, sending every ounce of love and compassion I can muster, and surge it towards her. I open my eyes when she gasps out loud, worried I've hurt her, I find her looking down in awe. Her skin previously covered in deep purple and blue, now has a healthy glow, her olive complexion returning to the surface. The nakedness before a sign of weakness now becomes her, she looks like nature intended, beautiful.

"Leave the scars," she asks quietly. I don't question her request and leave them be.

"What are you?" She asks curiously in wonder.

"She's a healer," answers Louise promptly, coming down to sit beside me, "aren't you Peri?"

I nod, grateful for her input. Truthful as it may be, I was about to let slip that I was an Elemental. Lying doesn't come naturally to me.

"How can I ever repay you?" the pregnant lady cries.

"You just look after yourself and that beautiful bump of yours," I smile.

"I will!" she cries before rushing over to the other women excitedly.

Louise looks at me with exasperation, "no chance they'll believe the dog set them free now," she rolls her eyes at me, "my boy said you were stubborn."

"Really?" My heart lurches at the mention of Euan.

"Amongst many things," she smiles warmly at me, "he knew you'd come for him you know. Was the reason he got up every morning."

I smile ruefully, he always believed in me more than I did myself. I miss him so much.

"What happened to him when he came back?" My eyes re-fill with tears, dreading the answer.

Louise goes to comfort me, then remembers her bare skin and goes for a back pat instead.

"They held him captive the first week, starved him until he'd tell them where he'd been. He convinced them he'd returned by choice, told them he preferred it here. No idea how he managed it, but they believed him, kept him on as a worker as a reward for coming back."

"Really?" I ask shocked, "that's a little gullible."

"We thought so too, but years went past and the punishment he was always awaiting, never came. Cows aren't renowned for their intellect, so perhaps they did believe him. Or perhaps they wanted to keep him happy to prevent him from showing others how to escape. Who knows? Either way, he had more freedom which meant we got to see each other again. He spoke of you often."

I smile wanting to hear more but knowing we don't have time. It won't be long until the cows are on the move again, and we're too close to be safe.

"We need to get out of here," I whisper softly, but urgently. "We can't rest here, it's too close to danger."

"I agree. Let's get that dog of yours and start moving," she rises to call over the women. I reach for her hand while she faces the other way, surging forth my healing powers before she can tell me not to. It's harder this time, my energy is low, making me exert myself to free her of her wounds. I grit my teeth to heal her further, but she pulls her hand away.

"Thank you, Peri," she pats my back one last time, "don't worry about me. I feel better than I have in years just for being out of that hell hole. Let's get everyone to safety and focus on getting your energy back, you're more important than I."

She surprises me by kissing my forehead briefly before gathering the others and heading up the hill to get Phoenix. She really reminds me of Euan, her mannerisms, her walk, especially her smile. Goddess I wish he were here. He'd know what to do. Scolding myself I sit up. I just broke free over thirty women, took down an entire herd of cows, replenished a stream and healed two women and a dog – I need to stop doubting myself. Shaking my head, unsteadily I get to my feet, my first step is a wobbly one. I need my energy back if I'm going to help these women.

With that in mind, I know what I need to do. Popping my feet free from the confines of my boots, I glance over my shoulder to check I'm alone and strip down to my skin. When I'm certain no one is looking, I wade out into the water and close my eyes. The effect is instant. It feels blissful. To be completely bare amongst the elements. I feel the earth beneath my feet, the water flowing over my body, breathing in the crisp morning air and feel the fire of the early morning sun warming my face. My body recharges and I feel my energy replenish, beginning at the tops of my toes and working its way with a delightful tingle up my legs, spine, throughout my chest, head and even to the tips of my hair.

I try to imagine I'm back home, at my favourite spot by the old oak tree, wading into the crystal-clear pool after one of my midnight strolls. The scents in the air are different, but if I focus on the sounds of the trees rustling above, I can almost feel the shadow of the great tree towering over me. I recite Joe's words, feeling hope return, in the end, everything is going to work out. Hearing my name called frantically, I open my eyes to Phoenix thundering down the hill towards the water.

"I'm fine – just recharging," I explain.

Before he has the chance to scold, I drench him with a spray of water covering him from ear to paw. I can't help but guffaw, he looks thunderous. I splash him again, this time aiming at his face, his spine goes rigid, and I know I'm for it. Ducking under the water before he can get to me, I hold my breath until I'm blue in the face. After a minute, I can't hold it any longer and come up, hoping to avoid detection, but no such luck; he's on me in seconds, dragging me back under by my foot. In a fit of giggles, I manage to get free and drench him again, to which he drags me back under without reprieve, making me squeal loudly.

We haven't played like this in years. We splash around in the cold water both equally covered in weeds, caked in mud, drenched through and through until we're out of breath and can water fight no longer. We sit in the shallows a moment while we get our breath back and enjoy this rare moment of normality. Moments pass when I get the feeling of being watched. Phoenix's ears prick up as twigs break behind us. I swivel around, palms facing forward ready to protect us, my heart hammers in my chest, petrified something may have happened to the others above, while we were playing unseen.

In the darkness I can make out eyes, small eyes, low down, not gleaming like foxes or large like cows. I wonder who they belong to. Phoenix's ears stay alert, but I stop him before he pads forward to inspect, I don't sense any danger. I faintly make out sobbing, followed by frantic shushing. I can't believe it. I think it's the children that escaped the A.I Station.

Using my magick I close my eyes and picture the first thing that comes to mind. I have no idea how, but before my very eyes, the water from the brook transforms itself into my best friend. The younger Euan that stood at my window caked in dirt and grime all those years ago now stands beside me, made purely from water. He grins at me, and I can't help but grin back, Goddess I miss that smile. Without my doing, he signals to the scared eyes hidden in the trees that it's safe to come out. I hear gasps, followed by,

"That's Euan!"

"It can't be?"

"He's young again!"

Sensing that they fear Phoenix I splash him lightly, he jumps startled by the cold.

"Play along," I whisper.

He catches on and splashes me back, using his paws to splash me rather than dunking me under like before. I splash the water silhouette of Euan's feet, he grins his cheeky smile then heads into the water, signalling again for the others to follow. Slowly, timidly, the youngest make their way forward, just as another boy steps forward to bring them back. I will my magick to splash him gently. He jumps back shocked, and I smile at him before running back to the water to play with the element-based Euan, now dancing freely atop of the water. He splashes me again with his feet and I splash back in retaliation laughing. That seems to do the trick.

The next thing I know, there's a pitter-patter of feet awkwardly charging towards us, their shackles making them stumble, but none fall. Some seem excited to play, others desperate to get clean, the majority confused and not wanting to be left alone. They squeal, as they reach the water's edge. I forget most of them won't have seen fresh water before. Surging some of the water back, I use it to coax them forward, splashing the odd one here and there. One of the younger girls' giggles and that's all it takes.

Suddenly the brook is a mass of children frolicking; splashing each other wildly, screams of delight sound throughout the early morning rising around us. I can't bring myself to quieten them, they look so happy, I let them have this moment. Closing my eyes, I break free their shackles and use the water to heal them as best I can. There's so many of them, mostly girls, only a few are boys, and whilst they're in better condition than the women, it's still a struggle to heal so many at once. I will as much compassion and healing energy as I can muster, borrowing the water's energy as I do so to replenish my own. It takes some doing, but when I open my eyes, the children are still playing, happily unaware – only looking more like children again.

The excessively overweight children, although still large, no longer struggle to stand or look as deformed, they appear to bear their weight more freely. Those that were malnourished no longer appear skin and bones, a healthy glow emits from them. Thoroughly whacked out, I collapse amongst the reeds, exhausted. I hear Phoenix join me and lean into him for support.

"What are we going to do? We can't leave them."

"I was worried you were going to say that" he answers wryly. Before I have a chance to question him further, cries of joy can be heard from atop of the hill.

"Amy!"

"Mumma!"

"Claudie!"

"Mummy!"

"Sarah!"

The morning air is a wild commotion of mothers running to grasp their children in disbelief and delight. The women of the A.I station thunder down the hill and into the water, embracing each other in pure joy. All are below except one, who comes alone to sit beside me.

"He always said you were worth waiting for," she sighs tearfully, "he was right."

Louise wells up and disregarding our bare skin, embraces me in a hug. Looking over her shoulder, I see the element-based Euan stop dancing to watch us from the water with a smile, I smile back before closing my eyes and let him cascade back down as part of the brook once more. I fear the sight would've been too much for his mother to bear.

"I'm going to get him back Louise," I promise.

"Oh, I know you are dear," she holds me fiercely, "but first, we must get everyone to safety. I hate to break up everyone's fun, but we aren't safe here. We best get going before the sun comes up."

Nodding, I grab my pack as an idea comes to mind and Louise goes to gather everyone from down below. I pull out the various clothes crammed into my backpack and begin ripping them into scraps of material. There isn't enough to keep everyone warm, but it will at least provide a little modesty. I change into shorts and tear my t-shirt in two, covering my chest, whilst leaving my tummy bare and adding another four strips of material to the growing pile to hand out.

"Are you sure you want to do this?" Asks Phoenix.

"I can't leave them, and I'm not going back home until Euan's safe with us. I understand if you must go back..." I trail off, I really don't want him to.

Nudging me with his snout he points me in the direction of the group gathering in front of us.

"I stand by your side always young Witchling."

"Earthling." I correct him with a smile, stroking his head before heading down to the others. Now that everyone has been in the water and had a little healing, they no longer resemble slaves, except for the bare skin on some and deep scars on others. Remembering my plan, I grab the pile of rags and start to hand them out amongst the women.

"It's not much," I explain, "but I thought you'd be more comfortable travelling with a little skin covered."

They take the rags gratefully and begin tying them on each other's personal areas. There's just enough to cover all the female's lower region, some of their chests remain bare whilst others manage to cover both areas. With their hair wild and their children clinging to them, I'm reminded of one of my study books from home, of the Amazonian tribes from across the seas. They look like they belong in the wilderness, we just need to find cover and come up with a plan. As if reading my mind, Louise steps forward and addresses our situation.

"Listen closely everyone. It's going to be hard to stay hidden, but it can be done. We need to travel quickly and quietly until we find cover away from the farms. Is everyone able to walk?"

The women nod collectively whilst some of the children whimper or grumble in response, the effect of being awake for so long beginning to show.

"I know you're tired, but we must keep going, they will be coming to look for us soon, we cannot stay here children."

"But where will we go?" Asks one of the elder children, I recognise him as the one that went to pull the others back from the water. The boys appear to have more scars than the girls in the group, his are the most severe.

"That I do not know Jack," replies Louise, "but we cannot stay here if we wish to remain free."

"What about the witch and her dog, are they coming too?" He eyes Phoenix and me warily.

"Peridot and her dog…"

"Phoenix," I interrupt, "his name is Phoenix and he's not my dog, just I am not his human, we are equals."

There is a confused response from some of the group, a babble arising.

"What if she's with them?" Asks one child.

"Animals are the enemy!" Cries another.

"What if he tries to eat us?" Questions one of the smaller children.

"Peridot and Phoenix," she nods in our direction, "are the reason we are free. They will be travelling with us."

"But why do they want to travel with us?" Presses Jack, not letting up, "they'll just lead us to the dogs that broke out the teenagers!"

"We aren't with them," I explain, "I came here to rescue my friend, we didn't come with the other dogs."

"You expect us to believe that the same night a pack of dogs steal all the teenagers, another dog and a witch just happen to be passing? I don't buy it." He stands firm, hands on his hips defiantly.

"I'm not asking you to buy anything, it's the truth!" I answer frustrated.

"Whatever. I don't trust witches. Or dogs." He spits.

I gasp in shock. It takes everything I have within me not to lose my temper, as I feel my hands begin to flame.

"Peridot," intervenes Louise stepping in front of me to hide my hands, "is not a witch Jack," she looks at me meaningfully for a moment. She doesn't trust the children to know of my abilities.

"She is a healer. If it weren't for her, none of your mothers would be here now. She helped us escape and healed us. She healed you too by the looks of it. She could have left, but she didn't. I trust her, and I expect you to try to as well."

The children look down realising their changed appearance excitedly, some look at me curiously, while others look at Phoenix with fear in their eyes. It's like our moment in the water never happened. I go to say something else, but Phoenix stops me.

"Let's head out, they can follow on after us, nothing you say will make them feel any different towards us. Not while they are tired, hungry, and afraid. We can get a head start while they sort this out amongst themselves."

He begins to make his way into the bushes heading back towards the thicker trees, leading into the forest. I trudge after him begrudgingly, this isn't what I wanted. The plan was to find the A.I Station, rescue Euan, and go home. We've found the A.I station but are further away from Euan now than when we started. Only now, we're travelling with a group of people, who don't even want us with them.

"What are we going to do Phoenix?" I find myself asking once again. I feel lost. For all my powers and gifts, I have no idea how to find Euan now, or how to keep these people safe.

"I do not know. This wasn't part of the plan," he sighs looking troubled.

"What are you thinking?"

"I am thinking that your mother is going to throttle me when we get home," he half smiles, half winces.

Back home. I hadn't even thought about that. They will be so worried if we aren't home in a few days. But if we head home now, I'll never be able to get Euan back. And I can't leave his mother behind with all these children and the other women defenceless. The solution comes to me in an instant.

"I have an idea," I begin, "but you're not going to like it."

"I have the same idea," he gains eye contact, "but it is not me that won't like it."

"You mean Mum?"

He nods. "She will never allow it."

"But, why not? Surely when she sees these people we've saved - she'll want to help them too?"

"It's not that simple when it comes to Vallaeartha. She cannot use the island as a sanctuary for humans. Not without jeopardising everything she's built there for you."

"I don't understand."

"The island is meant for you to grow old, safe and unharmed. A place where maybe you can one day bear children of your own. Bringing others there, changes all of that."

"But how? Surely, I have more chance of starting a family by bringing other people to the island? I can't make a child by myself."

"True, there is that. Although Euan fixed that issue."

"You've got to be kidding me? She let Euan stay thinking I'd never have to leave the island as a result? I can't live life playing happy families while all these people suffer Phoenix – it's not right!"

"I understand that. Vallaeartha, however, does not. She will always have it in her interest to keep you safe Peri. No matter what the cost."

"But it's not right!" I repeat.

"Right does not come into the equation, as far as Vallaeartha is concerned, she will do whatever she has to, to keep you safe. If we are not back in a few days, there is no doubt in my mind, she will be coming for you herself."

That wouldn't be such a bad thing. With Mum on our side, we can get Euan back, I'm sure of it. But at what cost. Leaving behind his mother? Louise will never agree to come live with us and leave the other women and children behind. And Euan would never leave his mother. The reality of the situation sinks in.

"I can't return home, can I?" I ask.

"Not if you wish to leave." Phoenix answers honestly.

His eyes momentarily have that purple glaze I've noticed before and he shakes his head repeatedly as if trying to get rid of a bad thought. Before I can ask about the purple flash, screams assault my ears. The women and children behind us can be heard clear as crystal, crying out in fear, a tirade of barks and snarls following them.

"Mother of earth what is it now?!" I cry out. There isn't a moments peace on this land, no wonder my mum didn't want me coming here. Still, that doesn't mean I can leave them and go back. I turn hurriedly, retracing our steps to the brook, Phoenix in tow signalling me not to use my magick.

The scene in front of us, however, makes my powers desperate to resurface. Our group is surrounded. By no less than a hundred dogs. How we did not hear them coming is beyond me. There are so many of them. So many different shapes and sizes. Brown dogs, white dogs, grey dogs, spotted dogs - no ginger dogs though.

"Who is your leader?" A large, long-haired dog with a protruding nose asks.

Louise steps forward before anyone can stop her, not a trace of fear in her eyes, "I am," she states.

"Where do you come from?" the shaggy-haired dog addresses her.

"We are wildlings," she replies.

"You haven't just escaped from the A.I station?"

"Do we look like we have been in captivity recently?" she scoffs, making the idea sound preposterous.

The large dog appraises her, giving her body the once over and concedes that she is telling the truth, my healing having made the group look almost normal.

"We haven't seen a group of wild humans this large in years, how have you survived?"

"We do what we must to survive," Louise replies solemnly, to which the dog nods in understanding.

"Well, your time as wildlings is over human. You are to come with us."

The children begin to cry, the women stand in front of them protectively.

"And if we don't want to come with you?" she counters.

"We don't intend to hurt any of you, but we will use force if needs be. Trust me, when I say this is for your own good female," the long-haired dog replies whilst scratching behind his ear. A marking of sorts is visible under his hind leg.

Phoenix whispers hurriedly, "are you sure you wish to help these people Peri?"

I nod, not taking my eyes off Louise, palms already warming, ready to fight.

"Follow my lead then. And do not under any circumstances use your magick in front of these dogs, they're part of The Resistance. Humans are safe but a witch would not be. You'll need to rip your clothes more, so you look like them, hurry now quickly," he uses his teeth to tear gashes in my top and I allow him, no questions asked. I trust Phoenix resolutely.

"Follow. My. Lead." He utters softly in my ear before shoving me forward with his head.

"Found another one hiding sir!" He barks, as I stumble forward in shock, not expecting him to do that.

"Good work soldier, good work," replies the dog in charge, before facing Louise again.

"Is that all of your group, wildling?"

She nods in stunned silence as I re-join them, other than my lack of scars I look just like the other women and fit in no questions asked. I choose to stand by the pregnant girl whom I healed first, she takes my hand for comfort, and I give it a reassuring squeeze.

"Do you have food?" Asks the younger boy Jack, stepping forward bravely. I can't help but admire his audacity, he doesn't fear the dogs. His contempt for them can be seen clearly across his face.

"Yes, we have food," replies their leader, giving Jack a once over before adding. "And for those of you that want it," he pauses for effect "a chance for revenge."

That receives a mixed response, some of the women look pleased, others troubled, the younger children don't seem to understand, except for Jack who looks thrilled at the prospect. A murmuring begins amongst the group.

"And for those of us that don't want that?" Questions Louise above the rising of voices.

The dog looks away in response, not meeting her gaze.

"That's enough chat for now," he asserts, "let's move out!" He nods towards his pack who begin to encircle us, herding our group together so that we're forced to move forward, back up the hill, out towards the open fields. A rising feeling of dread surfaces with every footstep. We're being taken back to where we started. To the A.I Station.

BONDED

I can't believe it, after so many years desperation to find this place, now I can't get away from it. They herd us together in the largest of the barns. The children huddle with their mothers for warmth while Louise and two other women hang back. We've seen no sign of the cows or foxes, but four large dogs stand guard by the door in silence, making sure none try to escape. I try to see through the gap to get a glimpse of Phoenix, but so far, I'm yet to see him.

"What do they want with us?" Asks one of the two females anxiously. She's tall, with short, ash blonde hair, fair skin and appears younger than the other mothers, perhaps not much older than me.

"They want us to side with them Marie," replies Louise grimly.

"They must be desperate if they're recruiting mothers and children now?" Gasps the other female, she appears to be around Louise's age, her deep brown skin a mass of scars, clearly visible, even in the dull light of the barn.

"That's exactly the case Dorothy," Louise watches the dogs warily, worry lines creasing across her forehead.

"I don't understand," I input, "who are they?"

"They're a branch of The Resistance, which branch I'm unsure. Rumour has it that they're creating an army to fight back."

"But that's good, isn't it?" I press.

"Depends on what they're fighting for. And whether we have any choice in the matter. Being a slave for milk is bad enough, a slave to fight could be worse, I fear. The children are too young to be involved in any of this. We need to break free as soon as we can."

"What if we want to fight?!" Exclaims Jack, who unbeknown to us, had been earwigging from the back of the group.

"You're too young to fight, you'll get eaten alive out there. Don't you want to taste freedom?"

"What's the point in being free? We'll only be captured and taken to a slaughterhouse. At least with the dogs, we have protection. And food. They said they were going to feed us."

It's then that I notice his scars. He's covered in lacerations from head to toe. My magick healed his pain but not his markings, I hate to think how he got them.

"I thought you didn't trust dogs?" I can't help but ask.

"I don't," he shrugs, "but if they plan on fighting back at the farm animals then I want in. I don't stand a chance in the wild, none of us does."

"Keep your voice down Jack!" Louise chides.

"But it's true! We're just kids and a bunch of broken mothers, there's no men amongst us. No weapons. We don't stand a chance!"

"We are not broken! We don't need men and weapons to survive out there, we have our wits. One day you will grow into a man yourself, do you not want a chance to be free of all this?"

"You just want more help getting your son back, you don't care about me. No one does."

Before Louise has a chance to reply he stomps off into the thick of the group, standing at the back with a few other children that stand alone.

"Where are their mothers?" I ask apprehensively. I can't believe I didn't notice some of the children were alone.

"When we can no longer produce children or milk, we're sent to slaughter. Jack's mother was sent off a few years back. He tried to stop them from taking her, he wasn't successful," Dorothy replies grimly.

"Is that what his markings are from?" I gasp.

She nods before heading towards the group, most likely to talk him around. I want to join her, but I know I'm not Jack's favourite person, I watch instead as Dorothy tries to comfort him, only for him to push her away. She tries again unsuccessfully, before coming back to join us.

"We have to get these kids out of here before they all end up like him," Marie groans.

"It's not his fault, no child should have to watch their mother be sent to her death." Dorothy sighs sitting down, "he's angry at the world and they're giving him an opportunity to get revenge. I won't lie, it's tempting to take it."

I realise now that Dorothy and Marie are both without children. I don't want to ask what happened to them. I don't think I can bear the answer. My eyes still fixated on Jack, I notice that many of the younger children still have spikes in their noses.

"What are they for?" I ask.

"Stops the children from nursing, we can't take the pain with the spikes, we try but it's too hard," Marie covers her breasts, ashamed of the scratches indented upon them. I don't know how to comfort her.

"Phoenix will get us out of here," I attempt to give a little hope back to the group, their fight noticeably diminishing by the minute.

"Perhaps. But Jack may be right," Louise concedes, "we cannot outrun the dogs - there are hundreds of them.

Even with one on our side and you to help us, it is not enough."

"You can't give up, we can get Euan back I know we can."

"I'm not giving up," she snaps.

I take a step back shocked.

"Sorry," she sighs, reaching out to rub my arm, "it's been a long night. I just need to get some rest. For now, at least, we are safe. We'll figure it out in the morning."

She heads over to the group, Marie and Dorothy in tow and suggests that everyone try to get some sleep. Feeling stung from Louise's snap and alone for the first time without Phoenix beside me, I try not to let anxiety take over. The barn is chilly, and I no longer have my pack. All my supplies, my beautiful cloak, my wand, everything was left behind. I begin to feel naked without my possessions, when I realise that for the first time in my life, my magick has been working fine on its own. No herbs were used for the last batch of healing, no crystals, no incantations. Just my will. And the elements. I smile to myself despite the cold and the awful situation I've got myself in. I can do this. I just need to get some rest as Louise suggested. Laying myself down close to the group and in eyesight of the exit, in case Phoenix should try to make contact, my tummy grumbles loudly. The only supply that would've been handy right now, is the last of Ann's cooking.

Twisting and turning, I try to get comfy on the gravelly stone floor beneath me. My skin is cold to touch, my teeth begin to chatter uncontrollably. Now the adrenalin of the night has gone away, the cold, along with my lack of clothes makes it impossible to settle. If only I could start a fire without causing a commotion. Or another blaze. It's too risky. Just as I go to sit up and move positions again, Louise comes to rest beside me. She motions apologetically for me to lay beside her, which I do, gratefully. Her skin is as cold as mine but after a while of lying beside each other, we begin to warm up. The exhaustion of the night finally sinks in and just as the sun begins to rise to its fullest, I fall asleep.

We wake a few hours later to the sound of buckets thudding down beside us.

"Breakfast!" Calls out a female dog, she's grey with short fur and a friendly face.

Groggily, I rise, my back stiff from the hard ground beneath us, warm rays of sunshine slice through the slats in the barns, giving a little much-needed warmth. Looking around, the children are hunched over the buckets, grabbing handfuls of what look like biscuits. Not the ideal breakfast choice, but better than nothing. Slowly I make my way over to the closest bucket, it's full of small multicoloured pellets. They don't look at all appetising but my stomach squirms uncomfortably and I take a handful. Taking a sniff, I try to work out what they're made from. The smell is peculiar, something I don't recognise and they're ever so hard, not soft or doughy like the biscuits we make back home. Everyone else is chomping away quite contentedly, so I follow suit and do the same, popping a collection of the strange biscuits into my mouth. After one bite I splutter in repulsion, spitting them upon the floor.

One of the children runs to me and begins patting me on the back, "Don't choke lady!" her brow furrows with concern making me smile through the coughing.

"I'm okay," I wipe my mouth vigorously, "I think these biscuits may be off though."

The girl takes one from my hand and pops it in her mouth, "Tastes fine to me," she chomps, "can I have yours too?"

"Emilia!" a woman scolds, I assume it's her mother, "let the poor girl eat in peace." She takes Emilia by the hand who giggles as she's led away.

Strangely, Jack comes to join me. "Not hungry?"

"Are these meant to taste like this?" Holding my hand out, I offer him my share of food. He takes it hungrily and smacks his lips loudly after swallowing.

"You don't like kibble?" He frowns, "do you prefer the wet stuff?"

"Huh?" I reply perplexed.

"I don't think Peri has had kibble before Jack," explains Louise coming to join us.

"What do you eat then? Do you eat animals like we used to?"

"No!" I exclaim, "I eat earth grown food."

"Huh?" Now it's Jack's turn to look perplexed.

"Erm," I try to explain, "fruit, vegetables, grains and so on."

"What's that like?"

"Delicious, you can make anything with earth-grown food; pasta, pies, soups, stews, sweets, anything you can think of."

"I've never heard of any of that stuff, is it nice?"

"Oh yes," I go on eagerly, "I had some with me in the forest, but I left my pack behind. I wish I'd snuck some in my pants now," I joke.

"Shame you didn't, I'd like to try it."

"When we get out of here, I'll show you how to make it if you like," I suggest, surprised he's being normal around me.

"No point. I'm staying here. I heard the big dogs talking. They chased the cows away and have control of the barns now. They're feeding us so we're strong to fight back."

I don't know what to say, so stay silent. I'm not from this world. I can't guarantee if he comes with me that I can keep him safe. It's his choice to make. Louise also stays silent, quietly chewing away on the remnants of kibble left behind by the children. My tummy continues to rumble loudly.

"You really should eat Peri; you won't be getting any earth grown food while you're here."

"What is this though?" I rub an individual pellet between my fingers, the scent making my nose crinkle.

"Pet food," she replies. Sensing my confusion, she continues, "before The Changing, some animals lived alongside humans as companions. They were called pets. Pets were given pet food. This is what's left of that."

"Animals ate this?" I sniff the tiny biscuits attempting to eat another morsel and fail, emptying my mouth upon the floor, quieter this time so as not to cause a scene.

"I can't eat that," I gag.

"You'll be going hungry then," says the grey dog coming back round to collect the buckets.

"I take it you were always a wildling?" She notices my lack of scars, unlike the others who are all covered in various markings of sorts. Not knowing what to reply, I simply nod uncomfortably.

"You did well to survive this long," she appraises, bending down to collect the remaining bucket with her teeth.

She catches my eye as she does and for some reason, I can't look away. Her eyes are the most beautiful, blue-tinged brown I have ever seen. Her fur, upon closer inspection, is an almost silver shade of grey, with mottled ginger brindled throughout. She is small in height, stocky and with floppy ears like Phoenix. Without meaning to, I reach out to touch them. She doesn't resist and leans into me momentarily, enjoying the contact before realising her action and jumping back startled, buckets falling to the ground.

She looks at me in puzzlement, I share her expression, not sure what's happening between us. My heart beats faster, my body feeling warm all over. The hairs on the back of my neck stand on end as I remain unable to break eye contact with the small blue-grey dog. The colour of her irises begins to shine brightly, her eyes before a mottled blue brown, now shine an avid sea-blue, brighter by the moment until I'm forced to squint to look at them. I don't know why but I can't look away.

Suddenly, images flash before me; a litter of puppies being tossed in a box then left by the side of a road. Humans one by one take them, except the smallest. She remains alone, cold, and afraid. A man with a kind face and a long beard covered in grime discovers the box with her inside and places a blanket inside. She snuggles upon the blanket, whimpering. The man smiles warmly, stroking her until she eventually falls asleep. Another flash of images, the puppy is larger now, almost fully grown, she ambles happily alongside the bearded man, people cross paths to avoid them but they carry on oblivious. Another flash, she rests beside the bearded man upon a flattened box, people walk past them, some dropping coins into a paper cup, others avoiding eye contact. It's dark and a group approach them. One takes the cup of coins, she barks in protest and is kicked to the curb, another of the group go to kick her but the bearded man steps in the way. They kick him instead. Repeatedly. They don't stop. The young dog howls for help but none comes. The kicks continue, I can feel her pain, it hurts so badly. With a struggle, I'm able to pry my eyes free. I can't watch anymore.

Falling to the floor I weep for the beautiful dog in front of me. To have been treated so cruelly. Reaching out to her, she shakily sits down, I rest my head upon hers and breathe her in. She smells of flowers, earth, and rain. The group begin to look over, she gives me a solemn lick before stumbling back to collect the fallen buckets and heading to the exit.

"Wait!" I call after her, she turns back, still shaken.

"What's your name?" I ask tentatively.

She looks behind to check she isn't being watched by the guards, then holds my gaze confused before answering faintly, "Freyja."

FAMILIARS

My head spins. I've never experienced anything like that in my life. It felt as though I was experiencing her life through my eyes, bonding with her somehow. I wish Phoenix were here, he'd know what that was about. I try shakily to get up from the ground, unsuccessfully, and remain planted with my head still in a spin. Jack strides over and sits beside me.

"You have a weird effect on animals," he observes.

I remain quiet not knowing what to say.

"What was that?" He presses.

Gazing fleetingly at him, I'm tempted to be open, but something inside warns me not to, "I have no idea," I reply, partly in honesty.

He returns my gaze dubiously before shrugging and walking away. I feel for him and what he's been through but something about Jack unnerves me. I try once again to get to my feet, needing fresh air. The smell within the barn is suffocating. Looking around, I notice a few of the children relieving themselves making me realise I need the toilet too. I can't pee in front of all these people. It may be normal for the others to live like this, but it shouldn't be. Craning my neck as best I can, I try to see past the guards outside, Phoenix must be out there somewhere. Even if he is, I can't just ask him to let me out without arising suspicion. The dogs on guard are both large, bigger than Phoenix. One is black and beige with long shiny fur, the other tall and thin with the same colourings, only short-haired with pointed ears and snout.

"Excuse me," I approach them timidly.

A few of the children scuttle away in fear of their response. The barn falls silent as everyone stops to listen.

"What is it human?"

"I need to go to the toilet..." I whisper, aware that the barn has gone still, and all can hear.

"So?" replies the pointed snout dog, "go to the toilet."

"Can you let me out please? I'll come straight back, I need a little privacy."

The dogs look at each other, then laugh. I remain still, partly bewildered by their response, but mainly annoyed. I need the toilet more by the minute, this isn't funny. When they notice I haven't moved, the longer haired dog turns to face me.

"Human, we can't let you out every time you need to pee. You can go in the corner like the rest of them."

"But - "

"I'll take her," interrupts a female voice. I look past the guards to see Freyja walking over. She is easily half the size of the two males in front of her, but she shows no fear. The two guards look at each other confused.

"Why?" Asks one.

"It's not allowed?" questions the other.

"How do you expect them to fight alongside us, if you treat them like the farm animals did? We want them on our side, not against us. I'll take her."

"Has Rider approved it?" The pointed ear dog looks wary.

"No, he hasn't," interjects a female dog, "the human-lover here would have us all back on leashes if she had her way," she snipes, glancing at Freyja. The female is smaller in frame, white with brown and black patches, various scars

210

and markings embedded in her fur. A low growl emanates from Freyja in response.

"Simmer down ladies," commands an authoritative tone as the leader from last night returns, "what appears to be the problem?"

"This pet over here," snarks the smaller female, "wants to let the humans out to roam free."

"Pet?!" Snarls Freyja lunging forward.

The leader steps in front just in time, blocking her from making contact, "calm down Freyja!" he demands, "Aria take that back, you have no right."

Aria looks taken aback for a moment, then skulks away muttering under her breath.

"How are we meant to take back control when we don't even have control amongst ourselves!" the leader barks.

"Sorry Rider," says Freyja earnestly. "They aren't going to trust us if we treat them like this though. They should be allowed to go to the toilet. And space to walk freely. There's enough of us to stand guard, it's not like they can outrun us or escape."

Rider sighs in exasperation but doesn't look annoyed. I notice the way he looks at Freyja, I think he has a soft spot for her. Turning towards the pointed eared guard he instructs; "Bane, get the other Dobermans and bring them here," then turning to the longer-haired guard, "Rolf, rally together the Alsatians, you can take turns rotating guard duty. An hour's free time to roam every three hours. None leave the compound. Any that try to escape, send to Aria, she and the other Beagles can stand guard of any fugitives in one of the smaller barns. Understood?"

"Yes sir!" They bark, heading off to get their packs.

Sighing again he looks at Freyja. "Happy?"

She grins up at him in response.

"Bloody dogitarians," he rolls his eyes woefully, "you may have had a good human, but not all of us did, remember that Freyja." Turning to face the barn he opens the gate with his snout. No-one moves.

"Humans!" Rider commands. "Whilst under my authority, you will be entitled to an hour's free time every three hours. Free time means you can roam the compound at your leisure. Your day begins at nine in the morning and curfew is at nine at night. Anyone out of the barns before or after that time or found trying to escape will be placed in a separate barn until I see fit. Anyone violent towards any dog will be eaten for dinner. Understood?"

The group nod uncertainly, excited until the dinner part of the command. I'm not sure if that threat was empty or genuine. I'll have to ask Phoenix if dogs eat humans. Bane returns then with a dozen or so other pointy-eared dogs, all tall, slim, with shiny coats and very pointy teeth.

"Okay – here goes nothing," mutters Rider under his breath, "rotate every three hours with Rolf and his pack."

Bane nods and steps into the barn.

"You heard him – out you come, walkies!"

The women shuffle forward, children in tow looking down, not meeting the dog's eyes. Once out of the barn they stand in a group, unsure of what to do with themselves.

Bane murmurs to his pack, "Humans are strange. What's the point in free time if they just stand there?"

"Get them some sticks they can play with," suggests a female.

"Good idea," he replies.

I watch bemused as he instructs two others to find some sticks for the humans to play with. Louise joins me then with the two women from yesterday.

"Where were you?" I ask, realising during the commotion they hadn't been present.

"Finding a way to get in and out of the barn," replies Louise, "not that we need it now. Well done Peri, this is more than we could've hoped for."

"It wasn't me," I look for Freyja who is no longer in eyesight. I want to find her and talk about our moment this morning. And to find Phoenix. But mostly – I need to pee.

"Back in a moment," I dash for the closest tree, one of the Doberman pack watches me go. As soon as I'm behind the bark I shimmy down my tattered clothing and relieve myself. How the others go in front of each other I'll never know – I need privacy to go to the toilet. Once finished, I re-join the women outside the barn, keeping an eye out for Phoenix, but to no avail. Where is he? I feel eyes on me and turn to find Freyja watching with acute interest.

"You're looking for the ginger one, aren't you?"

For some reason, I feel I can be honest with her and nod my head anxiously. "How did you know?" I take a seat closer to the tree.

"We had no ginger dogs in the pack until that night," she comes to sit beside me, "I'm surprised none of the others noticed. What is your relationship?"

"He's my friend from back home where I come from. Well, more of a brother actually, have you seen him?"

"Not since you arrived, I'm sure he'll be back soon."

I'm grateful for her words, but it does nothing to reassure me. Where could he be? He wouldn't try to get Euan back without me. Perhaps he's gone back to get Mum and the others. I'm not sure how I feel about that. I feel something wet on my arm and look down to find Freyja nudging me with her nose.

"Stop worrying," she squirms, "it's making me nervous."

"Huh?"

"I think I feel what you're feeling," she explains confused, "if I find him for you, will you feel better?"

"That would be great, but how would you find him?"

"I have a good nose," she replies sniffing the air, "I'll be back in a minute."

She dashes around the barn and out of eyesight. I sigh feeling alone once more as Louise comes to sit with me.

"Taken a liking to you that one, hasn't she?" She observes, watching Freyja as she comes back into view, sniffing around one of the smaller barns.

"Something happened while you were gone," I begin, stopping short as I watch Freyja intently. She appears to have found a scent and follows it, nose flat to the ground, bottom in the air, tail wagging slowly from side to side.

"What happened?" Urges Louise.

"Oh, sorry," I continue, "I saw flashes of her past and now I feel bonded to her somehow. I don't know, it's weird."

"You haven't told her of your powers, have you?"

"Not yet..." I trail off awkwardly.

"Peri! You can't tell her at all if you want to remain safe, if animals learn of your abilities, you'll be in danger."

"More than we are already?"

"Well, I wanted to talk to you about that," she sighs avoiding eye contact. "I don't think we are in danger here. The dogs want us on their side, and as much as I hate to admit it, for the time being at least, we're safer here under their protection, than we are in the wild on our own."

"Perhaps," I concede, "you have shelter and food, well, if you can call that stuff food. I can't stay, I need to find Euan, it's all I can think about. As soon as Phoenix returns, I'll be on my way."

"I wouldn't expect any less," she smiles.

"You're staying too, aren't you?"

"I can't leave the women behind, they need me more than Euan does, he can take care of himself. I trust you to find my son and keep him safe, I think you'll succeed where I failed in that department." She looks away ruefully.

"It's not your fault things are the way they are. I'll bring him back to you, I promise."

"I know you will," she smiles again, tearful this time.

I know she feels bad for not coming with me, but a part of me is relieved. The fewer that join me, the fewer distractions I'll have to keep safe on the way. It's better just Phoenix and me. And Freyja. If she'll come. The thought surprises me momentarily. I don't understand why I'm drawn so strongly to the stocky grey dog with the waggy tail. Perhaps it's the floppy ears. She bounds back over to join us then, tail lolling and panting slightly.

"What did you find?"

"He's left the compound," she pants, "but he's close, I picked up his scent back towards the trees. I'll find him after curfew."

Inwardly, I wonder what he could be up to, perhaps he's hunting for food. He mentioned the laws about eating farmed meat and I know he wouldn't eat human. Maybe he's off getting his dinner or something.

"No, that can't be it," says Freyja out of the blue.

Louise looks up in confusion.

"None of us eats farmed meat either," continues Freyja in explanation, "we're the Natures Alliance. We believe in restoring things to their natural order, we don't live by The Descendants rules."

Louise looks at me perplexed not understanding the seemingly random outburst of information.

"You can hear my thoughts," I gape.

Louise looks panicked for a moment.

"It's okay, Louise, we can trust Freyja. I can't explain it, but I know we can, I want her to come with me."

Freyja looks at me confused, reaching forward I place my hand on her skull, "Freyja, there's something I need to show you – "

"Peridot no!" Exclaims Louise going to pull my hand back. Freyja growls in response, stepping forward towards the older woman, placing herself between her and me.

I quickly rise to stand back in between them, "Louise, I'm sorry but I'm telling her. I want her to know."

"To know what?" Freyja tilts her head to one side.

"She's not like Phoenix Peri, you can't trust animals from our way of life!" Warns Louise, panic in her voice.

"How do you propose to ever fix any of this if we don't at least try?" Ignoring her, I step forward, gently placing my hand atop Freyja's head, looking into her eyes.

"See me," I whisper, letting her in.

I have no idea how. But I show her everything.

Every memory I can, from my earliest days to my most recent. I show her it all. The island, Mum, Joseph, Ann, Roland, Amy, Phoenix, Euan. My magick. The journey here. Everything. When I've finished, I release her from my gaze, gently removing my hand as she leans into me, breathing deeply.

"Are you okay?" I stroke her ears gently.

"You are of magick." She whispers.

"I am."

Louise walks away at that moment exasperated, but I let her go. I'm grateful for her concern but it's up to me to decide who I do and don't trust. And I trust Freyja. We stay sat in silence a while, both breathing each other in until a familiar voice breaks us from our trance.

"Well, this was unexpected."

Looking up I find Phoenix staring down at us.

"Phoenix!" I exclaim, hugging him joyfully. I pull away quickly before any of the other dog's notice.

"So," he looks to Freyja, "you've made a friend I see."

"I can explain –," I begin.

"No need," he interrupts sitting down beside us. He's not angry or worried which surprises me. Sniffing Freyja, he gives her an appraising look, "welcome to the family."

She stays quiet, but I notice her tail wagging and smile, "You're not mad I told her?"

"You couldn't hide it from her even if you wanted to," he chuckles, "you have just bonded with your familiar."

He looks at me meaningfully and I gasp in shock.

I've read about familiars in lessons with Mum, I didn't think I'd have one myself. Not for many years to come anyway. Familiars normally bond with their person of magick in their adult years.

"I'm not a familiar, I'm a Staffordshire Bull Terrier," Freyja looks to Phoenix confused, "you must recognise my breed, I'm not that different to yours?"

"Yes, I can see that young Staff, but you are as of this moment, also something else entirely. Let me explain –"

"Young?" she cuts in, "I'm just as old as you!"

"I sincerely doubt that, if you'd just let me –"

"You can't be older than eight?" She continues offended. I smile to myself again, she has a temper on her.

"That is correct," he agrees, also looking amused by her temper, "I am eight. And have been eight since The Changing, so you see Freyja; technically, I am older than you."

I look up at Phoenix startled. "You're a familiar?"

Looking at me briefly, I notice the purple flash in his eyes that I so often see. "Wait, you're Mum's familiar, aren't you?!" I jump up, the sudden realisation seeming so obvious now.

"Yes, Peridot. I am Vallaeartha's familiar. Just as Roland is Joe's, and Amy is Ann's."

"Why didn't you tell me?"

"You've only known I can speak since we left the island and I can honestly say that with everything going on since we got here, it's not occurred to me to tell you. What with being ambushed by foxes, burning down a third of the New Forrest, taking down the cows, rescuing the humans, and now being in captivity ourselves. We've had quite a lot going on."

I can't argue with that logic, but I can't help but feel annoyed, he should've told me.

"Did she tell you to come with me?" I accuse, my frustration building. I feel Freyja come to stand beside me protectively, sensing my anger.

"I came of my own free will. I knew you would attempt to do this alone and I came to help and protect you."

"Don't familiars have to do what their person of magick tells them to? Mum must've told you to come with me."

"In normal cases, you'd be correct but as always with your mother, nothing is as it seems. She didn't believe it was right to have control over me. She adjusted our bond, so I retain my free will and can do as I please. She is cursing herself for that currently I might add. And me."

Part of my anger dissipates. To have defied my mum is one thing, but to have defied Mum as her familiar – I can't believe he'd do that for me. Kneeling, I wrap my arms around his neck and hold him tight, "Phoenix. Thank you."

"No thanks needed. I love you as I love Vallaeartha, I will always do what I believe is in your best interest. Your mother is blinded by her need to keep you safe sometimes."

"Can she hear you?" I whisper, aware that a familiar's bond is strong enough to see and hear, as the other sees and hears.

"When I let her, yes. If she hadn't given me free will then she could see in as she pleases."

I let that sink in for a moment. Partly nervous, partly excited. This means I can speak to Mum! I feel Freyja shifting behind me and shake my head of the possibilities going through my mind. "Sorry, this must make no sense to you."

"I think I understand. He is bonded to your mother who is also of magick, and she didn't want you to come here?"

"That's right," I nod.

"And you came here to get your friend back who lived on the A.I Station? The boy from the window?"

I nod again.

"Okay. So, when do we leave?"

"You're taking this in your stride," Phoenix appraises, "do you not have any questions about being a familiar?"

She thinks for a moment before replying.

"Will I stop ageing too?"

"Yes. From this day forth, you will be the age you are now until Peridot passes. Then you will continue to age as normal."

"So, we can't die?"

"Oh yes, we can die. Although being a familiar, has certain benefits. We're able to withstand most injuries and don't get ill. An explosion or severe attack would still kill us, we aren't indestructible."

"And we can see as they see?"

"Yes and no," he lowers his voice as another dog walks past, "you are connected to Peridot, you will feel as she feels, it becomes second nature after a while. You will sense where she is, what she needs and want to be with her. Always."

"Are you okay with this?" I turn to Freyja concerned, I don't want to burden her life if she's happy.

"Yes, I'm glad for a chance to leave. The other dogs here didn't have a good human as I did, they don't like me much. Except for Rider."

"Did he have a good human too?" I ask curiously.

"He had a few families. Most were good, but his first was as bad as they come. He understands all sides of the story. It's why he's in charge. He's good at communicating with the other leaders of The Resistance."

"What is this branches purpose?" Asks Phoenix.

"To create an army to fight back. They want to use this as a base to train the humans. Once they have the numbers, they'll break into another compound, they'll keep going until they have enough to get The Descendants attention."

"And then what?"

"Try to negotiate a deal. The N.A want to be able to live in the wild. Free to roam and hunt as nature intended. They don't want to eat the farmed food."

"The Descendants will never agree to that," sighs Phoenix.

"Rider thinks they will if we have an army large enough, that they can't say no."

"There are trillions of farm animals, even if every dog came together and agreed to fight, it wouldn't be enough."

"That's why they're breaking the humans free. The Resistance calculated that after the farmed animals, the next species with the numbers is the farmed humans. They reason that humans will want to fight. They're just giving them the chance to."

"But not all humans want to fight," I input, "what will happen to them?"

"Truthfully. I'm not sure. Rider's a good leader. The rest of the pack is a mix of dogs treated badly by humans or pups that have only met farmed ones. They do what they're told. While Rider's in charge they'll be safe."

"Let's hope he stays in charge," I think of Aria and her scars, things would be different if a dog like her was in control. I sit back down feeling overwhelmed, there's so much hate in the world. Why must it be this way?

"It has always been this way sadly," says Freyja sitting beside me, resting her head into my chest. I stroke her, grateful for the contact and a contented snort escapes Freyja making me grin. Phoenix notices and grins back. He's as happy as I am that I've found her. It's hard to explain, but I feel like a piece of me has been missing all these years until she came along. I just need to save Euan and then I'll feel complete.

ONWARDS

Weeks pass and we're still in captivity. Although, it no longer feels that way. It doesn't even feel like the A.I Station anymore. Louise asked Rider if we could remove everything that reminded the mothers and children of being in captivity and he agreed. We moved all the restraints, cages, insemination devices and electric prods into a separate barn. We thoroughly cleaned out the barn, bringing in fresh bales of hay for bedding so nobody is made to sleep on the cold concrete anymore. We dug out holes at the very back of the furthest building to use as toilets and the smell of faeces is less each day. The taps on the side of the barns provide fresh water to drink and wash under - it's the closest to a normal life the group has ever lived.

I even used a little magick in secret to grow earth grown food in the back field. Root vegetables mainly, with a few tomato plants and apple trees scattered here and there. I've taught the children how to cook over an open fire, so that if they get separated from their mothers, they won't have to go back to eating pet food. The dogs haven't questioned the sudden influx of fresh food, Louise managed to convince them that it had always grown here. Some of the dogs eat dinner with us which has helped the atmosphere to feel less entrapped. If I weren't so desperate to find Euan, I'd stay.

Even the set rules of an hour roaming time every three hours seems to have been forgotten, the barn doors are open always, allowing us to come and go as we please. The only time the dogs stand guard is after curfew – it's the only reason I'm still here. When we leave, we need to do so during the day, as after dark, the guards don't move an inch.

Phoenix has joined the scouts within the pack, they leave the compound sporadically to check Descendants aren't on their way back. So far, no other animals have been seen. The urgency to leave is minimal, except for my constant worrying about Euan.

Freyja has assured me that he will be safe with the other branches of The Resistance, offered the same treatment as we are here. Only he would be trained to fight, due to him being an older male. They have little use for the women and children here. Yet. The main purpose of this base is to maintain control of the A.I Station as a dog compound, ready as a safety zone for when the time comes. The dogs are certain that war is coming. The mothers are aware but do not speak of it, trying to give the children a slither of normality before the harsh reality hits.

Looking around, the children are certainly enjoying themselves. Emilia, the young girl that helped during my choking incident, is currently throwing sticks, which the younger dogs' fetch and bring back for her to throw again. Some of the older dogs appear to have bonded with the children too, I notice one of the boys, Charlie I think his name is, rubbing a Dobermans tummy happily. I'm glad they'll be safe here when I go. It makes leaving less of a worry. We're just waiting for the right moment to move on. If we get caught, it may restrict the freedom of the group after we leave, so we mustn't be seen.

It's a cloudy morning, the sun flitting in and out from behind dark grey clouds, a chilly breeze flows through. I cuddle into Freyja for warmth, who in return makes her snorty noise. I've grown accustomed to it and snort back teasingly.

"Your fault for being too comfy," she licks my cheek with extra wetness.

"Hey!" I feebly protest, nudging her with my elbow.

Freyja retaliates pouncing lightly, landing on top of me, her tail wags ready to play. Aria walks past at that moment, uttering her disgust loudly for all to hear.

"Back to pet life already I see," she jeers.

"Go away Aria," growls Freyja, the hair on her spine standing on end in annoyance.

"No, I don't think I will," she taunts, "always knew you enjoyed being a pet. Typical Staff through and through."

"Ignore her Freyja," I whisper, climbing out from underneath her, not wanting to draw attention our way.

"Yes, that's right Freyja, do as your human says," she continues, not giving up.

"Give it a rest will you," hollers the Doberman I noticed earlier coming to join us, Charlie in tow. "Some of us like humans Aria, get over it."

"You can't be serious?" she scoffs.

"Look around, everyone is happy except you," he walks away shaking his head.

Taking a moment to look around, he's right. Both dogs and humans look genuinely content. A pack of mixed dogs' pad through the compound gate at that moment, Phoenix and the scouts returning from the day's checks. He gives me the eye to join him by one of the trees and I dust myself off and head over, knowing Freyja can handle any snarks Aria throws her way.

"Phoenix, we can't stay much longer," I whisper anxiously, "every day we stay, the more likely they are to notice we're gone."

"Sorry to be the bearer of bad news but they will notice we're gone Peri. I've just been asked to be the head counter. They do a headcount every night when the humans go in for curfew."

"How did we not notice that?" I try not to despair, "Phoenix if we leave, the others may be punished."

"That's a risk you're going to have to take I'm afraid."

"What do you think they'll do when they realise that I've gone?"

"Rider isn't cruel, but he won't be able to show any weakness either. He will most likely implement captivity and end roaming time."

I plonk myself down in frustration. Why isn't anything ever easy? Rescue Euan - he disappears moments before we get here. Save the humans - we get captured moments after setting them free. Now they're safe and I can finally get Euan, but it means jeopardising the other's freedom in doing so. I could scream with annoyance.

"Peri," Phoenix warns.

I look down to find my hands glowing a deep red. I shake them out and focus on water to calm myself, it doesn't work as quickly as before, my hands itch with pent up frustration. Phoenix stands in front of me to block my hands from view, but not quick enough – I look up to find another dog, like Aria, watching me. Quickly I sit on my hands but it's too late, the dog scurries over to Aria who stops berating Freyja to listen intently.

"Now that *is* interesting," she proclaims loudly for all to hear, turning in my direction gleefully.

Freyja looks my way startled; she can sense my growing apprehension. Thankfully, the shock of being found out has made my fire dissipate, only now an even bigger problem faces us, as Aria trots towards me with malice in her eyes. "Got a little secret have we *human*?"

"W - what do you mean?" I stammer nervously.

More dogs begin to look over curiously, I have no hope of leaving unnoticed after this, every dog within the compound has their eyes on us.

"Leave her alone Aria," Freyja comes to stand in front of me protectively.

"I think I understand why you've been sniffing around this one so much," leers the smaller dog, the other Beagles' grouping behind her.

"Don't pick on her just for being near me. It's not every human's fault what happened to you – "

"Don't you dare!'" Aria seethes, "you have no idea what they did to me. It's no secret that I despise humans, but this one isn't even human. Is she?" She glares at Freyja, eagerly awaiting as large a crowd as possible, before spilling my secret for all to hear.

I feel my hands clamming up, as my anxiety builds, more dogs look our way, Rider included. I need to alleviate the situation before I do something I can't control. I look to Freyja desperately for a way out. She gains my eye contact breathing in deeply, encouraging me to do the same. I follow suit and focus on my breathing, unaware that whilst she distracts me, Rider and his pack have made their way over.

"What's today's commotion about?" He barks, striding between us and the Beagles.

"Yes Freyja, exactly what is today's commotion about?" Aria smirks.

"Pack that in!" he snaps, "I'll only ask once, what's going on?"

I struggle to hold myself together, trying to maintain my breathing, I don't want to let any of my powers leak out in panic. I look around nervously for Phoenix, maybe he can get us out of this, but I can't see him anywhere.

"Well?" Rider barks, patience not an attribute.

Freyja sighs loudly, taking the focus away from me and onto her in doing so. "I was waiting for the right moment to tell you in private," she sighs again, stalling as the cogs whirr for an excuse to take place. She has a plan, her irises widening as she makes eye contact for me to trust her.

"This human," she pauses to look at me, "is a healer."

Everyone falls silent as that statement sinks in. No one says anything, except Aria who splutters incoherently, shocked at Freyja's explanation. I look up to see Louise and the other mothers looking my way anxiously, I try to signal for them to get the others to safety in case things go awry. Louise catches on and begins ushering the women and children together, my eyes finally locate Phoenix bringing the smaller children to the safety of the barn. He looks my way, his eyes flashing between his gold and my mum's purple. She must sense his anxiety and be trying to get through. I can honestly say Mum would be handy right about now.

"You can't seriously expect us to believe this nonsense?" Aria intervenes, snapping me away from my thoughts and back to the situation unfolding.

"It's the truth," insists Freyja to Rider, who still looks shocked by the revelation.

"That wilding isn't a damn healer – she's a witch!" exclaims Aria, causing an unsettling uproar amongst the crowd. Rider snarls at the mention of the word, cutting his eyes towards me, I look down to stop my eyes from betraying me, my heart beats frantically as I try to stay calm.

"Rider – "

"Be quiet Freyja!" Rider thunders, stepping towards me. She goes to leap in front of him, but I block her with my magick, stepping backwards in preparation to protect myself. I don't want any harm to come to Freyja because of me. Rider stands tall across from me, staring me down.

"Sit."

"W - what?" I stammer out.

"You heard me female. I said sit!"

I do as he commands and sit, flashbacks of the night with the foxes plaguing my mind. I mustn't show my power, or everyone here will be in danger. I feel his eyes on me as he approaches, my Elemental desperate to surface from within. The command of 'sit' appears to have awoken my powers, I feel them stirring to be freed. It takes every ounce of inner strength I have, yet I manage to force myself to submit, allowing Rider to tower over me. A low growl reverberates from his throat as he takes his time sniffing me over, his growl becoming more menacing as he approaches my face, daring me to gain eye contact. Freyja catches my eye encouraging me to stay still. It feels like an eternity battling myself to stay calm, but eventually, Rider stops, turning irritably to face Aria.

"This human is as much a witch, as I am a Chihuahua!" he proclaims, glowering down at the group of Beagles.

"But I saw her - I'm not lying, her hands glowed!" The male that saw my powers insists.

"He's not lying," Freyja intervenes, "her hands may have glowed, but she's not a witch. She really is a healer."

"How do you know this?" He advances towards Freyja, but she stands her ground, not an iota of fear in response.

"I saw her heal one of the children a few days past, I gained her trust and she's admitted it to me."

"And you didn't think it advisable to tell your leader something so important?!" he demands incredulously.

"She would never have admitted it if you asked her, I had to gain her trust first. Besides, it gave me an idea."

"What idea would that be?" he gripes.

"Well," Freyja treads slowly, I can see the cogs in her brain ticking as she voices her plan, "she could heal the troops that were hurt from the ambush. I could take her to the next compound. If you'd allow it."

She sits, her head slanted in question. I don't know how she's managed this, but if he says yes – I can get Euan, and nobody here would be punished for my leaving. I could kiss her. Rider paces back and forth irritably. He's annoyed this has been kept from him, but the appeal in my potential abilities is too great to pass up. Minutes pass with bated breath, the entire compound remains silent while he chews it over. After what feels like forever, he turns to us.

"If I say yes – and this is a big if Freyja, she will be your responsibility. And you would have to return once the troops are healed, your place is in this pack, do you understand?"

"I had no intention of leaving, I just want to help," she replies so sincerely, even I almost believe her.

"And you, healer?" he turns his attention to me.

"My name is Peri," I reply nervously, returning his gaze.

"Well Peri, do you agree to help our wounded and return here with Freyja afterwards?"

I had every intention of returning to Louise once I have Euan safe and sound, so I agree without hesitation, nodding my head vigorously.

"You can't seriously be allowing this?" Snorts Aria in disbelief, "you can't be letting them go?"

"You forget your place Aria. I am the leader of this pack, if this human can do as Freyja says she can, she will be an asset in the battle ahead. What kind of leader would I be to let such an opportunity pass? Our soldiers need aid, and she can give it to them."

"I highly doubt it, she'll run the first chance she gets!"

"I would never – "

"Quiet human, I wasn't speaking to you!" she growls interrupting me.

"Calm down Aria, it isn't your decision to make, it's Riders. He said we can go, so we're going." Freyja asserts firmly, giving me the eye to back away.

"Hang on a minute I didn't say you could go now," Rider stands, "I'm lenient, but not foolish, we need two others to protect you on the journey. Who will accompany Freyja and the healer to Compound Four?" he barks.

Phoenix doesn't waste a moment and steps forward briskly. "I would like to go, Sir."

"Why so eager?" Questions Rider, looking between Phoenix and Freyja suspiciously. I think he has feelings for her. Phoenix doesn't miss a beat and replies tactfully.

"I have a mate in the next compound. I would like to bring her back with us."

Rider visibly relaxes, "So be it. A Pit would be handy if you come into trouble, in fact, Fergus?!" he hollers loudly over the crowd of pointy-eared, wet-nosed canines in front of us. Over trots one of the largest dogs I have ever seen, he is pure muscle, with jaws big enough to fit my head in.

"Fergus are you up for a journey? I don't want any harm coming to Freyja or the healer, she will save many lives if she remains safe with us."

"It would be an honour, Sir!" Barks the beast of a dog in reply, causing me to flinch.

"Are you sure Fergus's the ideal dog for the trip, sir?" Questions Freyja tentatively. Fergus doesn't seem to have heard and sits to attention, awaiting Rider's command.

"There is no one I trust more to keep you safe," he replies firmly.

"I understand that Sir, but –"

"No buts! My word is final, and I have spoken. The three of you shall take the healer to Compound Four on the morrow. Get a good nights' rest, it's a long trip ahead."

With that, he heads back to his quarters in one of the other barns, signalling for Phoenix and Fergus to accompany him. Phoenix glances in my direction before padding after the two larger dogs. The crowds begin to disperse, all except Aria who remains.

"I've met many humans in my time female, only those of magick have hands that glow. I'll be keeping my eye on you when you return. Or should I say, *if* you return," she sneers, re-joining her group, noticeably infuriated.

Unsteadily, I sit down as a wave of relief crashes over me, Freyja leans up against me to support my rattled breathing. That was too close.

"I can't believe that worked," she whispers gleefully.

"Neither can I - you're amazing you know that?" I grin, I feel eyes on me and notice the Beagle's have their eyes firmly fixated on us causing the grin to fall from my face.

"What is their problem?" I gripe.

"Don't take it personally, they had an awful life before The Changing. It's why Aria's such a cow. Most Beagle's were test dogs," she explains.

"Test dogs?"

"Science experiments," she nods.

I continue to look baffled so she continues, "humans would test if their inventions were safe on animals. Beagles were the common dog breed used, along with other species. Monkeys, rabbits, rodents and so on."

"What kind of tests?" I ask, dreading the answer.

"Not nice ones," she grimaces, "not many survive as a test animal. Aria was only a pup when she changed and got her freedom, but the time she suffered was enough. It makes it harder to hate her. Which is annoying. I really want to hate her."

"Poor Aria, that's awful."

"She'd do it back to you given the chance. Her childhood made her bitter and cruel, she hates anyone that's not a Beagle… except Rider," she adds as an afterthought.

"That's why she dislikes you so much, Rider has a soft spot for you, and she likes him."

"Rider doesn't like me like that, he just knows me from my street days. He took me in after, well, you know…" she trails off looking away sadly.

I put my hand on her paw to comfort her, until I notice Aria still looking over with hatred in her eyes. I remove my hand but feel less agitation towards the group of dogs leering over at us. I can't imagine what they must've been through. Humans did such awful things. No wonder so many animals hate them. I begin to get lost in my own train of thought when Fergus ambles over.

"Commander wants to see you Freyja," he shouts making me jump.

"Coming!" Freyja shouts back, making me put my hands to my ears. She laughs when she notices.

"Travelling with Fergus is going to be a nightmare, I can't believe Rider chose him," she shakes her head.

"How'd you mean?"

"He's deaf, haven't you noticed?"

"Oh," I gasp in realisation, "that's why he shouts all the time."

"Yup, deaf as dung," she rolls her eyes, "will you be okay until I get back?"

"Sure, I best start saying my goodbyes to the others," I stand slowly, dusting myself off as I head back towards the barns. Louise and the others huddle together in the furthest corner, a collective sigh of relief exhales from the group as I approach.

"We thought you'd been found out - I was so worried!" Louise surprises me with a hug.

"Hey, it's okay," I comfort, hugging her back, "it's good news, looks like I'll be heading off tomorrow. I can finally find Euan," I beam.

"How did you manage that?"

"I didn't, it was all Freyja's idea, she suggested she take me to the next compound to heal their troops. It took some doing, but he agreed, we go at sunrise tomorrow."

Louise's eyes well up again, relief flooding her features. I think she was beginning to think she would never see Euan again.

"I told you I'd bring him back," I comfort.

"I know you will," she sniffs, "you'll be missed just as much though," she pulls me into another hug then steps back and shakes her head. "Pull yourself together woman," she scolds, before calling out, "tonight is to be Peri's last night with us. Let's make it one to remember."

"I don't want to cause a fuss – "

"Nonsense, you freed us, gave us hope, we will forever be in your debt." She holds my gaze sincerely.

Not wanting to seem ungrateful for her words I accept, allowing the women to begin to light a fire and prepare a stew for dinner. I can't help but smile, I'm glad I'm leaving them with a better way of life, I'll have some good news to share with Euan at least. Tomorrow I can finally get my hopes up again, I'm going to find him, whatever it takes.

COMPOUND FOUR

"Euan!"

I hear my name hollered across the field, causing me to come to an abrupt standstill. Time ran away from me. Sweat drips from my brow and my legs ache as I trudge back through the mud towards camp.

"Pushing your luck, don't you think?" David grins as I approach.

"Always," I grin back, taking the top from him gratefully, wiping first across my face, then pulling on over my head. He rolls his eyes making me grin wider. Clean clothes aren't top of my priorities, getting better conditioned for what's to come is. Being skinny and nearly six feet tall would've made me a weak link but training hard is starting to pay off. The top stretches tightly over my broad shoulders showing off my newly acquired athletic build. David in comparison, is shorter and naturally stocky, not having to train like me, having been raised for labour during his time in captivity. We reach the compound unseen.

"You're lucky they never catch you, there'd be hell to pay if they saw you leaving without an escort."

"Not been caught so far," I shrug.

"You do seem to get away with a lot," he muses.

"I thought that too. Earth knows why."

David looks at me bemused.

"What?" I ask.

"That's an odd phrase."

"I picked it up off a girl I knew once - kind of stuck with me," I explain, my mind wandering to the girl I think of often. Not a day goes by that I don't think of Peridot. Where she is. What she's doing. If she ever left the island. Part of me hopes she didn't.

As much as I was wary of Vallaeartha, I understood why she kept so much from Peri. It allowed her to be free from all of this. Looking at the compound in front of me, I realise just how lucky she is to not be a part of what's to come.

The compound is vast. What was a slaughterhouse, is now an army base of sorts for The Resistance. Row upon row of barns holds a mix of humans, dogs, cats, horses, and birds. All desperate for this way of life to end. We've been training to fight ever since we arrived over a month ago. Gruelling, brutal training sessions, every day, come rain or shine.

I remember the night we were taken, or 'liberated' as the dogs prefer to call it. Not that I don't appreciate them freeing us from the A.I station. I just wish they'd freed us all together. They assured us another pack was rescuing the women and children, but it is another matter whether I believe them or not. I may prefer dogs to other animals, but they're still animals. I don't trust them. They only want us while we're useful to them. At least they don't eat humans – that's one saving grace, I suppose.

There was a dog I trusted once, several years ago. He's probably long gone now. The thought makes me sad; I'd have liked to see Phoenix again someday. Our life span is one advantage humans have over animals, if we're lucky enough to live to the end of our days that is.

We come to a halt as we approach the furthest barn, the sounds of sloshing and chomping, a welcome sound to my ears. My morning run left me famished. David heads to a table near the back, away from the leaders prying eyes, my secret workout remaining unnoticed. He yawns loudly, discreetly nudging me before sitting down.

"Morning lads," greets John, one of the few men within the camp. Most of our number are my age or younger.

"Hey John, been up long?" I yawn, feigning tiredness.

"Not as long as you I doubt," he gives me a knowing look, reaching for a bucket of chow.

Averting his gaze, I take a seat opposite him, awaiting the feed to make its way round to me. Looking down the table, the buckets are being passed down, each boy scoops out a fist full of wet mush and swallows it down. As the bucket makes its way to me, I suppress a gag, the smell is foul. Taking a small handful, I hold my nose and swallow it down in one go. John sniggers loudly at my discomfort.

"Prefer the dry stuff lad?"

"Something like that," I grimace, the foul aftertaste of wet pet food pungent on my tongue.

"Has the water come around yet?" I pass the bucket of chow down to David, who, like the others, takes a large fist full and wolfs it down ravenously. For some, chow is a luxury. Many weren't fed regularly in their previous stations. Especially those kept by chickens.

"Water up!" Bellows a booming voice from the front of the barn. Several large brown stallions proceed to bring buckets down, thudding them down heavily upon the worktops. I'm the first up from our table, the others still eating the chow greedily. I waste no time, plunging my hands into the cooling water, slurping hurriedly to rid my mouth of the remnants of pet food. They rotate various brands, but they all taste as bad as the other. Although admittedly, I do prefer the dry options. Once I've drunk my fill and the taste is nearly gone, I sit back down, full of water as opposed to food.

"You'll have to eat it sometime you know," David glances up at me, "it's not that bad once you get used to it."

I nod my head distractedly, having had this conversation many times before. I'm aware to the others I seem strange for turning my nose up at what is a treat to them. The luxury of having eaten as Peri taught me all those years ago, left me with an advanced palette. If I could explore the outer woodland, I could rustle up some proper food, but there's not so much as a cornfield in sight from what I've seen.

I may have hated returning to the A.I station, but I came back with knowledge I didn't have before. Away from prying eyes, I'd managed to scavenge a small allotment of root vegetables away from the cows. I'd share it with Mum when I could, although she rarely took any, not wanting to have more than the others. She's stubborn like that. I hope she's alright.

They swore others were on their way to get the mothers and younger children. They swore. But why would they return for them? They're no use to fight against the animals, the women are worn to the bone and the children too small. They only took those of us with potential to survive the war ahead. I remain hopeful they returned, trying not to let doubt creep in. Mum's as tough as she is stubborn, she won't go down without a fight, she'll be okay wherever she is. David gets up from the table then, bringing me away from my thoughts as John slides in beside me.

"He's right lad, you need to keep your strength up. Foul as this might be, somethings better than nothing. You'll waste away if you keep that up."

"I know," I sigh, "taking me longer than I thought to get used to it again."

"Is the dry stuff that different?"

"The textures more tolerable, it tastes pretty much the same. Just doesn't feel like you're eating innards."

"Technically we are," he grimaces himself, "it won't always be like this, if we win this war though."

"You think so?"

"Got to have hope lad. Or what's the point in any of this? Freedom is something worth fighting for."

I nod. He's right there. Everyone deserves the right to freedom. "What were you?"

"Hmmm?" He answers distractedly, peering at the leader's table.

"Before you were liberated. What were you?"

"Oh, I see. Guess," he shrugs.

I look him over. He's one of the oldest humans I've met, outside of captivity anyway. Joseph was the oldest. I think of him often too. John looks a little younger than him. To have lived this long, he must have use to the farm animals, his flesh would be no good as meat now. His skin although weathered and worn, is scar-free in comparison to the rest of us who bear various lacerations and markings from our time in captivity. Many of the boys have brand burns, marking their time for slaughter, John, however, is brand free. He doesn't appear large enough to be a fighter, or lean enough to be a labourer, which leaves only one outcome.

"You were a pet?" I gasp, the surprise in my voice evident even for me to hear.

"Got it in one, yes lad, I was a pet. Of sorts anyway," he adds, looking away.

"What was it like?"

He sighs, "the herd that kept me were kind enough, I wasn't allowed near the other humans though. It was lonely at times, but better than what you boys have been through. That's some mark you've got." He points to the large welt that starts on my chest and makes its way up to the front of my neck, ending just below my chin.

"Hurt like hell," I nod.

"What happened?"

"Ran away from my A.I station when I was little, ended up back there by bad luck. I thought I'd end up as chicken feed, but after a few days roughing me up, they let me be. Let me stay on as a worker."

"That's some roughing up lad, cows were it?"

"Nah, a chicken, would you believe it? There was a coup that'd come and go regularly, their leader convinced the cows I needed punishing." I shudder involuntarily at the memory.

That was the first chicken I'd met face to face. Evil feathered fleabag he was. Never met an animal with as much hate for humans as that chicken had. I pray to the Gods I never have to see him again.

"What did you do as a pet?" I change the subject.

"Not much if I'm honest," he shrugs, "I was a musician, before The Changing. I had my guitar when they took me. It's lucky I did, everyone else that I was captured with is probably long gone, steaks and burgers by now. They liked to hear me play. Other than that, I was left alone."

"Didn't you try to escape?"

"And go where lad?" he scoffs, "get caught by another herd and end up chicken feed? Not worth the risk. I didn't like being on a leash, but better than being in one of their food bowls."

I can't argue with that. Besides, who am I to judge? I could've stayed on the island for who knows how long if Peri hadn't landed me back here by accident.

It's strange thinking back to those days. It was so long ago, and so brief compared to my time in captivity. If it wasn't for the coven marking on my wrist, I most likely would've convinced myself it was all a dream by now. That and the black stone Joe gave me. It's protection most likely the only reason I'm still breathing. I've gotten away with a lot that I shouldn't have. It's like he knew I'd need it. Hell. Maybe he did know. Wouldn't surprise me. I always felt like he knew more than he let on.

I asked him once, but he wouldn't tell me. "Mark of a good Seer," he'd say, "keep your sights to yourself."

I smile at the memory, he was funny was Joe. I'd like to see him again someday too. The stone digs into my wrist at that moment, wrapped in material, tied tightly to form a band, conveniently covering my coven mark also. If either were found, who knows what would happen. Everyone knows the pentacle is a sign of witchcraft, and crystals of any kind were forbidden as a mark of the craft years ago. I almost wish I did have abilities like Peri, maybe I could put an end to all this somehow. The scraping of chairs brings me back to the present, as everyone rises to get ready for today's training session. I follow suit, falling in line behind John, David at my side.

"Can't believe he was a pet," he whispers.

"Too old to be anything else," I shrug.

"But still, a pet?" he snickers.

John comes to an abrupt halt before I have time to answer, causing the rest of our line to crash into him, "Something funny about that lad?" he turns towards David.

"He didn't mean anything," I elbow Dave in the ribs to stay quiet as the line regroups.

"It's not like I had a choice," he grills further, "are you telling me you got a choice in your means of captivity?" Noticeably offended he turns back around, muttering under his breath when he doesn't receive a reply. We continue to herd outside, heading back towards the hills and open fields.

"Bit touchy about it, isn't he," Dave rolls his eyes once we're out of earshot.

I can't help but stifle a grin, typical David, always puts his foot in it. I've not known him long, but we bonded instantly, he's loyal to the bone and funny as the day is long. We come to a halt, reaching the greenest of the fields, the horses and dogs out front begin sorting us into groups for training. We're rounded into the same group as John and a few others I recognise from around the base.

"Humans!" Barks Merrick, the leader of our compound.

We turn to face him, a large beast of a dog. Mixed breeding has made him taller and broader than he should be, he's a Rottweiler mixed with something I'm unsure of. Whatever breed it was – he's huge.

"Train today like you've never trained before," he thunders, "comrades from Compound One will be headhunting recruits to join them on the human base."

A collective gasp draws from all within our group. None were aware there was a base run by humans – myself included. I glance over at Dave who's beside himself with anticipation, I give him a nod, we're getting one of those places. Craning my neck around, I try to see behind Merrick to get an eye on the human leaders, but they're out of eyesight in the shadow of the trees. How can there be a human branch of The Resistance if humans have no knowledge of it? A question that can wait. It's time to show them what we're made of.

A deep howl marks the sound to run. With no warning of the sudden start, we flag behind the group, needing to get to the front quickly or our hopes of being chosen are slim to none. Dave charges forward and I fall in behind him, dodging and weaving in between the gaps to get to the front. A lad to my left notices our gain and plays dirty, shoving Dave so he loses his footing. My height, for once being an attribute rather than a hindrance, allows me to balance him out, keeping the pace side by side, thundering forward. The early mornings of extra training work to our advantage, as we break through the front line to take the lead. My heart pounds as we accelerate, leaving the group behind with ease. With the finish line in sight, Dave winks, before giving one final burst of speed as he crosses the line first. I'm right behind him and surprised to see John come in immediately after, followed by the lad that shoved his way through.

"Good race lads," Maverick approves, nodding his head in our direction. Behind him follows three humans, all having their faces covered to conceal their identity. I make eye contact with one, who looks me over briefly before following behind the others as they make their way to the combat field.

"How'd you think we did?" Dave claps me on the back.

"If we keep it up, we're in with a shot, I reckon. Don't hold back in training – let's show them what we've got." An opportunity like this may never come again, we can't let it slip away from us.

Together we jog to the next field along with the rest of the recruits, some already puffing and wheezing. The years of being in captivity with no exercise hasn't been kind to many. Their scars and wounds are clear for all to see. Dave and I are amongst the lucky few, with wounds that don't hinder our performance. We can use this to our advantage if we get chosen for Compound One.

Maverick nods for the dogs to separate us into pairs. Dave and I annoyingly aren't paired together, but he's strong, I have no doubt he'll beat his opponent. I get paired with the feisty one from earlier, who eyes me with contempt. His face a mass of scars, a bright red number one hundred and forty branded onto his skin. He's younger than me, he must've been saved from a slaughterhouse, his brand a death sentence he luckily escaped.

"Shall I follow your lead, or you follow mine?" I approach him, not wanting our combat styles to clash and jeopardise our chances. I'm surprised when the younger male ignores me completely and turns away. Looks like we might be fighting for real this time. I may be fast, but my lack of proper feeding has made me small in comparison to the stockier lad, who no doubt has bulked up on chow. Silently, I curse myself for not just eating the darn pet food like the rest of them.

"When I give the signal – you will combat until submission of your opponent. As per your training, no weapons are permitted, use only non-lethal means to subdue your opponent. Am I clear?" Barks Maverick.

We nod collectively, each eyeing our opponent warily. There's never been an incident in training before, but the stakes have never been so high. The chance to leave and live on an all-human compound will be worth fighting dirty for, to some. Out of the corner of my eye, I spot one lad drop a sharp object he had concealed in his fist before Maverick's announcement. This could get ugly. I feel Dave looking in my direction and glance up, he gives me an encouraging nod before turning to face his opponent. I follow suit, wishing I could duel with him, not the angry lad before me itching to do some serious damage.

Maverick howls once again without warning, and I'm immediately caught off guard with a direct punch to the face. My nose explodes, crimson blurring my vision.

That hurt like hell. But it helped.

Now I'm angry. Time to fight back.

He swings again, but this time I'm ready and dodge moments before his fist impacts with my face. Ducking low, I turn back around and land a blow of my own to his ribs. He staggers downwards from the impact, allowing me to thrust my knee into his face, I hold back, not doing to his nose what he did to mine. He cries with rage before charging at my middle, a mistake in my favour that I don't waste, deftly reaching my arms around his neck to bring him into a headlock. He realises his mistake too late, struggling wildly, arms flailing, legs thrashing - he's got some strength in him, I'll give him that. I hold on tighter. Now I'm locked on, I won't let go. It's just a waiting game for him to submit.

Finally, he backs down, tapping my arm repeatedly to signal his defeat. Gratefully I withdraw, my arms on fire from exertion, my heart hammering with adrenalin. That's the first one to one combat I've had where I've been in real danger of getting my butt handed to me. Glancing around, I can see in many other cases, that's precisely what's happened. Non-lethal force still permits a lot of brutal contact. We are a mass of bloody faces.

A lad to my left spits a tooth out while his opponent claps him hard on the back. Looking closer I see that man is John. Blimey. For a pet, he sure doesn't mess about. His opponent's face is a mess. Maverick howls wildly again, signalling for the remaining combats to stop. A few scuffles appear to have gotten overheated and continue regardless. Years of captivity and torment being brought to the surface, some relish the chance to let their anger out at last. Maverick sighs irritably, signalling the dogs to break them up.

It takes mere seconds; a swift snap of their teeth is all that's needed to break up a fistfight. We're lucky the farm animals don't have canines, or we wouldn't stand a chance. Thankfully, it's the carnivores that are on our side, their teeth sure will come in handy when the war comes. The cloaked humans join Maverick and the higher-ranking animals, no doubt to discuss who they'll be taking with them. Dave hobbles over, holding his ribs.

"How'd you do?" he asks anxiously, seeing my face covered in claret.

"Took a cheap shot to the face, but I held out, he submitted. Did you win yours?"

"Course I did," he grins, "took a kick in the ribs though, hurt like hell. Glad we did the race first or I wouldn't stand a chance."

We sit down in the dirt, neither caring about the mud seeping into our clothes, Dave lifts his top to check his ribs and I follow suit, only wiping my face free of blood. My nose throbs to the touch, I dread what I must look like. Dave bursts out laughing, so I can guess it's not pretty.

"Is it that bad?" I grimace.

"It's not pretty."

I hear a laugh from behind and turn in disbelief at the stocky youngster that's revelling in having mangled my face.

"Didn't know losers were laughers, did you Euan?" Dave mocks loudly so all can hear.

The lad scowls in response and turns away.

"Little git," Dave scowls back.

I pay no bother. I've had worse done to me. Just not at the hands of another human. I was naive enough to think we were on the same side. It's each man for himself in this world. I hate what our circumstance has turned us into. Fighting like barbarians for a chance at freedom. It shouldn't be this way.

"Our comrades have made their decision," Maverick's voice brings our attention back to the front.

"You will be split into two groups. One group will stay here to continue training, the other, will accompany the humans to Compound One. If you're approached, move to the left. Everyone else, stay as you are."

Dave elbows me good luck. I elbow back, receiving a groan in response, I pat him on the back in apology, I'd forgotten about his ribs. Two Husky's sniff through the crowd, nudging some to the left, others to remain. There appear to be more chosen than not. They reach our group, sniffing over us one by one. Please I pray, let me be chosen, subconsciously squeezing my coven branded wrist tightly for luck.

I'm greeted with emptiness as David is selected and I'm left behind, along with John, my brooding opponent and a few others. I can't believe it. I didn't make the cut. Dave looks my way in shock, going to approach me, I shake my head, not wanting him to miss out on his chance because of me.

"Wait a minute," growls one of the Husky's, eyeing our exchange, "you there."

"Me?" I point at myself.

"No, your companion," he nods towards David.

The word results in a few sniggers from the younger boys. I can't help but roll my eyes. Companion to the dogs is another word for friend, not what they've taken it to mean.

"Back over here," he grunts, signalling with his head for Dave to join me. I look at him perplexed, that can't be right. He came first in the race and there's no way he didn't have a good fight, he's possibly the fittest of our group.

"Those of you on the left, return to base," instructs the Husky, "those remaining, transfer to Compound One."

Holy cow.

Dave grapples me in excitement as I shove him back exuberantly. I can't believe it. We're going to Compound One.

Terrain

We've been travelling for what feels like forever. My legs ache from trudging across country, up and down hills, through thick woodland and across rushing rivers. Thankfully, as we were close to where we had originally been ambushed, Phoenix had doubled back the night before to find my bag and supplies, it's strapped firmly to my back, and I couldn't be more grateful. I would never have made it this far without my boots or warm cloak. It's been amazing to see such beautiful countryside, but hard travelling without the use of magick. Fergus may be deaf, but he's got his eye firmly on every little detail around us. Nothing misses his gaze. I understand why Rider chose him for the journey – what he lacks in hearing he makes up for with his awareness. In any other circumstance, I'd be grateful for his company but given our secret mission ahead, it's hard not speaking freely to Phoenix and Freyja.

"Do you need to rest?" he hollers, turning around to face me from afront.

Freyja stifles a giggle as she often does at his lack of volume control, while Phoenix looks ahead to ensure no passing animals have heard us approach. Smiling at him, I shake my head and continue onwards, I'm itching to get there. Just the thought that I may see Euan later today if we keep up the pace makes my tummy flip. I'm so excited to see him. Also, a little apprehensive.

There's a chance that he may be angry because I landed him back in a war zone. He'd have been glad to be reunited with his mum, but he'd just come around to the idea of staying on the island with us. I think Louise watered down the animal's treatment of his return to the A.I Station to ease my guilt. I'd put it to the back of my mind, but out on the open plains, I can't help but dwell on it. After seeing the tools they had at the barn, there's a slim chance he wasn't punished with them. The electric prods and cages were there for a purpose. I shudder involuntarily at the thought and pick up the pace. The quicker we get there, the quicker I can apologise and get him back to Louise and onto safety, wherever that may be. I still haven't worked out a plan of action for when we're reunited. I'll face that issue when it arises, for now, we just need to get to Compound Four safely without attracting any unwanted attention.

We've been spotted by various animals on our travels, squirrels, ferrets and deer mainly, although they've kept to themselves. The odd rabbit popped up here and there but none that have caused alarm. Thankfully, no farm animals and no foxes - not yet anyway. We still have a day's travel ahead of us, and the journey so far, other than being tiring, seems to be going smoothly. Almost too good to be true. I had feared the worst, half expecting to come across bears or a pack of wolves on our travels. My magick may have taken down a herd of herbivores but carnivores, I imagine, will be a lot trickier. I wonder whose side they're on.

"Freyja?" I call out.

"What's up?" she bounds over, tongue lolling freely, enjoying the open countryside.

"Whose side is the other meat-eaters on?"

"The other meat-eaters?"

"The other carnivores I mean?"

"Oh, I see, I'm not sure. We don't have any in England anymore. They'll have them in some countries though."

"We definitely don't have any in England?"

"Not for many years, they were hunted to extinction by humans long ago," inputs Phoenix, padding over, "why do you ask?"

"Just wondering which other animals we have to worry about, is it only horses and dogs that are in The Resistance?"

"So far," Freyja nods, "along with some of the smaller mammals like cats and birds, but they gather intel mainly. We have recruits trying to sway other species onto our side."

"I thought the other species didn't care what's happening to humans, why would they get involved?"

"The recruits work it from another angle. Many want to hunt and roam freely, we appeal to that side of them, rather than the freeing of humans."

"You lie to them?"

"Not exactly, humans and animals join for their own reasons. For animals it's a chance at being able to live as nature intended, for humans, it's the chance to be free from slavery."

I guess that makes sense, "have many joined?"

"Some, but we need more. Each species will be in talks to decide who to side with when the time comes."

"What if they don't want to choose a side?"

"Many don't – but in doing so they're siding with the oppressors. Just because they're not doing the deed themselves doesn't mean they aren't complicit - turning a blind eye to it allows it to continue."

I can't believe no one's tried to put a stop to this already I think to myself as we continue forward, my legs beginning to ache from walking so far.

"It's punishable by law." Freyja answers my un-asked question as if I'd spoken aloud, "humans are classed as property, to free one would be stealing from the animals that own them. It's not worth the risk to most."

"But they're not property!"

"I agree, as do most dogs, horses and other species still loyal to humans. It's why The Resistance was created. To put an end to all this."

The terrain turns uphill, causing our conversation to stop as we push forward up the steep incline. Phoenix stalks forward to join Fergus upfront, checking the other side for any potential danger ahead. I'd completely forgotten about Fergus for a moment, that was the most we'd spoken on the trip, as a normal conversation anyway.

"You don't think he heard any of that do you?" I whisper in between pants as we reach the top of the hill.

"Doesn't matter if he did," Freyja replies breathlessly, "it's rare for humans of your age to know much about the world, outside of what they've seen first-hand. Few remember what it was like in their youngest years before The Changing. Most have been in captivity since they can remember, you're probably the only human in England that hasn't been in captivity."

Poor Euan. No wonder he was in such a state when he arrived. If only I'd listened to his ramblings all those years ago. If I'd believed him, maybe things would be different, and I wouldn't be scaling the country in imminent danger trying to find him. Fergus gives the signal that all is clear as we trek downhill, thankfully the decline is easier on my legs, allowing me to get my breath back. We continue onwards until the sun begins to set, fading lower into the sky, causing the skyline to become a swirled mix of pinks, purples and orange-tinged red.

"Shall we make camp?" Booms Fergus, coming to a halt.

Given his mass I expected him to struggle as I have, yet he's in better shape than the rest of us. I want to carry on, but my feet are begging me to stop. My ankles ache, the heels of my feet red raw, my toes squished in my boots. I've never hiked terrain like this before and as desperate as I am to see Euan, I need the rest. I'm exhausted.

"Yes please," I breathe, subconsciously resting a hand on his shoulder. He looks at the contact momentarily but sits quite contented as I gratefully lean my weight onto him whilst he surveys the land. His eyes scour for a safe place for us to rest. It's frustrating that I can't use my magick, I'm confident enough in my skills now that I could make a covering of sorts where we are.

"Over that pass should suffice," he points ahead, "can you walk that far healer?"

I grimace inwardly, I don't like being referred to that way. I nod rather than say anything, not sure how he'd react if I asked him to use my name.

"Her name is Peridot," says Freyja, having overheard my thoughts unbeknown to me.

"Popydot?"

"P-E-R-I-D-O-T," she enunciates each letter loudly for him. I turn my head to the side to stifle my giggles, Phoenix watches amused.

"Peri for short," I add.

"Peki?"

"Peri," I repeat, louder this time.

"Well Pepi, let's get a move on, we'll rest up and be ready to move at sun-up. Compound Four isn't far to go now."

"Would we make it tonight if we kept going?" I don't bother to correct him a third time.

"Speak up Pepi, I'm not a mouse."

I sigh exasperatedly.

"Would we make it if we kept going?!" Shouts Freyja on my behalf.

"Blimey Freyja, no need for that I'm not deaf!"

252

She looks at him incredulously, but says nothing, if she had arms, she would have thrown them up in exasperation.

"We could make it in three hours perhaps, more chance of foxes in the dark though. I don't mind if you want to carry on?"

I'm torn as to carry on or not, "could we stop to rest a while then try to get there before dark?" I ask loudly but not quite shouting.

"It bothers me none, what say you?" He turns to Phoenix and Freyja.

"Sounds like a plan," they agree, heading towards the spot Fergus pointed out to rest.

Gratefully collapsing on the floor fifteen minutes later, the boys check the perimeter while Freyja goes to collect firewood. I tenderly remove my boots to find my feet red raw and blistered. Phoenix shifts to help me, stopping himself as Freyja comes back, worry in her eyes.

"Sorry," she glances at him, "it must be hard letting someone else care for Peri when you've been with her so long."

"No need to apologise, I'm glad she has someone else looking out for her - Vallaeartha will be pleased too."

"Does Mum know?" I look up, I've wanted to ask about back home ever since we left, but with Fergus always within earshot, even with his hearing, it's not worth the risk of being overheard.

"She'll know you've bonded with your familiar – she'll have felt when it happened. She wants to see you, but if I let her in, she will eventually overpower me and know our location. We've been gone so long - she won't hold back from finding you. The only reason she hasn't already is that she doesn't know where we are."

My tummy squirms uncomfortably as guilt wracks my mind. She must be worried sick. Even though Joe and Ann approved of my decision, part of me wishes I'd confided in her before I left. I wouldn't be here if I had though. She never would have let me leave. Sighing I open my bag, I was hoping I could use Phoenix's bond with Mum to speak to everyone back home. Looks like that won't be happening. I begin sifting through my supplies for a lotion to apply to my feet. Locating a yarrow lotion at the bottom of the bag I give it a thorough shake before applying generously to each foot. It soothes instantly.

"Rats!" Startles Fergus from behind us, jumping up to smell the air.

"What –" I begin to question.

"Quiet Pepi," he shushes, pointless given the volume of his own voice, "I smell rats, we don't want them on our trail."

He begins circling the area, trying to locate the fiendish scent only to finish up at my feet in repulsion. "Great dogs human! What have you trodden in?" he falls backwards.

I fail to hold back my mirth, bursting into a fit of laughter. Yarrow lotion must smell truly awful for the giant of a dog to fall over himself to get away. I wipe tears of laughter from my eyes only to find him looking utterly perplexed, causing me to start all over again. "Sorry," I wheeze in between breaths, "the smell – it's a lotion. To heal my sores, look…" I lean down to show him my newly healed feet.

"Do all healing supplies smell so bad?"

"Some, they work wonders though."

"I think I'd rather the wounds," he wrinkles his nose, choosing to sit as far away from my feet as possible.

Chortling, I begin to make the fire, igniting kindling with pyrite then placing larger twigs on top to burn, surrounded by larger branches to keep the flames within. No magick is needed, Joe taught me how to make a fire when I was little, camping was one of my favourite activities. Moments later we have a crackling fire ablaze, we settle closely, enjoying the warming sensation.

"Do you mind if we carry on?" I ask Freyja, who looks like she could happily settle for the night.

"It's fine, we can make camp when we get there, I'm sure the other dogs will appreciate a fire also. Few humans know how to make one."

That strikes me as odd. It's in our nature to make fire as one of the first advanced capabilities humans mastered. In movies I'd watched back home, we had advanced technologies from televisions, phones, lights to cars … how could humans have all that, yet not know how to do something as basic as starting a fire?

"Humans lost touch of their nature over time," Freyja answers my silent question, causing me to glance up.

"Sorry, your thoughts are like my own, I can't seem to tune them out."

"Does it bother you?"

"Not really, I feel like I'm invading your privacy at times though, some thoughts you may not want me to hear."

"It's okay, it's oddly comforting. I thought I'd hear yours too though." I lower my voice as Fergus shifts to scratch his ear. We'll ask Phoenix later, I think to myself, Freyja hears and nods in agreement. Looking up Fergus's scratching becomes more vigorous, how that doesn't hurt I'll never know, he's scratching his ears raw.

"Fergus?" I question, he continues to scratch, not having heard, he looks up as I approach.

"Would you like me to take a look?" I ask, emphasising the words so he can understand.

"Not if I have to smell like your feet," he answers warily, "I'd rather the itches."

I don't take offence, the yarrow lotion is an awful scent, I wouldn't want it near my face either.

"I promise," I acquiesce, gently lifting his left ear.

"Is it just this one or both?"

"Both, but the left bothers me most."

Inspecting his ear, I see the infection instantly, a raised gash weeps freely, having scabbed over inside of the ear canal, causing irritation which has spread deep. I can heal it with magick, but not without arising suspicion, I'll have to take a longer course of action and use herbal lore to make an ointment - a scent-free one at that. Freyja brings my bag to me, placing it at my feet, I begin rummaging for the herbs required to heal him. Moments later I have the supplies I need; hyssop to quell the infection, chickweed to reduce inflammation and a quartz crystal to amplify their properties and make for quicker healing. It's lucky Phoenix thought to get my supplies as I wouldn't have found the herbs I needed on our travels. To keep up my façade as a non-magickal healer, I'll have to use my powers subtly to avoid detection.

Using a pestle and mortar from my bag I begin grinding the herbs until they resemble dust, adding water from my flask and sprinkling them into a tube along with the quartz. I give everything a good shake, turning my back to Fergus, stepping closer to the fire to avoid being overheard. Closing my eyes, I incant a hurried ritual to amplify the ointments properties. What normally takes a week to brew, is ready instantly, as I hold the tube over the fire. The ointment looks green and thick in consistency, pulling the cork, it has a slight aroma that I hope Fergus will agree is bearable.

"I'm going to apply this to your ears, it'll stop the pain and it should help improve your hearing too, providing there's not been damage further down."

Fergus looks at me not having understood a word I just said.

"Trust me," I mouth, he looks wary, but allows me to use the ointment, wincing when it touches the infected areas.

"How does that feel?" I ask.

He shakes his head, sniffing the air.

"Smells strange, but not like your feet, thankfully."

"But how does it feel?" I press.

"Better," he concedes, "thanks."

I nod, putting my supplies away. Out of the corner of my eye, I notice Fergus's ears pricking up each time the fire crackles, it appears his hearing has improved already. I smile to myself, glad I'd taken the extra time back home to learn how to heal without relying purely on magick. Hopefully, I can help more at the compound.

"Shall we head out?" I ask the others.

"We'll need to get there before dark if you don't want to risk running into scouts or poachers. The terrain ahead is different to the land we've covered so far."

"How do you mean?"

"We're leaving the A.I land and heading into slaughterhouse territory. The land here is flat and barren, there will be no fields of green or meadows to pass through."

"Why is it like that?"

"Natural land was destroyed to use as farmland, chickens cram as many humans as they can into this territory to stockpile their livestock. When an area becomes unusable, they move on to the next, then back around again. The land doesn't have time to recover."

"Where is Compound Four, is it safe?"

"It's one of the smaller slaughterhouses, made sense to stay there once we freed the humans, they need the shelter and we're further from the main stockpiles. It's away from any immediate danger."

"Do they know that The Resistance is there though?"

"Oh yes. That's why we're training the humans to fight, or they won't stand a chance in an ambush. We target the smaller facilities that we know we can over-run, get the humans as ready as we can and in the meantime, try to get the other species on our side. Once we have the numbers – we'll go to war. We daren't breach the main farms without the numbers to back it up, would be a massacre. We'll be ready soon enough if my brother's been doing his job properly."

He heads away in the direction of the flatlands below. Rising, I stamp out the fire to join him, using my boots to thoroughly disperse any remaining flames, then with my backpack securely upon my shoulders, we head back out.

Once over the other side of the pass, the terrain becomes flat and barren, void of plants and flowers. Fergus wasn't exaggerating, odd patches of grass sprout here and there but other than that, it's bleak and void of life.

Further ahead, buildings come into view on the horizon. Eerily they stand, like a grey wasteland, unearthly quiet, with no other signs of life. We continue in silence, each step a loud crunch on the crusted dirt beneath our feet. After an hour of walking, the buildings come into focus, it appears to be an abandoned town. I stop for a moment to take it in.

"There's no colour, no life," I observe, "does anyone still go there?"

"Herbi's live there now, they chose to live as the humans once did in their dwellings. Too unnatural for me. We should keep going Pepi, we don't want to be seen by the chickens, it wouldn't fare well for us."

The others quicken their pace and I follow suit, the idea of a town inhabited by chickens seeming almost humorous if it weren't for the dire circumstances.

"Why don't they let the humans go back to the towns, and the animals live on the land? That way no one needs to be in captivity?"

"That's what we're suggesting to the other species," Fergus agrees, "chickens aren't prepared to give up humans as leverage though. Whilst human is on the menu, they are not. Many of them eat human now themselves."

"But they're herbivores? Why would they eat meat?"

"They like the taste I suppose."

Revulsion creeps up on me, as mental images of chickens feeding on human corpses flash through my mind. I understand the hurry to get past the town and quicken my pace to match the others.

Anxiety builds again as I struggle to see a way out of the predicament we're facing. There are so many odds against us. Now I've seen what the humans are going through, I can't leave them to fend for themselves. I want to help. At some point I'll have to include Mum, she can't take me away from this life now that I've seen and experienced it first-hand. It was different when I didn't know what was going on, but now I've seen what's happening, I can't turn a blind eye and go back to the way things were.

The evening begins to turn cold, I wrap my cape around tightly, the previous cover of trees no longer blocking the wind. It howls wildly making it hard to walk.

"Peri," whispers Phoenix.

I look up to see him giving me the eye. I realise then that the wind howling is my doing, my anxiety causing the elements to stir to life.

"Sorry," I grimace trying to quell the increasing anxiety of what's to come.

Looking up I find Freyja looking troubled too, her eyes shining a vivid blue in the darkening evening night. Oh, earth, this is not what we need right now, especially as Fergus's hearing has vividly improved, I need to calm down.

Where's water when I need it? Looking around frantically, I try to find a stream, a river, anything water-based to soothe my anxiety, but all I can see is the endless row upon row of squared dirt fields. The saddening sight causes me to stumble, Freyja stumbles also as my panic rises - fear begins to take over. Phoenix rushes to my side to balance me as I try to make my way to Freyja.

"Peri," he whispers, "she feels what you feel. Your worry for her, makes her worry for you and vice versa. We're nearly there. Focus on finding the boy – that helps you."

I notice his golden eyes swirling with dots of purple making their way through, is that Mum talking to me through Phoenix, or is my mind seeing things that aren't there?

I do as he says and focus on Euan. Of arriving at Compound Four to find him rested, happy and well. The thought brings me peace and the winds begin to calm, the howling less frantic, the winds less erratic, my steps, in turn, become less faltered. Looking up, I find Freyja's eyes her normal grey-blue once more – no longer with a vibrant luminous glow.

"Thanks," I breathe relieved, "how did you know thinking of Euan would calm me?"

"Just an inkling," he replies avoiding my gaze.

That's odd, he never avoids my gaze. The winds begin to stir again, not liking the truth being withheld from me.

Freyja joins us, "it makes Peri anxious when you withhold things from us," she eyes him pointedly.

"I understand that Freyja, but now isn't the time," he emphasises his gaze towards Fergus, his huge mass barely affected by the winds.

Understanding his reluctance to answer my question I feel bad for doubting him, the winds continue to blow unsteadily, my mood all over the place.

"The winds are changing," booms Fergus from ahead, jumping at the volume of his own voice.

"Is that how loud I always talk?" He asks incredulously, many decibels lower.

We all nod in unison.

"Blimey, it's a miracle we've not been ambushed," he guffaws, laughing heartily.

It's the first time I've heard him laugh, it's deep, gravelly and surprisingly infectious. Within moments we've all doubled over laughing, it's hard not to as Fergus wheezes uncontrollably, rolling onto his back, legs in the air, tears of laughter streaming from his eyes.

"I – I've not laughed in years," he hiccups, rolling onto his front, "thankyou Pepi," he adds, "I feel like a new dog, my brother won't believe it when we get there."

"You're welcome," I smile earnestly, equally grateful for his presence as the winds calm to a complete stop, his interruption was exactly what was needed to extinguish my swirling mood. I don't have the heart to tell him he's still getting my name wrong though.

"Is your brother at Compound Four?" I ask instead, not having learnt much about Fergus on our travel so far.

"Yes, he's the leader there, would've been me if I had my hearing, glad it wasn't though, to tell the truth, too stressful making all the decisions."

"Do we have far left to go?"

"We'll be there within the hour I'd say, can't wait - I'm famished," he licks his lips in anticipation.

They'd hunted in turn on our journey, out of my eyeline, I understand their need to eat meat, but seeing it first-hand remains uncomfortable for me. Feeling peckish myself, I take the remaining root vegetables out of my bag and crunch appreciatively. Fergus's ears prick at the noise, he turns to watch curiously.

"Would you like to try some?" I offer.

"Sure, why not," he surprises me.

Passing him a carrot, which fits easily into his cavern of a mouth, he chomps away noisily.

"You like?"

"Surprisingly good," he nods, "what is it?"

"A carrot," I chuckle.

"Do you have any more?"

"That was my last carrot, but I've got some beetroot left," I peel back the skin to place the purple vegetable in his mouth.

"Tasty," he chomps, his teeth turning pink from the juice.

"I'll cook for you at the compound if you like?"

"Sure, my brother would approve, fussy eater he is, won't touch chow. Dogs think he's daft."

I wonder what chow is, but don't ask for fear of the answer. The sky is pitch black now, clouds scattering across an inky blackness, the odd star twinkling down, void of the moon. Having passed the town hurriedly, the cluster of buildings behind us get smaller, whilst looking ahead, another structure comes into view. It's immense. Not a town but barn, upon barn neighbouring each other, lights in many. Barks, chatter, and whinnying can be heard from the distance.

"Is that Compound Four?" I ask in awe, "I thought it was one of the smaller facilities?"

"This is nothing, wait until you see Compound One," answers Fergus, quickening his pace towards the vast structure ahead of us. My legs protest as I push myself further, never having walked so far, so fast in my entire life. Phoenix and Freyja each flank a side for support, their four legs much better at covering large distances than my two. Ten minutes later we finally arrive to approach a metal gate, manned by large brown stallions.

"Maverick?" Calls one confused, "Is that you?"

"Not quite," barks Fergus, his voice carrying across to them, "you can tell Maverick his twin is back."

"Fergus?" A female horse approaches.

"Gwyneth!"

"Is that really you?" she squeals.

Fergus runs the rest of the distance over to the female horse, jumping up at her front in greeting, "Good to see you Gwyn."

"But Fergus, your hearing?"

"Can thank this one for that," he looks my way signalling for us to join him, "this here is Pepi, she's a healer," he beams.

I manage to refrain from correcting him, not wanting to embarrass him in front of friends, looks like I shall be known as Pepi for the rest of our travels.

"You mean a doctor?" she eyes me warily.

"I mean a healer. She did this with nothing but a few herbs, I can hear for the first time since I was a pup."

"But she can't be?"

"What is it, Gwyn?" Another of the horses join us.

"This human, she's a healer," she replies.

"Impossible, they went into hiding years ago."

"Not this one," Fergus nudges me forward sensing my discomfort.

"Um, h – hello," I stammer feebly.

"What is your purpose here?" Asks the largest of the horses.

"I've come to help," I reply in earnest, "we were told you have wounded."

The horses turn to each other talking incoherently, I can't understand their mutterings.

"Fergus seems to trust you, so you may enter," he eyes me warily, "any funny business, and you're out. Do you understand?"

That wasn't the reception I was expecting. Why is everyone so wary around people of magick? The gates open before I have time to dwell, and my mouth drops open. There must be over a thousand dogs, horses, and cats here, and to the right, just as many, if not more humans. Somewhere amongst the hundreds of curious eyes in front of me, is Euan.

The H.L.F

The human compound is not what I expected. Everyone has their own groups and if you don't belong to one, you're an easy target. Gang rivalry is rife, everyone desperate to be seen as the toughest. Years of captivity has made this way of life normal to them, from what I've heard it was the only way to survive life in slaughterhouses. I'm almost grateful for being brought up at an A.I station, the scars on some of these boys put my scars to shame. Many are covered in them - some have limbs deformed or missing, you can't turn around without glimpsing something unsightly.

We've kept to ourselves, keeping our heads down to avoid the dramas that continuously erupt between groups. The lad that busted my nose left us a few hours after arriving, going straight to the males with brands like his. It seems that those with scars in common band together to form their own groups. The Branded, Castrated and Docked are the most volatile amongst those we've seen. The less violent of the groups are the Labourers and Pets, they all take some form of mockery from those that've suffered most, whilst those without a group are left to fend for themselves. The leaders don't seem to care, they're rarely seen, flitting in and out of camp, leaving everyone to their own devices. No training. No structure. A mass of disjointed, angry boys, cooped up in an abandoned slaughterhouse. Not a great environment to be in. I'd rather be back at Compound Four, at least they had a plan.

There seems to be no purpose to Compound One, other than it being a human base, everything about it feels morbid. The farming devices haven't been removed; hooks, electric prods, restraints, even the stun boxes and captive bolt pistols are displayed for all to see, it's carnage waiting to happen – I assume they're intended for us to use in battle. The more I witness what's to come, the less I want to be a part of it. I want to help others gain their freedom, but not at the expense of becoming as sadistic as our oppressors. I have no intention of putting any being in a cage or torturing them, whether that be human, dog, cow, or chicken. I want no part of that. I just want my freedom, although I daren't voice this out loud.

A bell rings out to signal dinner. As per normal we hold back, allowing the masses to fight it out, I'm in no hurry to get a black eye over a mouthful of kibble. The groups battle amongst themselves for who will get there first, buckets of feed falling to the floor in waste amid the commotion. I turn and walk away unable to watch, Dave and John follow behind me.

"Someone needs to get this under control, they'll kill each other before the war even starts. We're meant to be on the same side," grumbles Dave, irritable from lack of food. John nods his head in agreement, their previous squabble from Compound Four long forgotten, the three of us have become friends in the days we've been here. Alone, we'd have been targets for others to display their dominance over, together, we've remained safe. My height, Dave's frame and John's age have made us an interest to some, but not enough to risk a fight over.

The quarrel for food increases into a full-blown fistfight, the Branded and Castrated seizing any opportunity to let their anger out. They don't hold back, fighting brutally. Some watch, whilst others take the opportunity to seize their feed, leaving the commotion behind them. John stands to follow suit, Dave and I behind, unnoticed as the main gang's bait each other, their fights becoming out of control. Four lay fatally injured on the concrete, their blood splattered around them. A few fights continue, I notice out of the corner of my eye, the lad I fought from Compound Four is amongst the fights remaining. I can't help but stand and watch, I hold no sympathy for his plight, but concern for him makes my stomach turn. He reminds me of a boy from back at the A.I station, Jack his name was. Always angry.

The nameless lad from Compound Four gives all he's got but begins to falter, his opponent having the upper hand, his height and weight outmatching Compound Four's noticeably. A thorough hit to the face sends him flying, but he doesn't give up, slowly coming to his feet in refusal to back down. His nose is bloody, his eye all but sealed shut, claret pours freely from a wound to his cheek, and he holds his ribs, stumbling forward. The castrated opponent leers gleefully, enjoying his opportunity to inflict pain on someone.

I see the object glistening in his hand before Compound Four does, and against every warning signal rapidly firing into my brain, telling me not to – I rush forward, intercepting the boy's arm and launching him over my torso to land flat on his back. Compound Four offers me no thanks, shoving me forcefully before storming away. I watch after him dumbfounded, unaware of the crowd encircling me until the silence becomes almost deafening. The remaining fights have ceased, all gang members eyeing me with intent.

"You got a death wish or something lad?" Another member from the Castrated approaches his peer on the floor, the impact from his fall deeming him unconscious.

"He had a weapon," I explain.

"And?"

"And that boy is nearly half his size and could barely stand straight. He'd have killed him."

"Once again," the teen jeers, "and?"

I stare blankly at him in response. His eyes are almost black, no empathy can be found within. He would gladly watch the world burn. Looking around, many share his frame of mind, I need to remove myself from this situation and quick.

"I thought his life was worth saving, we're on the same side when the war comes," I shrug non-committedly, removing myself from the circle.

All eyes are on me, but none go to stop me, then slowly to my relief, the crowd disperses to have their fill of feed, only a few continue to eye me with suspicion.

"Bloody hell! I thought you were a goner for sure," David comes to my side, John in tow.

"Thought so myself for a moment."

"We'll need to be careful now mate, we'll sleep in shifts tonight. I don't trust these blokes for a moment. If I'd have known this was what it'd be like I wouldn't have tried so hard to be chosen."

"Tell me about it."

"One Forty wasn't impressed, was he? Ungrateful git, he'd be dead if you hadn't stepped in."

I stay quiet, the look he gave me when he shoved me, I think that had been his intention. To die. I don't voice it out loud, I could be wrong. He may just hate me for stepping in. Felt like there was more to it than that though. "We won't be making any friends here that's for sure." I sigh.

"Oh, I don't know, look around - the stragglers can't keep their eyes off you," observes John.

Raising my head, he's right. The youngest of the group, normally the targets of any unwarranted outbursts, are all looking my way. They remind me of the children back home, they'd always look to me when the slaughter collections came, like I could help them in some way from being taken. If only that'd been the case. I watched in tears along with their mothers and the rest of the kids as the boys were dragged, kicking, screaming, fighting with all their might to stay. I never understood why I wasn't taken with them. I was helpless then. Perhaps not now though. Sitting down, I motion for them to join us, I'm no saviour, but there's safety in numbers, I know that much.

One by one they gratefully join us, around fifty teenagers in total. Our group once the smallest is now large enough not to be tried with. The other groups look over with contempt. I don't know if I've just helped these lads or signed their death warrant.

"What's the plan?" Asks one.

He's around my age, sandy blonde hair, medium build, minimal markings. It's instantly apparent why the gangs would've targeted him, he looks almost normal in comparison to the horror story wounds that stand out on them. Looking around, every male that's joined has that in their favour. Or their hindrance in this compound. They are all young, bear minimum scars and lack the years of hatred for the world that the other gang members possess.

"There's no plan," I reply, "I didn't save that boy to be a hero, it was just the right thing to do. I've no interest in gang wars or being the man in charge, if it's protection you're looking for, I can't help you."

"They'll target you now that you've stood up to them, you have to make the first move or you're dead," he frets. Not in malice, but in worry. Whether for his safety or my own I'm unsure. He's right though. In saving One Forty I've singled myself out as a target. I put my head in my hands in frustration. There's always something. Always a drama. It's never straightforward. Overcome one hurdle just to have another thrown at you.

"That's their choice to make, I've no interest in it. We're meant to be on the same side." I get up to clear my head. Feeling eyes on me as I pace in a circle, I pay them no bother, they can look all they like, I'm not wasting my time on petty gang wars. The real enemy is out there, not in here.

"That was quite a spectacle," a voice close by surprises me.

"Not now lad, I need a minute," I sigh aggravated, not bothering to turn around.

A gruff chortle answers, causing me to turn around in surprise. Next to me isn't a boy, but one of the leaders. His face covered by a black scarf, only his eyes showing. He reminds me of something I saw in a film once back on the island with Peri. What was it called? A ninja. The thought makes me laugh despite myself. The man looks at me peculiarly as hysteria takes over. I continue to laugh, unable to stop, snorts wrack my body as a mix of deliria and genuinely not giving a damn takes over. He watches in silence. Neither confused nor seemingly bothered, more with interest than anything. As my breath returns to normal, the cackles slow and eventually my body stills. My eyes stream with tears, some of mirth, some of sadness, most of frustration. I needed that.

"Funny old world we're mixed up in, isn't it?" he muses. It's not a question so I stay silent, unsure of what to reply.

"Speak freely, you aren't in trouble."

"I should hope not!" I snap before I can stop myself. His eyebrow raises in response.

"Someone had to save him, nobody else was going to step in."

"Do you think we should step in?"

"Of course, even the dogs would on other compounds."

"Perhaps, but, we young man, are not dogs."

You don't say, I think to myself, but refrain from saying it out loud.

"You think we should act more like the canines?"

"It wouldn't hurt. It's chaos here. The boys need a routine, some sense of structure, a purpose. Without that – there's no hope to hold on to."

"Many here are beyond hope."

"Is that why you don't step in?"

"One of the reasons."

"Then what's the point of this? Why recruit us to come here, just to let us fight between ourselves? When the war comes, what good will any of this do?"

"We were waiting."

"For what?"

"For you."

Huh? What does that mean - how could he be waiting for me? That makes zero sense.

"Apologies. That was misleading, I'll rephrase; we were waiting for somebody *like* you."

Dumbfounded, I remain silent.

"We need humans that want to end this way of life. People that want to see a new world, a world of peace, where humans and animals can live in freedom alongside each other. A human that can encourage others that this is the way forward."

"But you're the leaders, you already believe this, what do you need me for?"

"I've lived a different life to you. If I bare my face to the recruits, they will not listen to me - nor my comrades. They can't take orders from someone that has not lived the way they have. We want peace. And we're going to make it happen. But we need humans that can work alongside animals without trying to kill them the first chance they get. The majority are either too damaged to ever comprehend the idea of peace between species, or too scared to make it happen. We need humans that are brave, but not reckless, and most importantly, they need to be someone that others are drawn to. I think we can both agree, that's you."

I don't know what to say. He wants what I want. I won't deny that. I don't want to go to war, killing all in my path. I want to help as many people as I can and then go back to my mum and the kids at the A.I Station. I hadn't thought past that.

"What would you want me to do?"

"We need people like you, to go out into the field and negotiate a compromise with the other species. Animals are in the field on our side doing this as we speak, but they can only get so far with assurances that not all humans are intent on revenge. They need to see it for themselves with their own eyes. We need humans that genuinely want peace to convince the animals that together, if they join us, we can make that happen."

"Do you have many recruits already?"

"You would be the first human negotiator. It's mainly dogs, horses, cats and birds that are in the field currently."

"I'd be the first human?"

"If you were to agree then you would be, yes."

"What if I say no?"

"That is your decision to make, I'm not here to force you to do anything you don't want to."

I'm not sure if I believe him, but he seems honest enough. There's just one thing that doesn't sit right with me.

"Let's just say I agree, how do I know I can trust you? You've let the boys here tear each other to pieces, how do I know the same won't happen to me out there?"

"We've allowed the compound to run like this for a reason. All of this was to find someone that would make a stand and step in, but not get power hungry and take command afterwards. You're the only person to have done that since we formed Compound One."

"How many years have you been waiting?"

"Six."

"Six years?!" I ask incredulously.

"It was necessary, you can't teach someone to be trustworthy. You either are, or you aren't. Animals can sense if someone is being dishonest. We need the recruits that we send out to be one hundred per cent genuine, or it's all for nothing. The animals have done the leg work whilst we waited. It would be your job to seal the deal, so to speak, if you agree to take the role."

It makes sense. Speak to the other species, convince them there's a better way of life than the one we're living, get them to join forces, then, when the numbers are up, offer an ultimatum. If enough agree, it could even bypass the war completely. A large part of me wants to do it.

"If I say no, what will happen?"

"Nothing, we'll wait long as it takes to find the right person. We're running out of time though."

"How do you mean?"

"The farm animals have plans to up production, we're unsure how, but the repercussions could be catastrophic. The land used to hold human livestock keeps getting bigger, natural resources are suffering from it. This whole thing is bigger than just freeing humanity, we're talking about life on this planet as we know it changing forever – unless we step in and make a stand."

No pressure there then, I think to myself. Six years they've waited for someone to come along that wants a better way of life, but not to hurt the other species in the process. I can't be the only one that wants this. But what if I say no, and they wait another six years for someone to come along? I can't allow that to happen. We could all be dead by then. He thinks I can make a change and maybe he's right. I need to at least try.

"Okay."

"Okay?"

"I'll do it."

"You'll be our negotiator?"

"I'll try my best," I shrug.

"Truly?" he asks seriously, making direct eye contact.

"Scouts honour," I mock salute, smiling ruefully at the memory of Joseph doing something similar all those years past. The motion doesn't go unnoticed, the scarved male eyes me intrigued, then shakes it off.

"We have an accord then."

He puts his hand out to shake mine. Following suit, I offer my hand in return, he grips firmly, placing his remaining hand atop of mine, looking at my band momentarily before releasing his hold. He reminds me of someone, but I can't place my finger on who.

"Thank you, young man."

"Don't thank me just yet, this could be a really bad idea."

"I have a good feeling about you."

"What makes you say that?"

"Just a feeling…" he tapers off his gaze wandering, "so, what do we call you?"

"Euan."

"Good to meet you Euan. I'm Lucky, welcome to the Human Liberation Front. Now's as good a time as any to introduce you to the others if you're ready?"

"Can I bring the guys that came with me?"

"How many?"

"Two, no - three," I correct, I'm going to ask One Forty to come, he's been alone since the fight, no longer with the other Branded. If my trying to save him ends up getting him shunned, he'll be good as dead when we leave.

"Three's do-able. Do you trust them?"

"Two yes, one, we'll see," I answer truthfully.

"He can stay behind - we can't take the risk."

"I've made him a target by helping him, he won't survive the night on his own."

"And this bothers you?"

"Of course it bothers me - I was trying to save him, not get him killed!"

He mulls that over a moment then nods, "So be it, he's got one chance though, if he's a liability, we'll send him back to Compound Four."

That seems fair, he'll hate me even more than he does already, but he'd be safe there. Lucky begins to walk away.

"Let's get a move on, it's time to make changes around the base now that we've found you, all this can stop at last."

"Are the dogs joining us?"

"Not yet, there'd be carnage, we need to give these lads structure before they can integrate with the other species. Training will start from tomorrow."

They need it, I think to myself. Half the compound can't stop fighting and the other half don't have a clue how to. They need to even it out if we're to stand a chance. Perhaps, if their plan works, it won't have to come to that though, if we can get enough species on our side, we could avoid going to war at all. The thought gives me a feeling I've not felt since my days with Peridot. Maybe there's hope after all.

INTRUSION

I want to scream. To physically open my lungs and scream my heart out. Euan's not here. Once again, I missed him by moments. Had we arrived the day prior, we'd have been in time. I curse myself for not leaving sooner, the only thought keeping me sane is that by leaving when we did, the mothers and children from the A.I station will remain content and well. Some good news I can relay to Euan, if I ever manage to find him on this earth-forsaken island.

The land has not been kind to members of The Resistance. Many dogs have severe wounds from their escapades freeing humans, the horses are malnourished, struggling to eat their keep on the barren wasteland surrounding us. They've resorted to eating kibble, much to their detriment. The canines don't seem to be affected, many having fed on this diet from an early age, the humans feed on it quite happily, chow being a luxury to them.

Although they show signs of brutality far worse than all the animals combined. Alike the children from the A.I Stations, many are severely malnourished and skinny, others bear mounds of excess weight from overfeeding. Some show signs of torture, having had their limbs docked to prevent fighting in the slaughterhouses. It appears many of the boys tried to fight back or quarrelled amongst themselves. It didn't bode well for them. Most are my age or younger, too young to have been through such pain.

I've healed as many as I can, being limited to how far I can help with the pretence of using only herbal lore. Their wounds are no longer infected, broken bones are on the mend, but questions will be asked if I attempt to regrow hands, arms, and other missing body parts. The castrated won't let me tend to them, ashamed of being made a eunuch. Part of me is grateful, not having seen that part of a male before. The other part of me still wants to help, the pity must be evident on my face as they shy away from me. Even after healing the injured, many of the camp remain wary, fear in their eyes. Mutterings of witchcraft can be heard frequently around the compound, suspicious glances watching my every move.

There are birds at this compound, crows and pigeons mainly. None that need healing, and they remain indifferent to my presence. Cats roam freely, keeping mainly to themselves. Only the dogs seem grateful for my being there. Having seen the effect of my abilities on Fergus, there was a queue as long as a field all waiting to be seen the following day after our arrival. My hands are raw from working, after three days of healing non-stop, my energy ebbs and the reality of our situation once again takes its toll. I wonder if I'll ever be reunited with Euan. The thought brings tears to my eyes which I blink away rapidly, I can't show any signs of weakness if I'm to stand a chance as their equal.

On my third day at Compound Four, I'm finding my energy nearly depleted. I wake to a pounding headache and my hands throb painfully. I need to recharge if I'm to help anyone else on the base, but with minimum sunlight and no signs of natural water close by, I have no idea how. It's times like this when speaking to Mum would be handy, it's frustrating being able to contact her, yet being too afraid of the comeuppance to try.

"You need to rest Peri," Freyja stirs next to me, feeling as equally drained as I, our bond has made us close in ways that neither of us was prepared for.

"My head hurts dreadfully," she gripes in discomfort.

"I'm sorry," I reply guiltily, I wish I could heal her, but it's pointless. Every time I do, she feels as I do moments later. It appears she will feel as I feel, until we learn how to control our bond. We've asked Phoenix in hushed whispers when we've had the chance, but someone is always close by, making it almost impossible to talk freely.

Fergus pops his head into the barn to start our day, we'd been sleeping separately from the others in the compound for our safety. Merrick, their leader has welcomed us openly, but fears what would happen if left overnight in a room full of those that fear me. Fear makes for irrationality he warned.

"Morning Pepi," Fergus greets.

I really must tell him my real name at some point, but we've become friends since I healed him and don't want to risk offending him.

"Morning," I yawn, wiping the sleep from my eyes.

"You look like you could do with more rest," he observes, not unkindly.

"I feel like I could too," I agree, stiffly rising from the floor to stretch my aching limbs, "are there any streams or rivers nearby?"

I'm hoping there is, ten minutes submerged in water would rejuvenate me more than a full night's rest ever could. I guess we're called Elementals for a reason.

"Not that I know of, there are pails out front though?"

"I was hoping to freshen up a little," I reply deflated.

"I see, I believe there are what you humans call showers in one of the cabins, I'll find out if they're still functional."

"Would you? That would be amazing," the idea of warm water sounds too good to be true.

"Leave it with me, I'll be back shortly."

Watching him leave, I lay back down to cuddle into Freyja who's fallen back to sleep with exhaustion. I hate seeing her like this. My body aches a little less and I can't quash my concern that she's taking the brunt of it for me, she whimpers in her sleep making my guilt grow. Where is Phoenix when I need him? Since being in the compound Merrick and the troops have taken a liking to him, involving him in the preparations of what's to come.

Apparently, the leader before Merrick was a red nose like Phoenix and they've warmed to him instantly. It will work in our favour in the long run I'm sure, but for now, I just want him back by my side. Just as I'm about to close my eyes, his large golden head appears through the doorway.

"Phoenix!"

"Have you missed me?" He smiles toothily.

"You know I have," I whisper, leaning my head into his to breathe him in. I don't know how, but he still smells of home. I can picture being back on the island, Ann cooking in the kitchen, Joe trudging in from the fields, Mum coming to join us at the table for tea. It hits me just how much I miss home. Choking back a stifled sob, I try to hold back my tears unsuccessfully as they begin to fall. My body shudders as I cry silently into Phoenix's fur. Everything has gone so horribly wrong.

Leave the island, find out the truth, bring Euan back home to safety. That was the plan, yet somehow, the plan has gone completely awry and I'm just as far away from finding Euan as I was when I left, only now, I'm equally as far away from home. What do I do next? I can't stay here healing everyone unless I have access to water to heal myself, and I can't just walk off to Compound One to get Euan without getting myself in even more danger.

"Tell me you have a plan," I sob quietly.

"I do, but you won't like it."

I know he means reaching out to Mum and part of me is tempted. But I can't. Not until I've found Euan.

"You know I can't. She won't let me carry on, it's taken me this long to get this far and I'm still so far from finding him. She'd never let me continue. I won't leave without him Phoenix, I won't."

He sighs looking away.

"Are you mad at me?"

"I'm not mad at you, I am mad at our situation. I too had hoped to have Euan back safe by now. I don't know how much longer we can carry on without getting too entangled in The Resistance. They're already asking me to lead one of the lesser compounds up north. I've said I'm searching for my mate and won't make plans until I've found them. That was before I found out Euan had been taken to an all-human compound – we have no reason to go there. We're going to have to leave unnoticed."

"Wait – he's at an all-human compound?" I look up startled.

"Yes. I didn't know there was such a thing. Apparently, The Resistance was started by a human. A free human would you believe it. Never been in captivity himself. Didn't know how to help the others so reached out to the dogs and The Resistance was formed."

"That's unbelievable."

"Yes, I think so too. Something doesn't feel quite right about it."

"Do you think he's of magick?"

"Perhaps. Although if that were the case, I don't understand his motive."

"Perhaps he wants what we want."

"Well, let's hope so, given he started all this. If it's all for nothing, everyone here is doomed."

Freyja whimpers then interrupting my next question. I stroke her head to comfort her, but she squints in pain at my touch, "Phoenix how do I help her?"

"What's wrong with her?" he asks with concern.

"She's taking my pain, I woke exhausted from healing so many, my head pounded, my hands nearly numb, I feel almost fine now though, yet she can barely keep her eyes open. I know she's taking the pain for me - how do I make it stop?"

"Can you not heal her?"

"I've tried, but I hurt after healing and then she takes the pain for me again. It's been a cycle like this since we arrived. It's the only reason I've managed to keep healing, I'm normally all out of power after a few sessions, let alone the hundreds or more humans and dogs I've seen so far. She's taking it all Phoenix - I don't know what to do."

He pads over to put his ear to her chest, sniffing around her face then sitting grimly, "she's a stubborn one your familiar."

"How'd you mean?"

"She's doing it purposely to keep you strong, but in doing so it's making her doubly weak. She won't last much longer if she keeps it up. You're of magick, your body can handle the exhaustion, as painful as it may be – hers cannot. Not this soon after coming into your bond anyway."

"What do I do?"

"You need to replenish the both of you, use the elements."

"There's no water source round here, I can't," I gripe.

"Peri it's not just water you can use, use the earth. I wouldn't use air or fire just yet given your emotions, they tend to run rife with you."

"How?"

"Was this not covered in your lessons?"

"We hadn't covered familiars in-depth, only briefly."

"I mean how to replenish your power, if you use too much?"

"Oh. No, I guess Mum didn't ever intend on letting me use my powers this way."

"Vallaeartha! How could she be so careless?!" his eyes flash bright amber fiercely, "I'm sorry, I had no idea, when I saw you replenish in the brook back at the A.I station, I assumed you knew how to recharge yourself."

"That was instinct, but I thought it was only water that made me feel that way," I explain, "I'm drawn to water, the other elements don't make me feel the way water does."

"That explains a lot," he nods, "well, from what I've seen your mother do, you can replenish using any element, but it's important not to take too much. If you take too much from the elements, it has an adverse effect."

"How do you mean?"

"Vallaeartha once took too much from the ocean, it backfired on her in the form of a tidal wave that she couldn't control. Take what you need and leave the rest to be. Work with the elements, or they'll work against you."

"Mum got hit by a tidal wave?" I almost giggle at the picture forming in my mind.

"As did a village full of innocent animals, humans and children, yes," he replies grimly.

"What happened?" I gasp.

"A story for another day young one, someone's coming. When you get a chance, go barefoot onto the earth, take what you need, and ensure to leave the rest."

He moves towards the door speaking loudly, "good idea Pepi, I'll see what they say," he winks as Fergus re-enters, they greet each other in passing.

"He seems chirpy?" He nods in Phoenix's direction.

"We had an idea to run by your brother."

"Oh? Do tell."

"When I'm finished here, I was thinking I should move onto the other compounds and see if anyone needs healing there too. Before we go back to Rider and the others I mean."

"I doubt Rider would like that very much," he shakes his head.

"It's not up to Rider though, is it?"

"You're too important to risk at Compound's One, Two and Three. They fear you here as it is, people of magick on a volatile compound won't be welcomed Pepi, even if you do mean well."

"M - magick?" I stutter avoiding eye contact.

"Yes Pepi, magick, I was deaf – not daft. That thing in my ear was my own doing from years of scratching, I was born partially deaf though. Your ointment may have cured the pain, but my hearing you brought back by other means. For which I am eternally grateful I might add."

"Does your brother know?" I ask worriedly.

"I've told no one, it's not my secret to tell. Over time, they will suspect though, some will see you as a threat, others an ally."

"What would your brother see me as?"

"Why is that important to you?"

I stall for a moment, debating whether to tell him the truth or not. I decide to go with my heart and trust him.

"Because I need to get to Compound One. My friend was taken there. It's the only reason we came, he was moved here after the liberation, but we've arrived too late, he's been moved again."

He looks momentarily shocked, so I continue hurriedly before I lose my nerve, "I'm not from this way of life Fergus - up until a month ago, I didn't even know animals could talk. I'm born of magick, but I have no idea how to use my powers properly and I'm scared. I want to help everyone, but I have no idea how to, and every time I try it backfires. The one thing I want more than anything is to see my friend again, but every time I get close to finding him – he's gone. I'm failing at everything." Tears threaten to fall as I confess my inner turmoil.

Fergus remains silent while he chews it over, "Well, Pepi," he placates finally, "that's a lot to take in."

"And my name is not Pepi," I add, "It's Peri."

"Is that all?" he asks dryly.

"Yes. I think so," I look away sheepishly.

Fergus paces back and forth lost in thought, I'm not sure if he's mad or not. He stops abruptly, "Does Freyja know?"

"Yes, she's bound to me, it wasn't planned it just kind of happened, and now she knows everything I know."

"And the Pitbull?"

"Phoenix is my family from back home, he came with me to keep me safe."

"Fine job he's doing," he says sarcastically.

"It's not his fault, it's not gone exactly to plan."

"You can say that again," Phoenix walks back in, surprising us both. He looks dishevelled, the hair on his spine stands on end, and his aura normally calm appears full of angst and uncertainty. Fergus notices it too.

"Settle down, I mean the girl no harm. I can't say the same for the others mind. Many will fear her. It would be wise to keep this a secret."

"I agree," Phoenix looks at me pointedly.

"I trust him Phoenix."

"Regardless Peridot - you can't tell everyone you trust on a whim what we're doing here. Someone will betray you eventually; they'll want to keep you for their own gain."

"It's not on a whim! I –"

"We'll talk about this later," he interrupts, his eyes briefly flashing purple. Before I have a chance to dwell, Freyja thrashes in her sleep, whimpering once again.

"What's the matter with Freyja?" Fergus goes to her, worry creasing his brow.

"It's because of our bond, she's taking my pain," I explain guiltily, my anger at Phoenix subdued.

"Why are you in pain?"

"Healing drains my energy, I need the elements to recharge. Once I'm better, she will be well again."

"Is that what the water was for?"

"Yes, I heal quickest in water."

"You're in luck then - the showers are intact, that's what I came over to say."

"Really? Can I use them?" Just the thought of feeling refreshed warms me from inside. I haven't been able to wash properly since we arrived, I'm covered in dirt and blood encrusts under my fingernails from healing so many.

"We could go now if you like?"

"I'll take her," Phoenix steps forward.

"One of us has to stay with Freyja, I don't want her waking up alone."

"Will you stay with her Fergus? It's not that I don't trust you – "

Fergus scoffs interrupting him mid-sentence.

"It's not – but Peri's in a weakened state right now, I'd feel better knowing I'm there to keep an eye on her."

Something about the way he's talking irritates me, he's acting out of character, but Fergus doesn't take offence, he sits beside Freyja agreeing to keep watch while we're gone.

"Showers are located past the barns, in the smaller dwellings towards the main gate."

"Peridot let's go," Phoenix heads out of the room, not giving a backwards glance. Giving Fergus a fleeting thanks, I head out after him.

"You're mad at me, aren't you?"

He remains silent, deftly parting the way between wandering humans, dogs, and horses, I struggle to keep up.

"Phoenix, will you at least speak to me?" I cry.

"Now isn't the time Peridot."

His clipped tone confuses me. This isn't like him. We continue in silence as I continue to fight back another flood of tears threatening to emerge. The sky begins to cloud over, a dull grey matching my mood. Phoenix glances up and quickens his pace, I jog to keep up with him.

"Phoenix, slow down," I breathe heavily.

"We're here," he nods towards a small building, separate from the main barns. Square in shape, made all of brick, it looks cold and uninviting. He nudges the door open with his head and I follow inside. To the left appear to be office rooms, a table and chair amid a selection of aged cabinets, tattered papers overflow the shelves. A light flicker's ahead, illuminating an open doorway, inside rows of shower stalls with lockers lining the adjacent wall. A lever to the left turns the showers on, I push down but it doesn't budge.

"I can't turn it," I gripe.

"Use your magick."

"I don't know how," I reply confused.

He knows I can't use my powers on impulse other than healing unless I'm emotional. Before I can question further, he jumps up to yank the lever with his teeth. The showers rattle and creak, then burst open amidst turrets of steaming water all at once. I can't help but rejoice, the sound of water music to my ears. Without a moment's hesitance, I shed my clothes and duck into the first stall. It's not as hot as the steam had me, but it's clean and it's refreshing. It does the trick.

I daren't peek downwards, the days of grime running down the drain, not a sight I wish to see. Closing my eyes, I try to imagine being somewhere other than here. It's a struggle at first, but eventually, my mind stops swirling and I'm able to relax, the sound of rushing water my only focus. I notice the welcoming tingle as my body begins to absorb the water, charging me from head to toe. I feel the best I have since I arrived, I'd almost forgotten what a warm shower felt like. Laughing, I open my mouth wide, taking a mouthful, then when he's not looking, squirt Phoenix with it playfully.

He jumps startled.

"Peridot Watkins!" he curses.

I gasp.

Phoenix doesn't full-name me. Only one person full names me. It can't be?

"Mum?" I utter, partly astonished, partly petrified.

Phoenix's head turns to face me, but it's Mum's eyes that look back, glowing purple ominously.

"Hello Peridot." Mum's voice rings out clearly from Phoenix's jaws. My mouth drops open in shock. How long has she had control of him? It feels alien, her voice coming from his body.

"H – how long have you been here?"

"Not long enough!" She clips furiously.

Her anger seeping through Phoenix's body makes his fur stand on end, his top lip curls back, teeth bared, claws tensed, looking murderous.

"But how? You promised you'd never control him? Mum, he'll never forgive you for this!"

"There are more important things at stake Peridot! It's taken me this long to get a hold and it's lucky I did - you were about to tell the leader of this compound what you are! Are you crazy? They will enslave you Peridot, you must come home now!"

"I can't come back, not until I've saved Euan, you must understand that?"

"This boy is not worth ruining your life over Peri, you must see the bigger picture! The longer you stay here, the more they find out about you, the more that will come for you. You must come back to the island now!"

"He's not just a boy, he's my best friend! He joined our coven, he is bound to us, how can you not care?"

"He is just a boy Peri! Do you think he would risk his life for you in return?"

"Yes, he would."

"For earth's sake Peri stop being so naïve - he is human! He will throw you to the wolves the first chance he got if it were to spare him his previous fate."

"You knew he was at the A.I station, didn't you? All those years, you knew the danger he was in, and you just left him to rot! How could you?"

"He is not my responsibility – you are! You will come home now Peridot or by the Goddess, I will come over there and bring you back myself!"

I cannot believe her. I've not seen her in months. I've been through so much, helped so many and she doesn't even ask how I am? She doesn't care about saving Euan, healing the wounded, freeing the humans, she just wants me where she can keep control over me. It's not right – for someone that is adamant the world will want to control me; she is the only one so far that's tried to do so.

"I'm not coming home Mother. I've seen too much to pretend this isn't happening. What they're doing to humans is wrong, I'm going to find Euan and I'm going to help The Resistance. We have magick - we can help."

"This is exactly what I feared would happen," she says more to herself than me. Phoenix's face looks torn for a moment, a strangled gasp reverberates through him.

"Peri – run!" his voice warns me too late.

Mum's magick seeps out of his eyes, swarming me in a purple mist. I attempt to block her to no avail, her power is too strong, I feel her will subduing my own, I'm bound tight as the mist coils around me, holding me tight.

"I didn't want to do this Peridot," she whispers, "but you've given me no choice."

Squirming uncontrollably, I scream in protest, but it falls on deaf ears, she continues regardless, even as I struggle to subdue her. I feel her in my mind, flicking through my memories like a picture book, discarding the ones she no longer deems worthy of keeping. My tears stream freely, I beg her to stop as she peels away my memories, one after the other; the dirty boy looking in through my window, watching movies weeks later in fits of laughter, holding hands on the summer solstice, one by one she flicks each lingering memory of the boy I want to see so badly away.

Next, the journey here, Phoenix talking, finding my power, I try desperately to will it forth to protect myself, but nothing stirs, her hold has my magick rendered dormant, I can muster not even a spark. She continues discarding my memories like pieces of litter to be thrown away, she doesn't hold back.

She reaches the A.I station, Louise is plucked from my mind, although I'm no longer sure who she is. Her name means something, her face reminds me of someone, yet I'm not sure who. Where was I? What am I doing sleeping on the concrete floor? I'm nearly naked? This is bizarre, what is that place and what am I doing there? There are partially bare women surrounding me, children huddled in corners looking afraid. Uncertainty fills me until a gentle face approaches, grey-blue in colouring, she distracts me from the women and children. Her eyes draw me in and somehow, I see into her soul.

Her life flashes before my eyes as my tears return, streaming in torrents. I feel magick that is not my own inside my head, trying to take her story from me. But I want to see. I know this creature. I know this story. It's my story. Why is it being shrouded from me?

Looking up I see the grey-blue dog in the flesh, she's here in the present, in this room with me, looking lost and afraid. Her face switches from fear to sadness, to anger, to defiance. Without hesitation, she launches herself across the room in a single bound, headfirst into a golden dog with purple eyes. He staggers back from the impact, his eyes turning gold momentarily, then resume their eerie purple to launch the female dog with fury across the room. She lands with a thud atop the concrete and moves no more.

Something within me stirs. She shouldn't have done that. My heart aches to go to the grey-blue dog lying limply upon the floor but looking down, I find purple vines coiled tightly around me. I turn my head curiously, following the trail. A lesser Elemental's magick courses from the golden dog's stare, attempting to encage me.

I laugh.

My gaze falls to the magick dweller before me, I barely contain my amusement at her attempt to keep me contained. Nothing can contain me.

I am the earth, air, fire, water, and spirit.

I am all and everything in between.

I feel her hold falter as a slither of fear radiates across the room. Her purple eyes lock with mine. I recognise this power, we've duelled before. I remove her purple swirls from my body with an effortless flick of my wrist, stepping toward the female stupid enough to ensnare me. A grin spreads across my face in anticipation.

"Hello Mother."

Freyja

My eyes open sluggishly to a droplet of water landing on my face. Glancing up, I find Fergus fast asleep on the bed beside me, belly in the air, head lolled to the side, a very wet nose about to drip down once more. I'm grateful it wasn't drool. That was a great sleep, I feel normal again, but where's Peridot? She was by my side when I drifted off. Her exhaustion from overworking herself is painful to endure, I hate seeing her worn down. I need to find her and check she's okay. Using our connection, I close my eyes to get a feel of where she is. That's odd, I can't sense her anywhere, I can always sense her when I try to. She has a turquoise beacon of green-blue light that leads me to her, but today, it's nowhere to be found.

"Fergus," I nudge him with my paw.

"Not now Beatrice, the pups can wait," he snores mid-sentence then rolls onto his front.

"Fergus," I repeat louder, using both my front paws this time, I try to roll him awake, but he doesn't budge. He's a mass of wet-nosed, snoring muscle. I'll have to find Peri myself. Leaving Fergus to slumber I head outside. The chilly air knocks any leftover tiredness right out of me, sniffing the air I feel fantastic, all my senses feel alert, I could run a mile in a minute if I tried. My energy level feels the best it has in months. I need to find Peri quickly, she must've healed me while I slept, she'll be exhausted again, for dog's sake, where is she?

"Hey –" I approach a fellow Staff, different in colour to me, her fur is the colour of sand, and she stands taller in size, "have you seen the female human?"

"The healer you mean?"

"Yes, have you seen her this morning?"

"Not since yesterday, she can't be far, shall I help you find her?"

I'm torn whether to say yes or not, two will find her quicker than one, but I don't want to cause a fuss. My worry must be evident as she eyes me intently, "I mean her no harm, she healed my hind leg, I'll help you. She's called Pepi isn't she?"

Amidst my worry, a chuckle nearly slips out, "Peri, actually. She's too polite to correct anyone."

"Ah, that'd be Fergus's doing I assume?" she gives me a knowing smile.

"How'd you guess?"

"I know the brothers well, I'm Merrick's second in command. Don't worry we'll find your human, I'll send out a pack to help search – discretely," she adds, sensing my worry.

I thank her as she heads in the direction of the dog's sleeping chambers, trying once again to find any remnants of the turquoise light that normally leads me to Peri, but it's no use. This is ridiculous, I'm her familiar, I need to learn how to use our connection properly. I could do with finding Phoenix - he could show me what to do. Using my secret sight again, I try this time to find him instead. Phoenix has his own trail of colour, only his is purple in colour, and less vibrant than Peridots.

Using my secret sight, I close my eyes once more. Paths of purple are visible instantly, they blind me with brightness, purple light radiates everywhere. Not in a trail like I normally see, but in a cloud, like an explosion encircling us all. The purple is deepest in the centre, with golden crackles fizzing and popping like lightning strikes. Something feels off.

Opening my eyes, I head in the direction of the purple explosion. The closer I get, the more anxious I feel, my heart beginning to race as my stomach twists with worry. I leap forward, running as fast as my paws will carry me. I'll never forgive myself if she's harmed. It would be like history repeating itself all over again. I blink away sadness as memories of my human come to mind, the man who saved me in more ways than one, dying in front of my eyes, whilst I was helpless to stop it. That won't be happening again.

I thunder forward towards the building surrounded by purple, finding Peri my only concern. Golden crackles strike repeatedly as the purple deepens, my heart continues to pound, but no one shares my panic, the others oblivious to the rainbow of destruction I hurtle towards. I glance back momentarily as the ground shakes violently, I push forward faster as my worries are confirmed, finally glancing a flash of Peri's light from within the doors ahead of me.

Around the compound horses whinny anxiously, the birds flutter to the air out of the way of the buildings, the remaining mammals rushing outside to make sense of the rumbling too late, as the buildings begin to shake and quiver. Slate tiles begin crashing loudly to the floor as the barns closest to the outhouse begin to crumble. Shouts and yelps cry out, as a mad dash of animals rush desperately to the exits, I want to help, but there's no time, Peri's inside the building that's causing this. I can feel her now, faintly, but she's there. It's all the persuasion I need.

I burst through the door to find the small building live with electricity, energy courses from room to room, bouncing off walls and back to the source in an almost violent motion – the air becomes void of oxygen, my breathing intensifies painfully, fur standing on end as I creep towards the furthest room where the source seems to be. Withstanding such potent energy is a struggle, but I pursue, dread fills me from ear to paw, my gut instinct telling me that Peri's in the middle of this energy storm somehow. I was expecting to find her surrounded by rabid humans out for blood, not whatever this is.

Peering around the corner my eyes bulge in shock. Phoenix has Peri entrapped in vines of purple power, holding her tight. She weeps uncontrollably, begging him to stop. But it's not Phoenix that replies – an eerie female voice comes from his jaws. It clicks then, he's being controlled by the purple inside him. I see now that the golden snaps are Phoenix fighting back, trying to get free from the purple's hold. Who could be doing this? Another magick dweller? It couldn't be Peri's mum. No mother would put her child through such pain. She cries out wildly then, solidifying my theory that another magick dweller somehow has control of our friend. I'm transfixed by the battle of lights, the golden bolts appear to be getting stronger when suddenly it's Phoenix's voice that cries out.

"Peri – run!"

I stagger backwards as Peri's memories come flying across my peripheral, just like the moment we first bonded, only instead of my own memories flashing before me, it's Peri's.

At first, they contain the boy – the one she's trying to rescue. From the moment they first met, to the moment she lost him, each memory fills my vision, then, just as quick, the visions are gone. I gasp in shock - it's erasing her memories! My mind flows as her journey here invades my mind, each vision dissipating into dust – until the day she met me. I sense the vision coming, and the magick's intent to destroy it. I lost my human - I will not lose my Elemental too.

I don't think.

I act.

I launch myself at Phoenix headfirst into his torso. He stumbles from the impact, shaking his head as his eye's fall golden once more. He looks at me with eyes his own, then – just as quickly – they're purple, his control faltering. I don't have time to act as the magick within him hurtles me across the room. I'm yelping in agony, hurtling sideways into the furthest wall as unimaginable pain wracks my body. I thud upon the tiled floor with a sickening crunch.

Then, everything goes black.

PHOENIX

Peridot's Elemental has taken over. I can see everything taking place in front of my eyes, but with no power to control it. I'm furious with Val right now, she swore she would never control me. She swore she'd never control Peri. Now the entire compound is in danger, Peridot's not in control, her Elemental is. Clothed once more, she saunters towards me, flicking aside Vallaeartha's vines of magick with ease, an otherworldly smile on her face, eager to release magick of her own.

"Val, give me back control!" I plead desperately.

"She's not herself, she could kill everyone here," she snaps, trying unsuccessfully to re-cage her daughter.

"She sees you as a threat – not me, I can get through to her, you have to let go."

"I won't – she doesn't know what she's capable of!"

"And whose fault is that? This is your doing! Your stubbornness to prevent her bonding with her Elemental has made everything you fear most come to pass. If you'd just held back and let her make her own decisions, we wouldn't even be here! For the love of earth Vallaeartha, let me GO!"

She falters for a moment, but that's all I need, shaking my head vigorously I push her out, my words cut her, I feel her heartache even so many miles apart, but it hurts me none, my anger at her actions outweighs any guilt at hurting her feelings. I use that anger to shut her out and regain control of my body. Surging power of my own, possessed through our bond, I seal my mind shut, she can control me no longer. It was a mistake to think I could ask her advice, even for a moment. Guilt arises from within when my eyes fall on Freyja, her body limp, almost lifeless on the floor. She needs healing urgently. If I don't save her, Peri will never forgive her mum or me for this. I dread to think of the comeuppance.

The Elemental within Peri is less than a meter away, gaining eye contact I step down, bowing my head in submission to show I am no threat.

"Who are you?" Her voice echoes curiously throughout the room. The question rattles me. She does not know me.

"A friend," I answer honestly.

"And the magick dweller?"

"One who means well - but makes terrible decisions."

"You tell the truth," she states.

"Always."

She cocks her head to the side, eyeing me curiously.

"May I ask a question?"

She nods.

"Who are you?"

She laughs. A tinkling, mystical sound, eerie to behold.

"I will tell you one day, friend. But that day is many moons away."

The breath I was holding subconsciously leaves my body as a relieved sigh. She looks up amused.

"I had no intention of harming you. The purple one, however, is treading on very thin ice."

Her eyes glow fiercely as she reveals this.

"To kill her, would kill me," I reply.

"I'll bear that in mind," she looks away in discomfort. Peri is still in there somewhere. I need to bring her back to the surface without enraging the Elemental before me. I was expecting her to be angry, but she's unearthly calm given what just transpired.

"Your familiar is hurt," I turn my head towards Freyja.

"We have a familiar?" she walks towards the fallen dog on the floor with concern. Upon closer inspection Freyja's chest rises and falls in short, rattled bursts, blood pours from her nose. Not a good sign. She needs help now.

"Can you heal in this form?"

"It's been a lifetime since I had a body of my own, and I was always better with our other gifts," she admits, tracing her hand sadly across Freyja's body.

"Please give Peri control again, she's an excellent healer, if you don't Freyja will die."

"Freyja," she whispers, a hint of remembrance coming to the surface, Peri can hear me.

"Peri, she'll die if you don't come back," I urge.

The Elementals eyes look back at me, not Peri's vivid blue, but a bloodstone swirl of red and green, the only way to tell the difference other than her mannerisms.

"Fear not golden one, I would never let our familiar die. I will give the young Elemental back control. You must make me a promise though."

"Anything."

She pauses.

"You didn't hesitate?"

"I trust Peri, so in turn I trust you. You are one, or you will be when Peri learns how to control the bond."

"Then I need not make you promise," she smiles, dusting herself off to stand, "tell her the truth of her power sooner rather than later, she will need me in times to come."

"You really won't tell me your name?" I prompt, curiosity getting the better of me.

She smiles her eerie otherworldly smile.

"Until we meet again friend."

She closes her eyes.

"Until then," I sit, giving her my paw in farewell.

She opens her eyes once more.

"A parting gift," she kisses my head, I feel a burst of power flow through me.

I look at her in confusion, what did she just do?

"Blessed be," she whispers, her swirling red-green eyes fading to Peri's blue once more.

Unveiling

I feel my body become my own again as the entity within relinquishes her hold. My vision returns, sending my eyes into a swirl of disorientation. Phoenix looks at me, concern etched across his golden features.

"Peri? Peri – can you hear me?"

Staying silent I nod, my throat feeling alien as the otherworldly voice leaves my body.

"What was that?" I ask shakily.

"That, was your Elemental."

"I don't understand – I thought I was the Elemental?"

"I'll explain everything I promise, but you have to heal Freyja first, she's hurt."

My gaze falls to find Freyja on the floor beside us, she isn't moving, blood drips from her nose, her jaw ajar, short, pained breaths shudder from her body. My heart jumps into my chest as panic threatens to take over.

"Freyja! What happened? I didn't do this, did I?" I cry, putting my face into her torso sobbing wildly.

"No, Peri. I –" Phoenix falters, "I did."

"What do you mean you did this?"

"Do you not remember anything?"

"I can grasp flashes, but I don't understand - it's like someone had hold of my body," I sob.

A thundering of paws and hooves echo down the hallway behind us, preventing me from explaining further.

Merrick and his lieutenants explode into the room, Fergus behind him along with three brown stallions close behind. "What in dogs name happened?!" Merrick barks.

"The water main burst," replies Phoenix, "damn near killed us."

"I – what? A burst pipe did this?" he asks incredulously.

It's then that I take in my surroundings, the room is a mass of destruction. The floor I lay on is an upheaval of cracked and shattered tiles, the walls show gaping holes, the ceiling threatening to cave in above us.

"It's common when they've been out of use for so long," Phoenix replies as if that explains everything.

Merrick's jaw hangs ajar for a moment., "well crikey, I'm glad I didn't use them!" he concedes, eyes still taking in the destruction, "we best get out of here pronto, the surrounding buildings have collapsed, the pipe must've burst further down too. It's a miracle this one's still standing."

"What happened to Freyja?" Fergus comes to my side, noticing her below me, worry prominent across his features.

"She got hurt trying to get to me," I sniff, "I need to heal her before we move, I don't know the extent of the damage."

"You may be a skilled healer, there's no doubt about that," Merrick joins us, looking over her injuries, "but broken bones won't mend with an ointment. She needs rest and plenty of it, there's not much else you can do I'm afraid."

"You don't understand, we can't move her - I need to heal her here," I cry, worry making my voice warble.

He turns away to whisper to his brother, "Poor girl. In shock she is. Take her outside and I'll get some of the humans to lift her friend out."

"No!" I exclaim, jumping to my feet.

All eyes turn to me in shock, Phoenix goes to step in, but I'm done with the charades. Hiding my true self is exactly what got us in this mess in the first place. The lies stop now.

"Merrick, I can heal her here. I am not an ordinary healer. I'm of magick." I confess, feeling the weight of a thousand woes lifting from my chest.

The horses gasp and a selection of dogs bare their teeth in my direction, one steps forward snapping her teeth towards me. Phoenix pushes me behind him, the fur on his spine standing on end, teeth bared also, a low growl reverberating in warning. The snapping dog goes for the attack, throwing herself in my direction, before Phoenix can intercept, I throw up a wall of water shielding us from her wrath.

"Stop it!" I shriek, "I don't want to fight – I want to help!" Frustration seeps from my pores, I feel the power within me wanting to bubble out, yet strangely, for once, that helps me gain control.

I don't know what took over my body earlier, but I'm not giving them back the reins again. Every time I lose control of my emotions, something else takes over and terrible things happen, well not anymore. I don't know who or what I am, or what I'm supposed to become, but in this moment I'm just a girl wanting to help my friend, I am the one in control. Nothing and nobody will get in the way of that – I don't care how many sharp teeth they have.

Keeping the wall of water held high with one hand, I kneel next to Freyja and place my other palm atop her chest. Taking strength from the water torrenting from my hands, I use its energy to heal her wounds. I feel her pain as if it were my own. It's agonising. Her ribs are cracked, one splintered directly into her lungs, causing her struggled breathing. She doesn't have long - her life force hangs by a thread.

Urgently, I will my energy towards her, wrapping it around each broken bone and moving it back into place, each becomes whole again with a sickening click. She feels nothing as I take the pain for her, my eyes stream in agony as each shattered bone repairs itself, the final bone slithers out of her lung causing me to cry out in anguish as her organs begin to regenerate, excruciatingly regrowing tissue until finally, her lungs are whole once again. I gasp in erratic, shaky breaths, the pain no longer present, but the after effect leaving me rattled.

Looking down, Freyja's breathing returns to normal, the blood no longer dripping from her nose and slowly, her eyes blink open.

"Peridot," she croaks softly.

"Freyja!" I cry with joy, throwing myself at my grey-blue friend, "I'm so glad you're okay," I sob, "don't ever try to save me like that again, I'd never live with myself if I lost you." Tears continue to flow from my eyes, only now tears of relief rather than pain.

"I'll always save you Peri," she whispers.

Closing my eyes, I don't berate her, taking the moment to breathe her in. I'm so glad she's okay.

An awkward cough brings my eyes back to alert as I remember the room full of animals. My wall of aqua protection no longer shields us, and before my eyes are a group of thoroughly stunned looking dogs and horses.

Merrick steps forward just as Fergus comes to be by my side, he growls in warning, Phoenix following suit. I can't help but smile as Freyja matches them, even though she faces the other direction with no idea what they're growling at. She turns to face the crowd, her growl growing louder to match Fergus and Phoenix's fearlessly.

"Stand down brother, I mean her no harm."

Fergus cocks his head to one side then steps back, allowing Merrick to face me, "it's not often that I say this, but I'm lost for words," he states.

Out of habit, I look down. Now that Freyja's healed, my inner fire seems to have left me, anxiousness returns. What have I done? I just showed my power to a room full of animals I don't know - it's exactly what I was warned not to do. If they deem me a threat, we're done for.

"You truly care for the Staff, don't you?" he presses, seeming to sense my worry.

"She's family," I reply honestly.

"And other animals?"

Sighing I glance up, I've shown them my true self, I may as well tell him the rest now too. It can't put me in any more danger than I'm in already.

"I'm not from this land," I begin, looking around for the growls to commence, oddly, none follow so I continue, "up until a month ago, I had no idea this way of life existed. A boy broke out of captivity and came to my home, he tried to tell me what was going on out here, but I didn't believe him," I pause as tears threaten to re-emerge and force myself to continue, "I came here to find him. My plan was always to find him, and bring him back home, but now I've been here and seen what's happening, I can't go back. I want to help. And to find my friend. Nothing more, nothing less."

Merrick sits back onto his hind legs and looks me over, "Brother," he turns to Fergus, "what are your thoughts on this?"

"I trust her," he answers without hesitation, "she healed me on our journey here, I didn't ask her to, she just did it. That solidifies her intent as far as I'm concerned. You just saw what she did for the Staff, she took on her pain like it was her own. We need Earthlings like that in the war to come."

305

"She's not an Earthling though," inserts one of the other dogs, a female alike Freyja, "what are you?"

Phoenix catches my eye then, practically begging me not to bare the words threatening to leave my lips. Knowing that dogs can sense dishonesty, I answer carefully.

"If I'm honest, I don't know what I am," I confess, "I was brought up as a human, then told on my thirteenth birthday that I come from magick, yet I've not had control of my power except for healing."

"But that wall you conjured - you did that with ease?"

"I get lucky sometimes," I shrug, "I don't know how I do it though. Sometimes my magick works, other times it fails me."

The dogs look between themselves, unsure how to feel about my revelation. They can sense I'm being truthful, but my gifts make them uncomfortable.

"I don't mean anyone harm," I go on, "I just want to find my friend and I'll heal whoever I can on my journey. I have no plan other than that."

"And the Pitt, what is he to you?" Merrick eyes Phoenix warily.

"My brother," I answer honestly, "he came with me to keep me safe."

"You see a dog as your brother?" Whinnies one of the horses confused.

"He is family, as is Freyja. I have horses that are family too," I add, "back home anyway."

"And where is home to you?"

"That's one thing I can't tell you. I'm sorry, my mum would never forgive me. It's a long way from here though."

The room falls uncomfortably silent as everyone contemplates what to say next. I no longer feel endangered, but the air in the cabin begins to feel suffocating.

"Can we go outside?" I aim my question to Merrick.

"Not until we've decided what to do with you."

Freyja growls again causing him to exasperate.

"Not like that, damn you, I mean here, at the compound. I can't just send you out into a war zone when you have the abilities you possess."

"It would be unwise to try to control her," inputs Phoenix, stepping forward, "those that have tried, did not survive."

"Is that a threat?"

"It is a fact. She means you no harm. But Peri's fight or flight instinct is too strong, she can't control it. A group of foxes found that out the hard way. She nearly destroyed the New Forrest, and they only asked her to sit."

All eyes turn to me in wonder then, some in fear which I think was Phoenix's intent, but others out of appeal, I can sense their desire to use my powers to win in the war.

"If you think you can use me in this war, you'd be wrong. I won't fight. I'll heal until I can heal no more, but I'm no soldier. I just want to find my friend."

"And where is this friend?"

"He was one of the humans taken to Compound One. We were planning to leave after I'd finished healing everyone. I wanted to get cleaned up before I started today and then all this happened," I signal to the room collapsing around us.

Merrick shakes his head, the overload of information too much to grasp, "You swear you tell the truth?"

"Scouts honour," I salute as I would back home.

"Scouts honour?"

"It's a saying from back home."

I sigh, I don't think I'll be going home anytime soon. One of the stallion's eyes me intently with interest.

"Merrick, I have no intention of deserting The Resistance and now you've seen my true nature, I can heal more wounds without having to stick to herbal lore alone – please can we get out of here, I need some air?"

He sighs, "Fine, but I think it would be unwise to show your gifts to the humans. It was people that killed your kind, not the other species."

"That was a long time ago, I'm sick of hiding who I am."

"That's your decision to make."

I nod, wearily I get to my feet. Freyja stands on one side, Phoenix on the other to support me. Together we trail out, my boots crunching on the shattered tiles. The air within the corridor is thick with dust from the commotion, causing me to put my hand over my mouth. I walk forward quicker, desperate to feel fresh air on my face. Practically throwing myself out of the broken doorway I breathe in deep lungsful of oxygen, grateful for each individual gasp.

Closing my eyes, I try to imagine I'm elsewhere, but a deep voice startles me, "I had a friend many moons ago that made promises as you do."

Looking up, the voice comes from the brown stallion that made eye contact back inside. He stands tall, a giant of a horse, although looking malnourished and in need of a good feed alike the rest of his species.

"Another horse you mean?"

"No, no, my girl, we have no hands to salute. This was a human. Of sorts," he adds, eyes twinkling, "his name was Joseph."

My eyes widen in surprise, but I remain silent unsure what to say.

"We fought together," he goes on, "during The Changing. It saddens me to say he fell ill, and we parted ways. You remind me of him though, your mannerisms. Uncanny."

"Were you friends?"

"Very much so," he nods his huge mane, deep brown strands billow in the wind, "He saved my life on more than one occasion, bravest human I ever met."

He waits for me to respond, but I remain quiet. After waiting a minute longer, he looks disappointed and heads off to join the horses as the silence becomes awkward.

"It's for the best," Phoenix re-joins me.

"I feel like I should've told him, that we know Joe I mean. I think we could trust him."

"Perhaps..." he stands beside me watching him go.

Watching the horses move further away, I'm tempted to go after them when once again, I'm taken back by my surroundings. The entire building adjacent to the cabin has collapsed, along with two barns on either side beginning to crumble. Bricks and rubble are everywhere. Groups of kids, dogs and horses work together to dislodge the fallen debris, amid muffled pleas for help. My gut wrenches.

I did this.

Once again, my emotions got the better of me and others paid the price. Guilt threatens to consume me, but I quash it down, I made this mess I can clear it up.

Stepping forwards Freyja intercepts, "are you sure you want to do this? Once they see, there will be no going back."

"I have to, I created this mess."

"No, you didn't, your mother did."

I'm taken aback for a moment, saving Freyja from her death completely threw me as to how we got in this predicament in the first place.

"Freyja I'm so sorry," I gush.

"Nothing to apologise for, it wasn't your fault."

"She's right," interrupts Phoenix, "it's mine."

"No Phoenix, she had control of you, I know you'd never hurt Freyja."

"That may be true, but it's my fault she gained control in the first place. I couldn't see a way of getting Euan back from Compound One, not without putting you in danger anyway. I hoped by explaining to Vallaeartha she would help, but she didn't give me the chance to explain. The moment I let her in, she took over. I was helpless to stop her... I'm sorry."

He sits with his head down in shame. Part of me is angry, but not enough to stay mad. This is not Phoenix's fault. He would never try to control me. Or try to steal my memories and force me to return home. Let alone throw my familiar across the room nearly killing her and bringing out the worst side of me. A side of me I didn't even know existed. No, this is all my mother's doing.

"I forgive you Phoenix, you were just trying to help. I know that" my brow crinkles, "she can't take control again, can she?"

"No, the ritual she did all those years ago means she can't take over my mind unless I let her in. It was stupid of me to think she would have done any different. She'll do anything to get you away from all of this," he gestures to the destruction around us.

"But I caused this," I whisper, "this is my fault."

My mind flashes then to the unearthly voice that flowed through me as I overpowered Mother, of my powers fighting back, being controlled by something else deep inside me. I realise then that it wasn't just me that caused this. My mother started it – but whatever or whoever is inside me played a large part too. But she also saved me. And let go of her hold so that I could save Freyja. She can't be all bad. I hope. Or my life just got a whole lot more complicated. If that's even possible.

Another muffled plea for help assaults my ears, shaking my head free of unanswered questions and lingering doubts I head in that direction. I can speak to Phoenix about all of this later, right now, people and animals are hurt, and I need to help them. My power ebbs from the exertion needed to heal Freyja so I kick off my boots to recharge, my bare feet impacting the dirt. Instantly

I feel a hum of energy beneath the soles of my feet. I can't believe it hadn't occurred to me to do this before. Always on the lookout for water when the elements are all around me. I must be the stupidest Elemental around. A jolt to my insides snaps that thought out of my mind.

"Hey!" I jump.

The others look to me startled.

"Someone's making herself known," I explain bemused. This is going to take some getting used to. I always sensed a stronger power inside me, but I thought of it as mine, not someone else's. More secrets and withheld truths for me to uncover.

Scowling, I refocus my attention on the scene before me. Everyone within the compound is present, trying frantically to move the heaviest of timbers that have fallen. Between the horses and the strongest humans, they've nearly lifted most of the rubble, while the dogs and those remaining pull out the many trapped inside. Cats tunnel in and out trying to locate those trapped further down. Many are injured, there's a lot of healing to be done.

Closing my eyes, I focus on the earth between my toes, the different textures, the softness of the mud, the roughness of stones, the energy of thousands upon thousands of insects burrowing beneath. So much life in something that looks to be dead. I draw in the energy slowly, taking little so as not to tamper with what lies beneath. I feel the power coursing through my veins instantly, it's almost intoxicating, the good I could do if all this energy were mine. The temptation to take more is hard to resist as I continue to draw more forth, I feel power within me, revelling in the excess energy flowing through my body.

Freyja nudges my side forcefully, bringing me out of my stupor, I stagger back power drunk as she steadies me, her eyes boring deep into mine, they glow a vibrant blue, almost luminous in colour. It appears she takes strength from my power also. I thank her internally for bringing me back to the present as we head towards the fallen recruits.

I can't believe how many are injured, there must be a hundred if not more that didn't make it out of the building in time. Guilt bubbles inside my tummy making my hands clam together, I wring them nervously, debating how best to heal so many. One by one? In groups? Kneeling to a male perhaps twice my age, I place my hand upon his head, a wound bleeds freely. With my other hand on the earth, I heal him. The remaining wounded back away in fear, my presence apparently not a comfort even though they need my help. I ignore the stares, the gasps, the hushed comments and whispers.

"What the hell?"

"Her eyes – did you see?"

"A witch!"

Irritation irks somewhere inside me. I'm not sure if it's mine or the other entities. Whatever happened between Mum and me, my Elementals presence is now very much intertwined with mine. It's both a blessing and a curse. A good thing, as I'm able to stay in control, I would normally have blacked out by now, but a bad thing as her reaction to my surroundings is affecting my own. The mutterings continue to annoy me as the human I healed comes around only to cower away in fear. Looking around, I notice all eyes are upon me, anxiously anticipating what I plan to do next. The compound grows uncomfortable as panic threatens to ensue. This is ridiculous. I'm here to help them – not hurt them. How can they not see that?

Standing, I don't ask if they want my help, I simply release the glorious tingling sensation at my fingers tips and will it towards those that need it. Unlike with Freyja, I don't take their pain. There are too many to heal for me to withstand the agony, they will have to endure the pain as I did earlier that day. They will survive, that is the main thing.

Across the compound shouts and cries call out, warbled yelps and an onslaught of curse words fill the air, as broken bones pop back into place, wounds seal shut and ligaments regenerate. It takes longer than normal, there are so many, it takes every ounce of strength I can muster, but I heal them all. Exhaustion finds me once again as the last of the cries die down, collapsing to the ground a satisfied grin spreads across my face.

"Peri!" Freyja rushes to my side.

"I'm okay," I pant, I'd held my breath without meaning to, "did I get everyone?"

"We'll check," Merrick's voice replies, but I can't make him out, my vision a blur from exertion.

A pack of dogs join Freyja, Phoenix and Fergus by my side. I assume an angry mob is forming, yells and shouts of witchcraft taint the air.

"Recharge Peri - use the earth again," Phoenix's voice finds me. I do as he says hurriedly, sensing the urgency.

A pack of dogs form a circle of protection, but it's not enough, there are perhaps thirty dogs standing to protect me – hundreds of scared and confused beings lie beyond, shouting their rage and profanities at my mere existence. Frustration and fury bubble beneath the surface as I struggle to contain my annoyance at being treated this way. I saved them. And this is the thanks I get. Fighting is the last thing on my mind, I almost wish I didn't help them. Attempting to shake my head free of disorientation I wearily get to my feet. Even with the help of the earth, I'm exhausted. There's no way I can hold off this many if this turns violent.

"If any harm comes to the healer, by hand, hoof, paw or claw - they will have the wrath of The Resistance to deal with," Merrick's voice carries across the compound with fierce authority as he re-joins our group, Fergus beside him.

They are with ease the largest dogs out of all before us, not that much smaller than some of the younger horses. They bare their teeth in warning as the crowd before me begins to reconsider their violent intentions.

His voice barks loudly for all to hear, "The magick dweller was sent here by the order to heal those who needed it. Now she has done that, she is to move on to the next compound. If any harm befalls her before leaving, you'll have us to deal with."

His growl even makes me shudder as he bares his teeth fully for all to see. The crowd shifts with uncertainty, none individually strong enough to take on the two beasts protecting me. After what feels like a lifetime, the crowd finally settles, and they begin to disperse. I exhale in relief, there are so many of them, they'd have got the upper hand or claw eventually.

Watching them go, some look back in my direction gratefully, but the majority look to me in fear. A frustrated sigh leaves my lips. After all this, all I've done to help them, all those I've healed, they still see me as a threat, just because I'm different to them. Looks like Mum was right after all; people fear that which they do not understand. I hope with every fibre of my being that she's wrong about everything else.

Hidden Power

What a day, I think to myself, laying upon the ground of the dog's quarters. We're to sleep with Merrick and his lieutenants and leave first thing in the morning. He doesn't trust the recruits in the outer barns, even from our separate dwellings, the air of unsettled stirring is fraught. As exhausted as I feel, I'm going to struggle to sleep, the nervousness of an ambush has my tummy in knots.

"Hey, it'll be okay," Freyja comes to my side.

I'm grateful for her words, but I know they are for my comfort only. Six large dogs stand watch by the barn door and Fergus hasn't left my side since the crowd dispersed earlier that day. Grumblings around the camp of evil witchcraft and sorcery fill the night. Forbidden magick, omens of plagues and the end of the world can be heard in hushed whispers throughout the recruits. I'm reminded of my history lessons back home, it appears humans kept their fears and prejudice of magick-kind, even from all those hundreds of years ago. And not just the humans. Many of the dogs and birds feel the same. Oddly, none of the horses or cats. They chose to sleep directly outside the dogs dwelling for extra security - the only thing keeping me sane. Thirty dogs could not keep the thousand plus humans, canines and birds at bay that wish me harm. I'd hate to think what would happen if we didn't have their added protection right now.

I doubt I could summon even a spark of my power to help in a fight, the healing of so many having rendered my gifts impotent. My hidden entity is quiet also, having lain dormant since the commotion earlier today. Not so much as a tell-tale sign from within to suggest that some other power dwells within my grasps.

"Phoenix," I call out softly.

He ends a conversation with some of the other dogs and comes to join me, "How are you holding up?"

"I'm okay, too anxious to sleep though."

"We have a backup route planned, if any try to break in, we'll escape out the back. The others will say we left earlier in secret which should prevent any fighting."

That quells my worry a little, but not my annoyance.

"Why do they hate me so much?"

"They don't hate you Peri, they fear you. And fear, unfortunately, creates irrationality and acts of stupidity."

"But I healed them Phoenix, can't they see I mean them no harm?"

"You also brought down three buildings," he whispers so only we can hear, "their fear overshadows any gratitude."

Looking around to check we're not being eavesdropped upon, I whisper almost inaudible, "that wasn't just me though, was it? That was Mum and the entity inside me – who is she?"

"Not here, we can't risk being overheard."

"But I can't wait any longer, I need to know what's going on inside my own body or how can I ever be expected to control it? If we get ambushed, I can't control what happens if she takes over again."

He looks torn, then nods before heading back to the group he was with moments before. They discuss something in hushed tones then he returns hurriedly.

"We have five minutes, come quickly."

"Where are we going?"

"Toilet break, if we're not back in five, they'll send help," he answers, leading the way to the back of the barn.

In the furthest corner appears to be a hole in the wall, just large enough for us to crawl through. Phoenix goes first, then Freyja, then I, rising to my feet as I come out the other side.

"Quickly we don't have long, ask your questions."

"Why didn't you tell me my powers were from another Elemental?"

"I thought you knew, I was aware you struggled to control your powers, but I didn't realise it was because Vallaeartha had told you so little of your heritage."

"What else didn't she tell me?"

"Well, a lot from what I can gather," he exasperates.

"Phoenix I need to know."

"I know you do - I know. How do I explain this?" he tapers off, lost in thought.

"Hurry Phoenix, we don't have long," I look over my shoulder anxiously.

"Fine, okay. I'll just come out with it," he concedes, brows pinching together.

"Peri what makes Elementals different to other magick dwellers is that they inherit their ancestors' powers. It's what makes you so strong. You have another Elementals power residing within you, along with your own. With that power, also comes a part of that ancestor themselves. That's why your powers are so hard to control, sometimes the ancestor takes over and controls them instead."

I reel from shock. It's absurd.

"You're telling me I have one of my great grandmothers in my head, battling for control over my body?"

"Not quite, they only show their presence when you use their power. When you use your own power, they stay dormant. When you tap into their sources, that's when their presence joins yours."

"How am I meant to know which is which?"

"I thought Val would've helped work that out with you, I can't believe she didn't. You need to bond with your Elemental so that when you use her power, she works with you, not against you."

"That explains why I black out all the time!"

"Exactly," he leans in to support me whilst I continue to reel in shock, "from what I've seen, your healing ability is your own. You have no trouble controlling water or earth either, which suggests that your ancestor's powers were fire or air, they're the ones you struggle with."

I nod in agreement. It makes so much sense now. I'm not a terrible Elemental, I can use my powers fine, it's the powers that aren't my own I can't control.

"Are you okay?" asks Freyja, having been silent up until now.

"I think so," I answer truthfully, gathering my thoughts.

"You're sure?" prompts Phoenix, still looking worried.

"Honestly, it's made me feel better if anything," I explain, "I've felt like a failure not being able to control my powers but knowing it's someone else powers that I can't control, I don't feel so bad about it. I didn't know they were in me before, now I do - I just won't use them."

"It's not that simple Peri," Phoenix sympathises, bursting my bubble.

"Why not?"

"You're a Pisces, you're ruled by your emotions. When you feel emotional, you reach to all the elements, not just those you control, it's why your ancestor comes forward without you calling to her. I think it'd be better to reach out to her and try to work as one."

"Is that what Mum did with hers?"

"Vallaeartha's a Taurus, stubborn like the bull. She opted to block out her ancestor, but at a great cost, it's one of the reasons she's the way she is. She lost part of herself the day she blocked them out."

"Why did she do it then?" There's so much about Mum I don't know.

"That's for her to tell you, it's not my tale to tell."

I hear frantic scurrying behind us to find a huge head stuck in the hole we crawled out from.

"Great dogs Peri!" Fergus's voice finds its way to us, "come back inside, you nearly gave me a heart attack!"

He tries unsuccessfully to pull his head back in, his huge skull well and truly wedged tight, he curses absurdly causing dogs on the other side to howl with laughter.

"Hold still! We'll get you out," we amble to his aid.

After pushing hard to no avail, he remains stuck. The laughing from inside the barn becomes almost contagious as I struggle to hold my own mirth at bay.

"Glad you think this is funny, I thought you'd been taken," he curses once again, "if my brother sees this, I'll never hear the end of it."

"Sorry, we needed somewhere private to talk," I explain quietly kneeling to help him free.

I'm tempted to use magick, but with my new knowledge of the elements not being completely mine to control, it's not worth the risk. After thoroughly chipping away at the rubble, the gap is finally large enough for Fergus to heave his way back out again. We follow through after him to find the room full of dogs watching with barely suppressed laughter. None are brave enough to laugh to Fergus's face, not with his huge jaws and teeth at the front of it.

"Not a word of this to my brother!" he warns, skulking off to the other side of the room.

Chuckling we get seated amongst the other canines that offered to watch over me. It warms me to see that at least some of The Resistance trust me. A sand-coloured Staff comes to sit beside us, I've seen her around camp with Merrick often.

"What a day," she sighs, "do you know your way tomorrow?"

"Not a clue," admits Phoenix, grimly.

"You'll be needing a guide then?"

"Are you offering?" his ears prick up.

"Sadly, I'm needed here, or I would accompany you. I'd opt for one of the Pigeon's, less conspicuous than a horse or cat and too many dogs will be deemed suspicious if any scouts see you. Best way to get there is under the radar."

It's good advice, but I'm yet to speak with any of the birds - we didn't have birds back home. Too close to chickens' Mum would say. Seemed bizarre at the time but makes sense to me now. Her words stick with me, although I wish they didn't. I don't want any preconceptions from Mum to bias my decision making.

"Are there pigeons you trust?"

"Many," she nods, "I'll introduce you in the morning. You should rest it's a long trip ahead."

She pads outside, off to find birds I assume.

"What do you think?" I ask Phoenix and Freyja.

"She didn't hesitate to help me find you earlier. And she's Merrick's second in command, that speaks volumes. It's rare for females to hold a position of power."

That's something I'd noticed at the various bases we'd visited, "why is that?"

"The strongest rule within a pack, it's that way with most species. Other than humans."

"She must pack a bite to be second in command," inputs Phoenix, glancing in her direction.

"Her name is Nala," Freyja informs with a knowing smirk.

"Thanks," he grins, heading after the lieutenant with a bounce in his step. Freyja laughs to herself.

"What's funny?" I ask puzzled.

"I think our brother has a crush."

I look after him bemused, the thought hadn't even crossed my mind.

Freyja comes to lay beside me, turning one way first, then the other, and back around again before plonking herself down, half on my torso, half on the floor. I lean back as she rests her head across my chest. The familiarity of fiddling with her ears soothes me, as it used to with Phoenix back home. Home. How different my life is now to what it was back on the island, what I would give to be under the old oak tree, the scents of Mum or Ann's cooking wafting over to us on a light evening breeze.

My mind begins to wander, thinking of Joseph, Ann, Roland, Amy and all the others we left behind. Thoughts of Mum crop up once or twice, but I swat them away, not wanting any anger to seep into what is becoming a mix of comforting thoughts. Freyja breathes heavily upon me, her lips flapping with every exhale, the motion making me smile, my love for her swells inside, warming me further. I can't believe how close I came to losing her earlier today. Holding her tight, I cherish the moment we have together and moments later, I fall into a comfortable, much-needed sleep.

Hours later, as I doze contentedly in a deep slumber, a dream finds me. It's been years since I've dreamed as vividly as the images that flash across my mind this night. Even in the full moon, the dreams that once woke me as a child no longer invade my sleep, having lost those when Euan left all those many moons ago.

Tonight's dream is peculiar. I walk a path that is not my own. Looking down, the ground looks to be further away from my eye line than normal, my steps stronger, more assured, confidence radiating from me. Putting my hands to my face I realise with a gasp that they are not my own. These hands are nearly twice my size and lead into muscled forearms, they appear to be male which is equally peculiar. I walk assuredly towards a group whom I assume to be friends, a mix of both canine and human.

"Davey boy," I greet another male who grins at my approach. My voice feels familiar even though I've not heard it before.

"You sure you want to do this mate?" he asks anxiously.

"We're here now, I've got to at least try," I nod.

"No going back now anyway," inputs another male, older than the other, perhaps nearly Joe's age, although he's aged well in comparison.

"How do you mean?" the male I occupy asks.

"They wouldn't let you go back even if you wanted to. Something dodgy about that Lucky fella if you ask me."

The room falls silent as awkwardness fills the void left by that statement.

"It's not that I'm worried about mate," Dave pulls me aside changing the subject, "Chickens used to rule here, I'm willing to bet my next meal there's still some scurrying about. If chickens are in there, you shouldn't go in alone."

"I can't go in with a calvary behind me, it sends the wrong message," I sigh, having thought the same thing but not voiced out loud, "they need to see me as trustworthy, that's the whole point of this. If I waltz in with a pack of dogs at my bidding, they'll think I'm just like our predecessors and never sign the treaty."

Dave remains anxious, but says no more as the older male re-approaches, "Who is this Lucky fella anyway?" he continues where he left off, "he just waltzes in, sends us over here to do his bidding. Why isn't he here with us if he believes in this damn treaty so much? Must be why he's called Lucky if you ask me, gets everyone else to do the dirty work."

I sigh inwardly whilst Dave walks away not interested in hearing more, "We've been over this John, part of the mission was that I don't ask questions. I don't like it, but if enough species sign the treaty we can end the war before it starts. I don't want to go to war, do you?"

John huffs and says nothing, he clearly has more thoughts on the matter but knows it's pointless airing them.

"Well, what about you One Forty – what do you think about all this?" he changes tactics, asking a fourth male who sits alone in the opposite corner of the room.

I hadn't noticed him until now. He's covered head to toe in bruises, one eye completely black, a busted lip and a bright red one hundred and forty branded upon his chest, even with his deep brown skin, the brand is clear as day. Bright green eyes stare back at the older man as he glances back in response, choosing not to reply, turning away from his gaze. I'm transfixed momentarily by him, his presence radiates across the room, making the atmosphere even more uncomfortable.

"Would it kill that boy to speak, just one bloody word?" gripes John under his breath.

I shrug my shoulders not acknowledging the question, "Do you mind if I have a minute? I need to get my head around what I need to say tomorrow," I begin to pace, nervousness for the day ahead beginning to surface.

John nods, acquiescing defeat and heads to the doorway, the branded male already by the door. Dave claps me on the shoulder before grabbing me in a brotherly hug. I hug him back, wishing he could come with me.

"Look after One Forty while I'm gone," I request quietly, "don't let John keep on, he's close to losing it with him."

He nods with a knowing eye-roll, I think he's close to losing it with the older male himself. I watch him retreat as they leave the room before turning to the window behind me.

Seeing through his eyes I look across the terrain. We're in a town, at the top of the tallest building, overlooking deserted fields and what appears to be an army base of sorts. Further ahead a large bunker rises from the ground, a semi-circular dome, sprouting from the earth. My destination for tomorrow. My tummy knots with apprehension at what's ahead, but I'm determined not to quit before I've begun.

The early morning sun rises in the skyline, shining through the glassed windows I now stand before. As the blinding rays of sunshine are eventually met with clouds, I'm left staring at my reflection, mirrored before me. I'm tall, broad-shouldered, dark tousled hair covers my eyes, I move it aside to see clearly and deep, sea-blue eyes stare back at me. I wake with a start. I'd know those eyes anywhere.

It's Euan.

ALLIANCE

Shooting up from the floor I inadvertently start a panic, Fergus wakes abruptly, launching himself in my direction barking like mad, which in turn sends every other dog into a frenzy. After a minute of thorough barking and searching they conclude there's not an ambush lying in wait, turning to look at me in question.

"What in the blazes Peridot? I nearly bit half the packs head off!"

"S - sorry," I stutter, half in shock from the commotion, half from my dream. Only that wasn't a dream. That was a vision. Clear as day. I can feel it in my bones, Euan was about to do something terribly brave and judging by his friend's reactions, terribly stupid.

"Well?" Fergus exasperates still awaiting an explanation.

"I –" I stammer again, all eyes in the room upon me, "I had a nightmare," I reply meekly, only with-holding part of the truth, as opposed to lying.

"Humans," a dog tuts, "wouldn't stand a chance in this war without us."

Others follow suit, rolling their eyes in my direction before twisty turning in semi-circles, all one way, then the other, then back around again before settling to snooze a little longer. Seriously, what is that about?

"What happened?" Freyja's voice startles me, her mouth remaining closed. Her voice is inside my head. That's new – we've not done this before. This must be how it feels for her, my thoughts constantly invading her mind.

"I saw Euan," I say in my mind, for her to hear only.

She looks shocked, unsure what to reply.

"Where's Phoenix?" I ask out loud feeling Fergus's eyes watching us curiously, "I need to speak to him."

"He went off with Nala ten minutes past to gather the birds," he answers slowly, he can sense I'm hiding something.

"Can you take us to him - but stay with us," I add, "you need to hear this too."

"Let's head out now before the compound wakes for breakfast," he leads the way hurriedly towards the door, I follow behind, wiping the sleep from my eyes as we go.

The dogs from guard duty last night have swapped shifts with another six, equally large canines. It appears Compound Four has no shortage of ferocious-looking beasts. Although if what Euan spoke of in my vision is true, perhaps their ferocity won't be needed. My mind reels at the possibility of ending all this without any bloodshed. I understand his friend's trepidation, it sounds too good to be true.

"There he is," Fergus points his head to the left, towards a cluster of trees.

Phoenix and Nala appear to be surrounded by a mix of twenty or so pigeons, crows and blackbirds. I can make out their squawky voices as we approach, it's bizarre hearing a human voice coming from their beaks, like a cartoon I'd watch back home.

"Peri, what's wrong?" Phoenix notices my worry instantly. I look towards Nala, debating briefly whether to voice this in front of her before continuing.

"I – I had a vision. Of Euan."

"What happened? Where is he?"

"Not at Compound One. Someone called Lucky sent him on a mission and he's trying to convince the other species to sign a treaty."

"A treaty? What kind of treaty?"

"He didn't say, but from what he seems to think, it could end the war before it starts, if enough species agree to it. It would end all this."

Our group look to each other unsettled, but excited, the idea of being free from this way of life sounding too good to be true. A flutter of wings draws my attention downwards, I just voiced all of that in front of the birds!

"Worry not," Nala notices my panic, "these are my comrades. Flock, this is the girl I spoke of, the healer."

"It's a pleasure to meet you," tweets one of the crows, the pigeons and blackbirds bob their heads up and down in greeting.

"Please, you can't repeat what I just said to the compound, not yet anyway. So many of the humans want revenge, if they get wind of this, they could revolt."

"Not a word shall leave our beaks, we have no interest in war either. We want an end to this as much as you do."

I smile gratefully at the crow addressing me as she continues to introduce herself, "I'm Florence, this here is Sal and Doe my second and third in command," she gestures to two birds, Sal a blackbird, Doe a pigeon. They nod their heads in greeting.

"Will you help me find my friend?"

"Where was he?"

"A tall building, many storeys high, overlooking a military base. There was a circular dome jutting out of the ground."

"Hmm," Florence tilts her head from side to side, "I don't recognise the description. Flock – have any birds flown past a place like this?"

A babble of tweets fil the morning air until a pigeon comes forward. She's smaller than the others, nearly all-white in colouring, with red eyes.

"I have," she caws softly, "I can show you, but it's a long way by foot, nearly two days walk as the crow flies."

"We'll never make it in time," my hand flies to my mouth.

"What do you mean, what is his mission?"

"To persuade the pigs and sheep to sign the treaty. He's going to the dome, but his friend was adamant chickens would be there. Euan's in danger."

I must get to him in time. But how?

"The horses!" I exclaim, rushing back towards the dog's chambers. The thudding of paws tells me the others are right behind me. I need to find the horse from yesterday. I find him amongst the others, attempting to graze on feeble patches of grass, they must be starving, but they refuse to eat chow. He cranes his large neck in my direction as I approach but says nothing. I hope I didn't blow it with him yesterday.

"I know Joe!" I blurt out, not knowing what else to say.

"I gathered that," he replies, looking back down at the floor for any remnants of grass that remain.

"Y – your starving," I observe feebly.

"I gathered that also," he replies with a hint of irritation, still offended by my hesitance to confide in him yesterday. I knew I should've been honest with him.

"I'm sorry," I apologise, "Joe always told me to follow my heart. My heart told me to trust you yesterday and I didn't. He's still alive, back home where I came from. He helped bring me here to find my friend."

"Joseph would never abandon someone as young as yourself, to a place like this," he grunts, about to leave.

"I'm not lying - he thought I could look after myself."

"Preposterous," he scoffs, losing interest in my ramblings altogether and heading to leave.

"I can help you!" I call after him desperately.

"I don't doubt that," he eyes me, "I've seen your powers, perhaps you can, but what do you want in return?"

"For you to take me to my friend. He's two days walk away, but I need to get there by tomorrow. I'll never make it in time, I'd need to ride with you."

The other horses hear my request and neigh in outrage, one steps forward indignantly, "we are not pets female, not even to people of magick."

"I know, I live with horses back home, they're family, I'd never heard of pets until I came to this land."

"A likely story," she snorts, about to leave also.

I had no idea horses were such proud creatures. If only Roland and Amy were here, they could talk them around. About to give up, an idea comes to mind and with trepidation, I kneel to the floor. The horse I had planned to ask has wandered off with the female in tow, but the remaining horses watch me curiously. Here goes nothing I think to myself.

I call to the earth, preying she hears and does my bidding without anything going a miss. What I'm attempting to do is unlike anything I've done before. I can heal with ease and occasionally my other abilities kick in when I need them to, but I have no emotion to help me with this one. Only desire, which I pray to the Goddess is enough.

"Hear me".

I call out to Mother Earth in my minds-eye.

"Feel my presence. Understand my need.

Their need.

Your subjects are dying, starved from the land.

Help me heal them. Help me feed them.

Mother Earth, if you hear me, show your true nature."

At first, I'm met with silence. I remember Mum's advice many moons past and continue to keep my intent strong, never wavering in doubt. That's when the rumbling starts. Around me, horses neigh anxiously. The barns shudder as they did yesterday, the occupants rushing out to avoid a calamity like before. I hear shouts and cries of confusion until their eyes find me crouched on the floor. There is no hiding that this is my doing, but I refuse to budge. They need this, the land needs this - it will work.

A mix of warning snarls nearly breaks my concentration as my group encircle me in protection. Stones are launched my way, some making contact, but still, I hold tight, waiting for the Goddess to do her bidding. The ground shakes violently. Opening my eyes, I see cracks in the earth begin to form. It's working!

Just as my plea is answered, I bring down the rains. That part I have no trouble in accomplishing. My joy at the ritual having worked a glorious emotion to behold. Rising to my feet I open my mouth wide taking in the falling droplets.

"Healer, what have you done?" Merrick thunders towards us, pushing those that wish me harm out of his way.

"Look," I smile.

"At what – have you gone completely mad?!"

I say nothing and simply point at the ground, no amount of fear or potential harm can bring me down from this high. Perplexed, he looks down, as do the angry mob launching stones in my direction. The earth, once bare of life, now flourishes with greenery. Grass grows rapidly, daisies and dandelions rushing from the ground amongst a mix of earth-grown food and shrubbery. There's everything you could ask for. Apple trees, tomato plants, root vegetables and cruciferous greens sprouting, bizarrely as we're in the wrong continent, even a pomegranate tree blooms before me.

I close my eyes, speaking to Mother Earth once more. "Thank you."

I send as much love and gratefulness as I can muster.

"Thank you for hearing me."

"Peri, we need to get out of here," Phoenix's voice jolts me back to the present moment.

The mob ahead although stunned, are still being ruled by fear, their group rapidly growing as more join their number. They wish me harm regardless of what I do for them. I give up. I healed them, now I've helped feed them. I can do no more. The land is no longer barren, providing them with a smorgasbord of plenty. My work here is done, it's time to do what I planned to do from the beginning. I'm going to rescue Euan. My eyes relocate the horses as they trot back round to us.

"I can't stay here," I address the brown stallion as once before, "I need to find my friend. I can provide you with food no matter where we go. Please, will you take me?"

"Any friend of Joe's is a friend of mine," he nods, my display of magick having swayed any doubt from his mind.

"Scouts honour?" I attempt to joke.

"Indeed," he lowers his mane for me to rise upon him. Many of the horses whinny in protest and re-join the humans, but a few remain to fare the horse well. The female who doubted me earlier appears to be coming with us, standing beside her mate in support.

"Are you leaving now?" Merrick approaches.

"It's for the best. I'm not welcome here, and I really must help my friend. Thank you for everything Merrick."

"It's I that should be thanking you. Off you go now quick before this lot get out of hand. I don't know – humans!"

He rolls his eyes before bounding towards the angriest of the mob, some still with stones in their hands. They drop them hurriedly as Merrick gets closer, each blaming the other for throwing them. Fergus approaches next, I feel overwhelmed with sadness at the thought of parting ways with my newfound friend, it must show on my face as he laughs softly.

"Don't be daft, I'm not leaving your side. Wait a moment while I say farewell to my twin."

I smile gratefully, glad he's coming with us.

"It's going to be hard to stay under the radar with a group this large," asserts Nala, also coming to say her goodbyes.

I had thought the same thing, but at least there's safety in numbers. There's no way we'll make it in time without the horses, I'm a hindrance to our group with only two legs.

She shares a glance with Phoenix, and I look away to give them privacy, it appears she's taken a liking to him also. We begin to head towards the exit, the others can catch up.

"I don't even know your names," I voice to the horses.

"I'm Ralph," replies the stallion, "and my partner is Grace." Grace bows her head in my direction, having warmed to me since my display.

"Do you not want to graze a while before we leave?"

"Oh yes, we're heading to the good stuff," he comes to a halt by a sprouted mix of greenery and wildflowers. They both tuck in ravenously on the fresh grass a mix with dandelions, their teeth grinding appreciatively with every mouthful. Some of the other horses join them, all grazing happily. Many nod in my direction gratefully, causing me to smile. I'm glad to have helped them.

The bell rings across the compound indicating breakfast, the humans and dogs head back into the barns for chow. I realise then that none have so much as touched the earth-grown food that now grows a plenty before them. Some of the younger males eye the fruit with curiosity only to continue towards the barns, oblivious to the goodness around them.

"Wait!" I call out, instantly wishing I hadn't. Some glance toward me, fear remaining present in their eyes. This is so frustrating! Jumping down from Ralph, I head to the closest apple tree. Those in my path back away like I'm covered in dung, afraid to get too close.

"Look –" I demonstrate, plucking an apple from the tree and taking a bite, "it's fruit. Human food. You don't need to eat chow or kibble anymore. If you look after the plants, they'll provide you with food for a lifetime," I take another large bite for emphasis, "it's delicious, try it."

Pulling another apple from the tree, I hold it out to the boys closest to me. None come forward. Some snicker and others clearly think I'm crazy.

"You want us to eat trees?" one sneers.

"Not the actual tree obviously, what the tree provides – it's earth grown food," I explain irritably.

Many burst out laughing and head back towards the barns for their normal breakfast, whilst others look tempted to try. None step forward for fear of being mocked by their peers. I throw my arms up in frustration. This is ridiculous. Fergus re-joins us then, Merrick in tow.

"This is what I was telling you about, the colourful food," he shows Merrick who peers at the apple curiously, "Peri, do you have any of the orange-coloured ones?"

"Carrots you mean?"

"Yes, that's the one – carrots."

Looking around, I locate the root vegetables sprouting from the dirt, their green leaves just visible. I walk over and pull a bunch free, handing one to Fergus and another to Merrick. Fergus doesn't hesitate and crunches into his loudly, nearly swallowing it whole. Hesitantly, Merrick takes a nibble of his, then, liking the taste, wolfs the rest down in one bite.

"Dogs alive – that's tasty!" he declares.

I laugh at his response - his tail wags and his ears are pricked up. I've only seen Merrick as the leader, always sorting something out, never relaxed, this is the first time I've seen his tail wag.

"Wait until you try it cooked," I beam.

"Cooked?" He asks between chomps of his second carrot.

"Yes, you boil certain foods in water, or roast over a fire and it changes the texture and taste. Some foods are nice hot, others cold. Some you can do both. I wish I had longer, I could show you how. Well, the humans, but I doubt they'd listen. They all hate me."

He sighs, "they'll come around in time. I'll get them to try this food, many hate the chow as much as I do. I'm sure they'll have warmed towards you if you ever pass through again."

"I hope so."

Phoenix, Freyja and Nala re-join us then.

"Well, I guess this is goodbye for now," he chomps, a third carrot between his teeth. Sitting, he places a paw on my shoulder, "good luck – I hope we meet again healer."

I place my hand on his shoulder in return, "me too."

The birds fly overhead, ready to show us the way.

"See you soon brother," Fergus bumps heads with his twin, Phoenix and Nala do the same, their heads lingering for a moment longer. Ralph lowers his mane for me, once I'm seated steadily upon him, as a group we head out. Two horses, three canines, a flock of birds and an Elemental. What could go wrong?

ALAN

Filthy humans. They repulse me.

Passing my way through the barns of livestock, I can't help but show my disgust towards the dirty creatures. How they ruled the lands once is beyond me. They're strange to behold. All skin, no fur, no feathers, no claws. They resemble no other form on earth. History tells us that they evolved from the monkeys, but that's absurd. Humans are vermin, a plague scourging our planet. Well, no more. Not once I'm done anyway.

I hear the canines have rallied together a resistance.

A resistance? Preposterous!

Only a pet would want to help the humans. Traitors the lot of them! They've sealed their fate in siding with the two-legged freaks I walk upon now. Many cower away in fear. Good, they've learnt their lesson. The last human that laid eyes upon me has eyes no more – I made sure of that. Clawed them out myself while the cows held him down. A smile graces my beak sadistically. That was a good day.

"Sir!"

"What is it?"

"They made it to the town. We'll need to leave soon - we don't have long."

"They made it there unharmed?" I rasp with annoyance.

The other chicken wisely steps back, "Y – yes sir, we lost our best poachers in the New Forrest fire. We had other packs looking, but they're not in the same league as Vixen."

I curse with impatience. Losing Vixen and her skulk was a blow we could've done without. Fires don't just break out in that magnitude for no reason. We aren't in Australia or the Amazon. English weather does not cause fires. Humans do. I curse again. It's the last thing I wanted, but I'm going to have to see to this nuisance myself.

"Get the clan ready, we move at nightfall," I instruct.

If they think they can get the pigs and sheep on their side, they're sorely mistaken. That would be a blow we'd struggle to recover from. If ex-farm animals show compassion towards the humans, then the other species will eventually follow suit. Stupid herbivores. Too soft they are.

And they had it worse than most, second-worst I'd say, after my own kind. Then the cows. They weren't tortured as bad as we were, but humans should've known better than to take their calves. Never mess with a female. Especially females that weigh over a tonne and hold over half the world's population. Worked in our favour though. We'd never have broken free without them. We may have had the brains, but their brawn made it happen.

And now The Resistance wants to undo all we've worked for? All these years it's taken to get the other species to agree to eat only human. The years of intensive breeding, intensive feeding to get their meat to be sufficient for the carnivores. It's taken a lot longer than we expected, but we finally have a system that works.

Ironically, we learnt from the humans. Their left-over farming manuals gave in-depth descriptions on how to bulk up a small animal into one large enough to feed from. Their devices sure came in handy too. What can be done to one mammal – can be done to another.

The scars under my wings start to throb as they often do, but I pay it no bother. I'm getting my revenge every day as I ensure the same treatment is inflicted upon them. No animal, no matter how many teeth or claws they have, is ruining this for me. Oh no, I'll go to the dome, I'll tell them some home truths and they'll never sign this blasphemous treaty.

As for the larger carnivores that grow restless, itching to hunt as nature intended, I think it's time we added dog to the menu. Filthy pets – they're as bad as the humans. Teach them to rally against me. Yes, that's what we'll do.

Herbi's can't catch dogs, so the restless Carni's can hunt them. That'll quell their need for the chase. A plan forms in my minds-eye, causing me to squawk with glee, it's brilliant. I cluck out loud to myself, my eyes bulging with delight. They'll have no idea what hit them.

"Sir!" Another chicken invades my moment of joy.

"What is it now?!" I screech.

"Th - there's a m - magick dweller at Compound Four!"

My stomach drops.

"What. Did. You. Say...?"

"It's everywhere, the birds saw it first-hand, it's a female one too."

That's impossible. She's long gone, not been seen in years. She went into hiding when the laws were being made. She wanted no part in it, left before the slaughterhouses went into production. Why would she come out now?

Unless...

"What did she look like?"

"A girl they're saying. A teenager."

Oh, this is too good to be true! It's not her – it's her kid! What I would give to have one of her kind on my side. I've been scouring the land for years trying to find humans with magick. Unsuccessfully, I might add. Well, except for that one time… but that didn't go to plan. This time around, I won't make the mistakes I did with the last one. This one's young. Impressionable. The younger humans are quicker to break. They have less resilience than the adults. Much easier to train. The damage she could do. All would fall to my feet. My beady eyes gleam.

"Send the army. Bring her to me!"

"B – but Sir – how?"

"Any means necessary! Do not kill her, harm her if you must, their type can heal. Send the message to kill all who get in our way!"

"Yes Sir!" off he clucks, spreading the word to all on base.

I cluck again to myself with barely contained glee, tomorrow I destroy the treaty, and soon after, I'll have my very own magick-user at my disposal.

Oh yes.

Today is a good day.

Ambush

We've travelled for hours, thundering across the terrain like our life depended on it. Although that's not far from the truth, all our lives will be affected by the outcome of tomorrow if this treaty is what Euan believes it to be. My backside throbs painfully from riding so long, my hands aching from gripping Ralph's mane so tightly. Looking ahead, a river comes into view.

"Should we stop to rest?" I shout.

"Thought you'd never ask," pants Fergus, starting to lag. Looking back, Freyja and Phoenix are struggling also, they can't travel at the same pace as the horses. As the river approaches, we gratefully slow down to a halt, Ralph lowering to the ground so I can dismount safely. My legs wobble as they impact the dirt, Phoenix coming to steady me. I feel wearier than I should, having taken some of the burden from Freyja so she could keep up.

"You may have to go on without me," she collapses to the ground breathing heavily.

"I'm not leaving you behind, here, I'll heal you," I place my aching hand upon her chest and with the other draw up energy from the earth, letting it flow through her. Immediately her breathing becomes less laboured, and I feel her energy levels rise. Getting up from the ground wearily, I go to do the same for the others.

"Recharge yourself first Peri, we can wait a while," Phoenix nods towards the creak with concern furrowing his brow.

"I'll do you first, then I only have to recharge once, don't worry, I'm fine," I assure him, placing my hand upon his back. Ralph and Grace head over to graze on the shrubbery surrounding the water's edge, both seeming fine from our journey so far. After healing Phoenix and Fergus, I take off my boots and head over to join them. The water level is low, barely splashing over the rocks and pebbles.

As I paddle in, the water feels cool and refreshing on my aching feet, relieving the weariness without having had to use any magick. Closing my eyes, I try to imagine I'm at my favourite spot back home, but to no avail. My worry for Euan is all that runs through my mind. I need to know he's safe.

I've tried tapping into another vision to see where he is, but it's pointless - it appears the visions only find me in my sleep. I have no idea how to use this kind of ability, having had no training or realisation I could do it in the first place.

Sighing, I sit down in the water, forgetting that I'm clothed. The coolness soothes my aching behind, so I remain seated a while, until my clothes begin to feel uncomfortable, clinging to my lower half.

"Peri?" Freyja joins me, "are you feeling alright?"

She paddles in to sit beside me, resting her head on my shoulder. Absentmindedly I stroke her ears, taking comfort from her presence.

"I'm worried," I confess, "every time we've found Euan's location, he's moved onto somewhere else. I guess a part of me feels like I'm never going to find him."

"I understand, it's hard being away from the one's you love," she empathises.

I'm grateful for her acceptance of how I feel. The reality of our situation is that we really don't know what's going to happen. Attempting to plan ahead is not viable on this journey, we have no idea what other troubles face us, or who may be lying in wait when we arrive. We'll face those dilemmas when we get there. My gut instinct foretells that we need to get there quickly. Something about that building sends shivers of trepidation up my spine.

The birds circle back once again within eyesight, having flown forward numerous times on our journey to check for danger. They're flying in fast, presumably looking forward to freshwater too. I best hurry and recharge so they can have the space to themselves. The river may have looked big from a distance, but what little water remains is feeble at best. A trickling of water, rather than a flow. Just as I finish replenishing my energy, the small pigeon with red eyes plummets down landing at my feet, tweeting shrilly.

"They're coming – you must hide!"

Fergus and Phoenix stand immediately to alert.

"What, who's coming?"

"Descendants! Hundreds of them – too many to count! We must've been seen, they're less than five miles away!"

"What do we do?" I ask frantically.

"I'm so sorry Peri, but I have to go back to the compound," Fergus looks behind urgently, "I can't leave my brother, he'll need me."

"I understand," I throw my arms around his neck, "promise me you'll be careful!"

He rests his head for a moment against mine, then, just as quick, he's gone, running as fast as his hind legs will push him, back in the direction we came from.

"Where can we hide?" I look around frantically, the winds stir with my anxiety.

"This land is flat," answers Ralph, "we have nowhere to hide other than the riverbed on which we stand. Even with your powers, it'd take a miracle to not be seen, let alone survive."

My mouth goes desert dry. I can't ask them to risk their lives like that for me. Not when I can't guarantee my magick will keep us safe. I'm beginning to understand how to control my abilities, but not enough to take on an army. A field of cows was one thing, hundreds of murderous mammals' intent on destroying us is another reality entirely.

"We'll go back," I decide, rushing out of the water quickly.

"Peri, are you sure?" Freyja feels my need to find Euan.

"No, but we can't take the risk of being seen. What good am I to Euan if I die trying to find him?"

"You're doing the right thing," Phoenix nods sympathetically. The remaining birds circle above us, "Florence, hurry – you must warn them, they're not ready for an attack of this magnitude."

She salutes with her wing and flies on ahead, sending Doe, her third in command and her unit to remain with us.

"How long until they're upon us?" Whinnies Grace.

"They're travelling with speed, we don't have long," Doe answers hurriedly.

"Climb on, quick!" Grace lowers her mane towards me. I clamber on, panic starting to quell in my tummy.

"We can't run back as fast with the dogs on paws," asserts Ralph, "Peri can you bind them to me somehow?"

"I can try," I nod, "catch up with Fergus, the boys can ride with you, Freyja on Grace with me."

"So be it," he turns with speed, cantering in the direction of Fergus whose now barely a spot in the skyline.

"Fergus – wait up!" I yell.

"Thank dogs you decided to come back!" he turns as we catch up to him, "tore me in two leaving, you'll be safer back on the compound."

"We won't get there quick enough on foot, you'll need to ride with Ralph," I instruct.

He looks taken aback for a moment but doesn't argue, his worry at reaching his brother over-powering any unneeded pride at excepting help.

"Woah, wait! How do you expect us to stay on – we don't have hands?" he wobbles atop of Ralph almost comically.

"Leave that with me," I help Phoenix clamber on behind him, "if you can sit so your hind legs flank either side, keep your front paws on top to balance."

They look uneasy but do as I request, whilst I help Freyja climb on Grace. Looking ahead, the land is mostly barren, but from behind towards the river, a few trees are dotted sporadically here and there. I call to them, urgently in need of their help. They answer without hesitance, their roots burrowing at the speed of light, blasting through the ground at my feet. I thank them before breaking some free, using them to bind each of my friends as best I can to Ralph. It's not ideal, but it's the best I can do under the circumstances. They look uncomfortable, but it holds them tight. Re-mounting Grace, I sit behind Freyja for added support.

"Hold on tight!" instructs Ralph.

We do as we're told as they canter back towards Compound Four, praying to the Goddess we make it in time.

We arrive an hour and a half later, Ralph and Grace wheezing from having run so far, so fast. They toppled many a time, I barely kept them safe with my magick. The trek has left us bruised and lethargic from the frantic, bumpy ride, but there's no time to waste - the ambush is perhaps less than an hour behind. Bursting through the gates we find the compound to be in mid-stages of chaos. Merrick struggles to keep control of his unit.

"Brother!" his relief clear as day when his eyes land on Fergus. He does a double-take as he takes in the ridiculous sight of his giant of a brother woven tight onto Ralph's back by tree roots.

"I suppose that's your doing?"

"It was the best I could do," I grimace in explanation.

He roars with laughter, unable to contain his amusement.

"We should've stayed at the bloody riverbed," grumbles Fergus as I hurry to set him free from the bindings. My legs throb painfully, my hands once again almost clenched shut from holding on so tight. Ralph and Grace head off in the direction of the horses to plan for what is to come.

"What's the plan brother?" Fergus asks now comfortably back on all four paws.

"Don't get me started," he exasperates, "half the humans are trying to desert, our kind and the horses are as prepared as they can be, but the cats and birds are undecided."

"But this is meant to be The Resistance?"

"You're telling me," he rolls his eyes angrily.

I can't believe it. I just rushed back here to help them, yet they're not even prepared to help themselves. I gave up on what could be my last chance to reach Euan to help save these people, they need to try to save themselves too.

"Listen!" I scream, as loud as I can for all to hear.

The compound turns to look upon me.

The fear is still there, but not aimed at me in this moment in time. Knowing that an army is fast approaching seems to outweigh their fear of my abilities.

"You cannot desert now!" I yell.

"You're one to talk!" An older boy hollers back.

"I came back to help you!" I try to remain calm, "I just gave up the last chance I may ever have of finding my friend to help win this fight - how can you not have it in you to fight for yourselves?"

"We're not like you," another cries out, "we don't have powers to protect us. How are we expected to fight off claws and teeth with our hands?"

"Use the weapons," Merrick steps forward, "we've been training for precisely this moment. It may be sooner than we'd planned, but this is what you've all been waiting for. You wanted revenge on those that hurt you, this is your chance to have it."

The crowd shifts awkwardly, each itching to leave, but none brave enough to make their move first. I decide to try another tactic.

"I know you're afraid, I'm afraid too. I've seen your wounds, felt your pain when I healed you. If we don't make a stand here today, even if you manage to hide, they will find you and put you back in captivity. If you're ever to stand any chance of freedom, you're going to have to fight for it."

They mutter amongst themselves, knowing I'm right, but still being ruled by fear. Who am I to blame them? I've not lived their life - I don't know what they've been through.

"I'm no soldier, but I'm going to stand for what I believe is right, we can't force you to stand with us, but we'll stand a better chance of winning if you do."

Turning away, I head towards the gate still open from our return. I feel my ancestor's presence re-join me in frustration as a gust of wind slams it shut.

"Thanks," I think in my head.

"Should've slammed it harder," her voice replies.

"How are you here, I didn't call to you?"

"You are ruled by your emotion's child. I feel what you feel whether you summon me or not, we share the same body after all."

The way she speaks doesn't sit right with me, it's my body, not hers. We don't share it. And I'm certainly not a child. A tinkling laugh glitters in my head.

"Until you see us as one, you will never truly control the elements young one. I have more experience fighting, you'll need me in the battle ahead."

"Get out of my head, I need to think!" I shout aloud in annoyance, squeezing my eyes shut for emphasis. I wait a moment and hear no more, the voice is gone. For now, anyway. This is the last thing I need, my great-great-grandmother or whoever she is trying to take control of my body. She could set the entire compound ablaze. No, I'll have to work with what I can control myself, earth and water. Freyja joins my side, Phoenix and Nala in tow.

"The twins are rallying the troops - some have decided to stay. Good idea to slam the gates, that helped," informs Nala. She looks confused when I scowl in retort.

"Sorry, it's not you, I was hoping my words might have had an impact," I explain, not wanting to voice out loud that the gates closing so forcefully wasn't my doing.

"It got at their consciences, but whether it gave them strength to fight, is another thing. They need to believe that we can win this. Any display of power will give them hope."

A display of power... I can do that. And I don't need my stupid ancestors help either. My tummy rattles as she tries to show me otherwise, but I shut her out. This is my time.

"Stand back," I warn the others.

Not knowing exactly what I plan to do, I call to the earth to protect us. She answers with gusto – the surrounding trees creaking ominously, the ground rumbles violently as the floor beneath our feet begins to rise, then –

as the noise becomes almost deafening, roots come to my aid, breaking free from the ground once more.

All around the compound gasps and shouts of surprise ring out. Some run away fearfully, thinking the roots are to bind them. To their surprise, the roots shoot past them, heading straight for the gate, binding it shut with coil upon coil of added protection. I smile triumphantly as the gate is well and truly sealed shut. That should buy us some time. Murmurs rise as more deserters are tempted to stay.

"They'll break through eventually," scoffs one, still heading in the other direction.

"How do you expect to leave now that she's sealed the exit shut?" asks another.

"Same way they'll come in - over the fence," he shrugs.

A few boys have already left, deftly climbing over the fences and running as fast as their legs will carry them when their feet land on the other side. There's nothing more I can do to help them now, they're on their own.

"Anyone else wanting to leave needs to leave now," I inform, realising I need to barricade the fences too.

I call again to the earth for added protection and once again she answers my calling without hesitance. The roots holding the gate begin to change colour, from their earthly brown to vine green, sharp elongated red thorns protruding in warning to any who may approach. The vines begin to lengthen quickly, spreading over the surrounding fences.

"If you're going – go now!" I shout, knowing the entire compound will soon be ensnared in the lethal protection.

"Don't touch the thorns!" I warn those continuing to leave. It appears earth means business, having used thorns from a euphorbia bush, they drip with toxic poison.

"That was pretty impressive," Fergus stands to my side.

I can't help but grin having thought the same thing myself as others come to join us. My ancestor inside isn't as impressed, but I pay her no heed. I can do this alone.

"That should hold them out long enough for us to get in position," asserts Merrick, "and hopefully take some of their number too."

"What do we do when they break through?"

"My kind will hold the front line, horses can hold the middle, humans and cats the rear. Peri, what offensive magick do you have?"

"Truthfully, I'm not sure. I've never had to plan to use it, something always comes to me when I'm in the moment," I confess.

"Do what you can from the sides, they won't be expecting a magick user, try to take out any that get through. The rest of our number can get them back out. It's not going to be easy, but it can be done."

His words spread encouragement across the compound, as the plan makes its way from ear to ear.

"I've moved those less able to fight to one of the further barns. They have protection, hopefully, they won't be reached," Nala informs us.

I look at her quizzically.

"The docked," she explains, "the humans with missing limbs can't be expected to hold their own in battle."

I'd forgotten just how disadvantaged many of the humans are. I can't blame any for leaving. Those that remain hold a weapon of sorts, a mix of metal batons, electric prods, and wooden planks. Enough to do damage, but only if they're strong enough to wield them. Most are only boys, too young to have to fight for their freedom. The ground begins to rumble, only this time it's not my doing. Phoenix and Freyja flank my sides, both looking fiercely ahead, all hoping the gates hold tight.

"Incoming!" various birds caw loudly in warning heads.

Nervousness and trepidation fill the air as the rumbling gradually gets louder, the sound of hundreds of paws, hooves and claws careering towards us. At this moment in time, I'm positively petrified, but I stand strong. The humans are influenced by power, if I stand strong, they'll take strength from that and follow suit. Sure enough, many look to me before taking their stand, comforted by the added protection of a magick dweller. The irony that my abilities are both what sets us apart and what brings us together is not lost upon me, but now isn't the time to dwell on it. We stand together in this moment and that's what counts.

"Be careful," I whisper to our group, rubbing both Freyja and Phoenix's heads before taking my stance.

"Always," they answer in unison, standing tall as Nala and Fergus rush to join Merrick out front. The thundering approach reaches a climax, the stones at our feet pitter-patter, wildly, across the floor as we tense in anticipation of impact. This is it - no turning back. I pray to the Goddess we survive.

THE STAND

The hoard collides into the gate with a deafening crunch. Thankfully, it holds tight, serving its purpose. Howls, cries and wails ring out across the land, as those that made contact are stabbed by the euphorbia thorns. Even though they are the enemy, each cry of agony stabs guilt into my mind, knowing I caused their pain.

"Now's not the time to be weak," my ancestor breaks into my thoughts.

"Go away!" I yell in my mind to her.

"Then toughen up! If we're to survive this, you must accept that many will fall at our hands. If you cannot attune to that, let me free, or your friends will not make it through what is to come," she berates.

She's right, I know she's right, but that doesn't make this any easier. It was never my intention to get caught up in any of this, my plan had only ever been to rescue Euan and help any on our path that we could. I wanted to help – not hurt. More screams assault my ears as the enemy fail to realise the thorns are their undoing. I feel sick with guilt as friends of the fallen cry out for their comrades, no doubt writhing in pain on the floor before them. There's nothing I can do. Not without endangering those that stand with me on this side of the gate.

"You can't think like that child," my ancestor scolds.

"I am not a child!" I snap, out loud this time.

Some hear and look to me in confusion as I shake my head, desperate to be free of the frustrating presence within. Think of Euan, I tell myself, he always calms me. I do just that, blocking out the screams of agony with thoughts of the one person I wish I could see more than anything else.

His face graces my mind vividly. Not as a child, but as I saw him in my vision the night before. He's tall, broad-shouldered, long dark hair falling almost to his shoulders, a deep laceration visible from under his shirt across his neck, ending at his chin. I'm fixated by the scar, dreading to think how he received such a marking. I shake my head from dwelling as bizarrely in my mind, I follow him, seemingly alone, making his way down a long dark corridor. His steps echo with each foot, he's as nervous in his situation, as I am in mine. I realise then that this is a vision, only watched from an outsider's perspective, rather than from his own. He opens a door entering a brightly lit room, filled with pigs and sheep.

"Peri!" Phoenix's voice jolts me from the vision, "are you alright?"

"It's Euan! I can see him!"

"Now isn't the time for a vision – we have a problem!"

I turn to him hurriedly, "what's happened?"

"They have fire," he shouts, causing me to look up, I don't know how long I was out for, but thick smoke rises from behind the gate.

"That's impossible how do they have fire?"

"They brought pets with them," informs a horse out front.

"Pets? You mean humans are helping them?!" I cry alarmed.

Sure enough, through one of the barbed fences, humans can be seen, leashed to a Descendant, starting fires ablaze from fence to fence, burning through my protection.

"What do we do?"

"Use water Peri," Freyja's eyes find mine, her voice soothing the panic threatening to rise, bringing back clarity, my heart beating less erratically. Make it rain, I can do that. Closing my eyes, I summon the element of water. The once clear sky billows with wind as clouds rumble, the promise of rain at my fingertips when suddenly Euan is in my minds-eye again.

"You?!" He gasps incredulously.

"Hello, Euan - is it?" answers a voice from below.

I look down to find a chicken at his feet. He squawks gleefully as he jumps atop a table to be at Euan's eye line, landing claw first upon a pile of papers, kicking them aside as he does.

"Shall you tell them the truth, or I?" he glares.

"What truth?" Euan replies confused, holding the welt on his chest subconsciously.

"Yes, the truth boy, not the lies you attempt to spread so callously," the chicken spits.

"I'm telling the truth – I swear!" Euan attempts to gain eye contact with the pigs and sheep, but the damage is done, they look back suspiciously as the chicken's presence fills the room.

"PERI!" Phoenix's voice frees me from the vision.

Shaking my head free, I try to regain focus on the present moment, but the clouds above have parted, floating away from my grasp. The fire afront now roars rapidly, the winds that brought the clouds having aided their blaze. Cheers and applause can be heard from the other side as a mix of hands and hooves can be seen batting away at the fallen timbers to make room for their number to come through. My stomach drops, what have I done?

"Let me free child, I can keep them out!" my ancestor thunders in my mind.

"Go away!" I scream. That bloody woman, if she hadn't tried to interfere, this wouldn't have happened in the first place.

The gate shatters as a stampede of bulls tear their way into the compound, heads low, sharp horns swiping through the front line. No, we weren't expecting bulls. The dogs are thrown aside before they can get so much as a claw in. Merrick and Fergus are the only two that land on their feet, the others all impacting upon the dirt with sickening crunches, Nala included.

"No!" Howls Phoenix, wanting to rush to her aid, but refusing to leave my side.

Quick as I can, I throw forth my healing power and mend her shattered bones, I take her pain in the process, crying out as the sharp crunches reverberate throughout my body.

"Peri no! You can't take their pain, not now – you need to stay strong!" Freyja cries.

A skulk of foxes makes their way through, veering straight in our direction. Freyja launches herself, jaws wide open for attack, taking down one, then moving on to the next. More of the hoard stampede towards us, Phoenix jumps upon a bull mid warpath, taking down many of our number on his way. I'm torn whether to heal the fallen or help Phoenix and Freyja. Nala rises, rushing to my side.

"Thank you Peri, but Freyja's right – we need your offensive magick if we're to survive this!" she launches herself onto the bull Phoenix has managed to latch onto, both tear at his flesh repeatedly, taking him down by the neck. I look away, unable to bear the strangled cry that escapes the bull's mouth.

"You must toughen up child – this is war! Now fight!" orders the voice in my head.

She's right, I know she's right, but I don't want to kill anyone – why does the world have to be this way? I scream with frustration, power flying from my hands as a mix of anger, fear and disarray take over. Without my meaning to, the next wave of animals that make it into the compound are hit by an invisible force, thrown back into the remaining thorns. They flail uselessly to get free as the poison takes over, more estranged howls and whines echoing throughout the compound. I try to make the next wave less forceful, to send them back without killing them, but another force is in control now. Her power exceeds my own as I struggle to keep hold of her powers unleashing from within. A fox manages to sink its teeth into my ankle, causing me to yell out loud, the pain throbs. I try to keep a hold of my anger unsuccessfully. The all too familiar feeling of fire warms my hands, a blaze threatening to blare free.

"No!" I cry, "don't do this!"

An unearthly, almost manly laugh, is the only reply as the element of fire flares free, taking down all in its path. More screams assault the air as bulls, foxes, cows and badgers find themselves engulfed in the flames. The fire strategically takes them down, harming many, but keeping our own unit flame-free. Then out of nowhere, to my complete disbelief, the next wave of animals forces their way through, led by a pack of wolves. They take down all in their path, snapping and swiping as they go, their grey fur instantly tainted red.

Another flash consumes my mind, Euan running as fast as he can up a seemingly endless stairway. Flock upon flock of chickens are at his heels, one manages to sink its beak into his ankle, he yells in pain, but it doesn't hinder his pace as he throws himself forward with more exertion. He bursts through a door opening out onto the roof of the dome. It must be four storeys if not more, with no way of escape, except the door from which he came. The chickens catch up with him, the one from my previous vision leading them gleefully.

"Time's up Euan," he sneers, slowly clawing closer to him.

"PERI!!"

My name being screamed frantically brings me back once again. My hands once ablaze have now gone cold, I've taken down many, but more continue to charge through and the wolves have given the enemy the upper hand. Our troops struggle to keep our number intact as they battle their way through the compound. I try to bring the flames back, but my vision seems to have rendered my ancestor dormant. I call on my own powers, urging the earth to our aid, roots of old surge upwards from the ground, holding back the army of teeth and horns battling their way through.

The humans fight with fury, their weapons stunning, battering and crippling those they manage to contact. Just as many lay injured or dead, blood spills everywhere, the lush greenery from my hands now tainted crimson. The dogs and horses fight steadily, but many are taken down, one tries to limp to safety just as a bull breaks free from my roots hold, his horns tear through the stallion from end to end. Tears nearly blind me as I struggle to withstand the carnage. So much death.

I hear Fergus cry out wildly as a wolf manages to get the upper paw over his brother, Merrick's body goes rigid between the wolf's teeth, his savage jaws held tightly around our friends' neck. I stagger backwards in shock. No. Not Merrick – I must save him. I try to throw my healing abilities towards him, but as I do, the roots holding back the remaining army begin to shrink away. Merrick's eyes find mine, he shakes his head, telling me it's okay for him to fall if it saves his troops.

"No!" I wail, "No, no, no!"

I try desperately to aid him, but it's too late, the wolf shakes his head violently. Merrick's neck snaps loudly for all to hear. My healing power doesn't reach him in time. Merrick's eyes roll back as his final breath leaves his body, his body falling limp, tongue lolling from his mouth, into a pool of his blood upon the ground. A strangled sob leaves my lips. This can't be happening. The wolf licks his lips indifferent to our turmoil, moving on to his next victim. Fergus howls wildly, throwing himself at the much larger canine as their battle continues.

My heart thumps wildly. My hands shake as I struggle to maintain any form of control. It's too much. I can't bear it. I scream. I scream loud and hard for all to hear. Merrick's dead. They took my friend. He was kind, he didn't deserve this. They'll pay. They'll all pay. My hands burn desperate to rage free, only this time I'm in control, I throw it towards the enemy in short sharp bursts. Enough to burn and injure, but not enough to kill.

"Leave!!" I shriek wildly at them, "Leave now or you'll all burn!!"

Some listen and retreat, but many still stand before me, I can't show any weakness. My ancestor was right. I must toughen up if I want my friends to survive this. Screaming with frustration, I unleash the flames directly at them, I hear their cries and close my eyes, not wanting to see the pain I cause. I keep screaming to drown out their wails as my flames rage into the enemy, turning all in its path to mere cinders and ash. The flames spiral out of control, engulfing more than the enemy. I struggle to reel it back as the blaze begins to latch onto our own, their cries of pain spurring me into a panic.

"Peri!" Freyja's voice reaches my mind, "Peri stop!"

She feels my pain, my fear, she knows I don't want to kill, she barges me hard, causing my flames to falter as I fall to the ground. My head hits the floor harshly causing my eyes to rush open, only, once again, it's no longer the battle I see.

I'm back on top of the dome. Euan stands by the edge.

He's surrounded by chickens. Hundreds, upon hundreds of chickens. He has no way of escape.

I realise then that I've seen this before.

The familiarity of the stairway, the roof and now what is to come, rushes to my mind with clarity.

Every nightmare I ever had of the scene in front of me, rushes to my brain in one moment.

All this time.

The nightmare was a vision.

Only not my own.

Euan's.

"Time's up boy," the chicken rasps.

Euan stands still, contemplating what to do. I see the moment he decides his fate, looking at the chicken with contempt before baring his cheeky grin that I miss so terribly. I know his retort before he says it, miming the words as if they were my own.

"Suck eggs Al."

I watch helplessly, unable to stop what happens next.

He jumps.

I reach out – desperate to save him. My hands clutch the air, he falls too quick for me to grasp. I falter, tipping dangerously over the ledge, then, before I can stop myself, I fall from the dome, tumbling after him.

PHOENIX

The battle wages on with no promise of reprieve. There's so many of them. Blood drips from my jaws from those I've taken down. I've witnessed too many fights in my day, mammals go down by the jugular; long as you reach their neck, it doesn't matter how big they are - they'll go down. Eventually.

I hold my current opponent down tightly as he writhes desperately to get free. Part of me wants to let go, but we're at war and he is on the opposing side. If I let him free and he kills someone I care for – I'll never forgive myself. Closing my eyes, I hold tight until the deed is done. As the bull's neck finally goes limp within my clutches, I sag in relief. This brings me no joy. I spent years protesting that I was not like my predecessors who had been bred to fight - only to be dragged into fighting regardless. I'd do anything for the ones I love though. Anything.

Looking around, I try to make out the rest of our group, Nala holds her own alongside Freyja, the two of them taking down as many foxes, cows and badgers as they are able. Fergus and Merrick make the ultimate combating duo. Kill after kill, they take down more than most of us combined, until the wolves arrived – that was a shock to all of us. Wolves haven't lived on this land for centuries. They're wild and know how to fight, never having lost their hunting instincts like the rest of us. Peri is wielding her magick as best she can, but she struggles to maintain control, her roots hold back the hoard of enemies desperate to get inside the compound. How long she can hold, I do not know.

Fergus howls wildly then, turning my attention in the twin's direction, his brother is in the clutches of a wolf, held tight by his neck. No, this can't be happening, one wrong move and he's done for. I rush to help, only to be struck from the side, two foxes throwing themselves at me venomously. They snap and bite at my legs trying to take me down, I'm able to dodge successfully, impacting damage of my own as my jaws clamp shut on ones' hind, she screeches wildly causing me to let go. It bothers me that she's female. It shouldn't, I know that, but it does. She looks at me quizzically, confused as to why I let go as her mate makes his second attack, almost making contact – then out of nowhere, we're blasted backwards.

Every animal within the compound, Carni's, Herbi's and humans alike – all of us – are thrown back by an unseen power as a terrifying scream fills the air. Frantically I look to Peri only to find rage has become her. I notice then that our leader has fallen. His body a pool of blood on the floor. There will be no saving him, he's lost to the other world now.

Silently, I say a prayer to the Goddess for his soul, then run as fast as my paws will carry me towards Peridot. If her ancestor has taken control, I may be able to talk her down. Only as I approach, her eyes are her own ocean blue. This is Peri's doing. Her hands flame as she shoots deadly bursts of rage, each one making contact. She closes her eyes, unable to bear the wrath she inflicts upon the enemy. Her wrath builds momentum, taking down our own number in the crossfire.

"Freyja!" I try to locate her familiar frantically.

Her eyes find mine as she launches herself at our friend, taking her down by the torso. Peri's body impacts the dirt with a thud, only for her expression to go vacant. Another vision has her held immobile once more.

"Peri!" Cries Freyja, "Peri – get up!"

The battle continues to rage amidst the burnt remains of charred mammals surrounding us. It appears there is no end to their numbers. They just keep coming.

"Peridot, please – you must wake up!" We both urge but she doesn't budge, the vision has her mind fully.

"There!" A badger cries, pointing in our direction, "the magick dweller, she's down – now's our chance!"

They head in our direction, more follow in pursuit, Peridot their only intent. Snarling we stand either side, protecting her as best we can, but we're outnumbered, twenty to one.

"Hand her over dog and we may let you live," the largest of their clan asserts.

"Never," we growl in unison, Freyja's spine goes rigid as does mine. I give my most ferocious snarl, they're not taking her anywhere. The badger laughs.

"AMURAQ!!" he summons.

A deafening roar responds as their clan parts to give way to the largest wolf I have ever laid eyes upon. Even crouched low, ready to pounce, he is easily, five times my size, if not more. His jowls still drip with our leader's blood. Freyja's stance doesn't waiver, neither does mine, we're prepared to die for Peri, but dying is the likely outcome. We do not stand a chance against a beast of this magnitude. I howl into the night as loud as I can, Freyja joining my call. We're answered as those that can, come to our side, Fergus and Nala the first to arrive. Nala limps, her front legs gashed and bloody. Fergus seems to be in good shape, led by the rage of his brothers' demise.

The wolf tilts his head, licking his lips before giving a bloodcurdling howl of his own. At first, none come, then all at once, he is flanked on both sides, all remaining wolves coming to his aid. Snapping and snarling, they itch for blood, revelling in the hunt and eager to get to their prize. We will not survive this. I have no choice, if we're to live, I must do what I vowed I would never do again. Peri will be furious, but she will understand, it is the only way.

I call to my Elemental.

"Vallaeartha!!"

She answers immediately, not so much a second's wait.

"Phoenix where the blazes are you?"

"Compound Four – we're in trouble."

She goes silent for less than a second.

"Phoenix I won't make it in time. Give me control."

"Promise you won't take Peridot back with you."

"Are you mad? There's no time!"

"Promise!!" I demand.

"Fine - I promise! Now give me control before you perish!!"

I submit my body willingly, praying to the Goddess it's not too late.

Vallaeartha

What the hell has my daughter got herself mixed up in? My presence fills Phoenix, taking hold of his body as if it were my own. I open his lids to find a pack of wolves snarling and snapping meters before us.

"Give. Us. The. Girl." Growls their leader.

I look behind to find Peridot fallen upon the ground.

Big mistake.

I unleash my power directly at him. His eyes bulge as unfathomable pain wracks his body from the inside out, causing him to convulse violently. Foam builds around his jowls as he fights to contain the agony unsuccessfully, a high-pitched whine escapes his lips as he succumbs to my fury. I look upon him with pure contempt, pushing my magick to harm him further, blood now weeps freely from his eye sockets, then, as he can withstand no more, he gives a final pained guttural whimper, before falling limp to the dirt.

His pack howl in outrage, stepping past their fallen leader to snarl in anger at his demise. I can't help but smirk. Is that the best they've got? I prepare to take them down also, my purple swirls form within Phoenix's eyes, ready to unleash my wrath upon any that seek to harm my daughter. The wolves show no fear and stand their ground, unlike the other species that back away and begin to retreat.

"The dog has magick!" A clan of badgers scurry away fearfully, skulks of foxes in their wake.

Traitorous little fleabags. The effort I went through to save their kind before The Changing, and this is how they thank me. By trying to capture my daughter?! They must have a death wish. Well, I'll grant it. Gladly.

I unleash my powers with malice, killing many whilst ensnaring the lucky few that manage to escape, entangling them in a cage of vines. I have questions that need answering, they will serve a purpose later. Turning my attention to the remaining wolves, I warn, "I suggest you leave. I won't offer twice."

They look upon their leader, a heap upon the ground. My words have no effect, they step closer towards me in anger, seeking retribution. I'd send them away, but they'll only return for my daughter, I know it. I warned her this would happen, but would she listen? The wolves continue towards me, deadly intent clear in their eyes. It's a shame to kill a pack so beautiful. But so be it.

It brings me no joy, but they shall fall also. My purple mist engulfs them. They try to fight it in vain. Snapping and biting as my deadly poison makes its way into their lungs. They begin to falter, my power crippling them one by one, when out of nowhere, I feel another presence battling my own. No, it can't be – not now. I've not felt my ancestor in decades, why choose this moment to break free of my hold?

"Now. Isn't. The. Time." I hiss.

"I won't let you kill the sacred animals," she breathes, her otherworldly voice causing me to shudder subconsciously.

"They are trying to take my daughter!"

"You must let what is foretold to be, come to pass. It is not for us to tamper with the worlds will."

"I will not let them take her!" I shriek.

"Yes. You will," she sighs, rendering my powers useless for the pack to regain composure. Rising slowly, they begin to approach Peridot, their prize within reach.

"No!" I cry, but I'm helpless to intervene, as magick that I have never been able to control, seeps from my familiar's eyes, into the eyes of the wolf pack.

Their eyes now consumed with darkness, the females lift Peridot without causing harm, whilst the males retrieve their fallen leader. They look upon me without emotion, their eyes no longer their own, a swirling empty blackness in their place. I know that darkness. Many a time I've glanced at my reflection only to find those unearthly death-black swirls looking back at me. The curse of an Elementals power. The never-ending battle to have true control. A battle I thought I had won until this moment. A spine-tingling howl erupts from the pack as they call for the battle to cease and begin to leave the compound.

"What are you doing?!" Peri's familiar wails, trying and failing to go after them. My ancestor keeps her rooted to the spot, unable to reach Peridot whilst unable to come to harm.

"It is what must be done," her voice leaves Phoenix's lips.

"No – Peri – wake up!!" Peri's familiar screams.

Panicking, I try to move, only to find myself trapped by her will, I manage to regain my voice and join her familiar in screaming, desperate for my daughter to wake.

"Peri! Wake up!! Please - snap out of it!!"

If anyone stands a chance at overcoming my ancestors' power it's my daughter, she's shown that on more than one occasion. If only I'd not interfered. In trying to keep her safe from this world, I've only solidified my fears into reality. I should've known better than to try and undo a vision. What has been seen, is always what will come to pass. There can be no changing a true Seer's vision - no

366

matter how hard I tried to do so. This was always going to be the outcome. Tears stream from Phoenix's eyes as he shares in my anguish, each second Peridot getting further from our grasp.

The wolves signal to their troops to follow, all eyes fall to them as they leave the compound, my daughter remaining held in their clutches. We continue to scream as loud as we can, but our pleas fall on deaf ears. Peri's eyes are vacant, glossed over, lost to another world completely, as the fear I've held for all these years unfolds in front of our eyes. If only I'd done things differently, she would be more prepared for what she is to face, out there, alone. With none other than her ancestor to guide her. Fear of her ancestor bubbles in my stomach, but it's not only my fear I feel. My own ancestor fears hers also. That can't be good. Who does Peri have within her?

The thought pushes my ancestor from my mind, she relinquishes her hold, releasing Phoenix's body into my control. I rush to the gate as fast as his legs can run, desperate to catch a glimpse of the hoard, but it's too late. They're long gone. My daughter gone with them.

Euan

As I plummet, fully aware that these last futile moments are all that's left of, let's admit, a pretty depressing life, I think back to the one time I was truly happy and her face pops into my mind. With seconds left, I do the last thing I thought possible in this moment. I smile. Opening my eyes one last time to look upon the world before I meet my end, I choke back a startled cry as my eyes behold something utterly impossible. Falling in my wake, a silhouette tries frantically to reach me. I'd know that face anywhere.

No. It can't be.

It's not possible.

It's a hallucination - my mind playing tricks on me.

I reach forward to take the ghost-like hand that tries desperately to grasp mine. Our eyes meet in confusion when our hands join. Her name leaves my lips with less than a second left before I impact upon the dirt.

"Peridot?"

END OF BOOK ONE

ABOUT THE AUTHOR

Ray's passion for writing comes hand in hand with a passion for animals and the environment which prompted the creation of the Earthlings trilogy. It is Ray's dream to open The Peridot Animal Sanctuary and Wildlife Reserve and that dream inspired this trilogy to life.

When Ray isn't writing, she is happiest spending time with her children, partner, family and friends, or walking with the real-life Phoenix and Freyja spending time in nature. Often found stargazing under the light of the moon, with a tarot deck in one hand, and a strong cuppa in another.

Like the book, all things 'Peridot' is in tribute to Ray's father, a beautiful, brave man, loved dearly by those who knew him, who sadly passed away in 2017 from pancreatic cancer. He was happiest when in nature with his family.

P.T.H – A man like no other. Loved, always.

A Note From The Author

Thank you for taking the time to read Peridot's story, I hope you enjoy reading her journey as much as I enjoy writing it. There are two more books in the trilogy to follow, with a prequel to be released shortly after with Vallaeartha's tale of how the Earthlings world came to be.

I hope you stick with Peri and her friends in their hardships to come, they will need you. I implore you in the meantime to watch the documentary **Earthlings** via Nation Earth - if you can bear it.

Every endeavour has been made to ensure that Earthlings is printed on recycled paper where possible, and I pledge to plant a tree per book sale for my published works, future, past and present. You can keep up to date with the Peridot Forest via my website.

For Mother Nature, always,
A fellow Earthling,
Ray x

Join me on social media @RayStarBooks

To contact me or join the Earthlings mailing list, you can reach me on my website: www.raystarbooks.com

ACKNOWLEDGEMENTS

To my wonderful friends and family, with extra special thanks to my mum, partner, brother, sister-in-law and four closest friends, I am endlessly thankful for your unwavering support in all I do.

The love that surrounds me from each of you, reminds me that there is good in this world worth fighting for.

To Taryn and the amazing team at Chronos Publishing, thank you for helping Peridot and me share the Earthlings tale with the world. I will forever be grateful to have found such supportive and like-minded women to work with. Here's to many magickal years ahead.

To my dad whom I miss more than words can say:

I wear your peridot ring every day.
It is with me always.
As I know, are you.

COMING SOON TO 2022

EARTHLINGS BOOK 2

DOMINION

Peridot has fallen.

Taken to the one place a magick-born does not want to end up. The Descendant's headquarters. Alone, she must learn to embrace her magick in order to break free.

Elsewhere on the mainland, with the treaty unsalvageable, The Descendant's new plans hold dire consequences for all who remain loyal to the humans. The Resistance have no choice other than to prepare to make a stand and fight.

Whilst all hope may seem lost, with the help of her friends, Peridot may be the saviour humanity needs to end The Descendant's tyrannic way of life, or the catalyst that could kickstart a war, deciding the fate of the Earthlings world, once and for all.

#DominionIsComing